TRAVELLER'S GUIDE TO THE MIDDLE EAST

A travel companion to
Bahrain, Cyprus, Iraq, Jordan,
Kuwait, Lebanon, Oman, Qatar,
Saudi Arabia, Syria, Turkey,
United Arab Emirates, Yemen Arab Republic,
People's Democratic Republic of Yemen,
Egypt and Iran.

Fourth Edition

TRAVELLER'S GUIDE
TO THE
MIDDLE EAST

Editor
Pat Lancaster

an **ɩꞓ** publication

Publisher	Afif Ben Yedder

| Editor | Pat Lancaster |

| Cover Design | Alison Perry |

Published by   IC Publications Ltd
London Office P.O. Box 261
69 Great Queen Street, London WC2B 5BN
Telephone 01-404 4333
Fax 01-404 5336
Cables Machrak London WC2
Telex 8811757

US edition   Hunter Publishing Inc
published by   300 Raritan Center Parkway
Edison, N.J. 08818

Typeset by   RSB Typesetters
Bagshot Road
Worplesdon, Surrey

Printed by   Page Bros (Norwich) Ltd.

Cover Photograph   Ministry of Information, Qatar.

© 1988 IC Publications Ltd
ISBN 0905268 53 9
ISSN 0140-1319
ISBN (USA) 1-55650-036-X

Travel in the Arab World

The countries of the Arab world offer vast scope and astonishing diversity to both tourist and business traveller. A country's potential for tourism depends on its climate, beaches, and other attractions such as historic sites, birdlife, flora and fauna. The realisation of this potential however, depends on the provision of certain physical facilities and a number of less tangible factors. Accommodation, catering, entertainment and transport facilities are among the most important of the physical facilities. Less tangible considerations such as government policy towards tourism, internal politics, the quality of service offered to tourists and the overall attitude of the indigenous population, should not be underestimated.

Regrettably, there are countries in the region, Lebanon is a prime example, where the government is unable to offer security to either tourist or business visitor. Bearing in mind the still uncertain fate of the foreigners and Lebanese nationals, taken hostage in the country, would-be visitors to Lebanon are strongly advised to take every precaution to ensure their personal safety – with the most effective precaution, postponing a proposed visit, usually the favourite option.

In terms of the numbers of visitors involved, the tourist trades of the Arab countries are at very different levels of development. At one extreme are Egypt, Jordan and Syria which for years have attracted visitors seeking both business and pleasure. At the other end of the scale are countries such as the two Yemens and Oman, which attract few visitors from either category.

The three main markets from which the Arab countries draw international tourists are Europe, North America and the Arab world itself. About half of Egypt's tourists are from Europe and North America and are either on business trips or tours of the country's historic sites. The majority of visitors to Syria and Jordan are Arabs engaged in family and business tourism. Moslem pilgrims, many of them from Arab countries, predominate amongst Saudi Arabia's tourists.

While business travel has long been acceptable in the Arab world, attracting the tourist hordes is an alien concept to some of the more conservative states. Even though Saudi Arabia deals with more than a million religious pilgrims every year, the government authorities would be unlikely to give the seal of approval to a foreign tour company wanting to sell "bucket and spade" holidays in the kingdom. However, Saudi Arabia is not by any means alone in this, most of the Gulf states employ a stringent vetting procedure on people wishing to enter their country.

Meanwhile, mindful of the precious foreign earnings tourism brings in, others have gone all out to attract more and more visitors. Turkey is one of the most recent to enter the arena and, thanks to vigorous marketing strategy, is recording the profits of a bumper year.

Contents

Introduction and Acknowledgements

This fourth edition of the Traveller's Guide to the Middle East has been completely revised and updated, following the total sell-out of the third edition. It is designed to help and inform tourists visiting the region for both business and pleasure. And, with the obvious exception of the Middle East's most noteable "hot spots" it is an area where much pleasure can still be had. For the most part, a region of beauty and tranquillity.

Despite the discovery of oil and the enormous amount of development that followed, there remains a peculiar timeless quality in many parts of the Middle East. In Qatar, home of the world's largest natural gas field, it is not unusual to see a Mercedes limousine pull off the multi-lane highway, in order that its owner may kneel at the roadside for the sunset prayer. In Saudi Arabia, wealthy businessmen and bankers regularly leave the comfort of their air conditioned villas to spend the weeekend in a tent in the desert, returning – if only for a short time – to the life led for centuries by their forefathers. And, watching the slow progress of a felucca on the Nile, one could be in almost any century.

For those who can find the money and the time I hope this guide will be an encouragement to explore some of the countries of the Middle East.

My thanks go to the many people who assisted in the compiling of this book especially to Mr Sami Badr of the Saudi Press Agency, Ms Leila Fannous of the Qatar Embassy in London and Dr Issa Kawari and his staff at the Ministry of Information in Doha. Mr. Walid al Khobaizi at the Kuwait Embassy in London and Sheikh Nasser Al Jaber Al Sabah and his staff at the Ministry of Information in Kuwait.

My acknowledgements go also to the many people who have assisted and helped in the production of this book, including Rhona Wells and Alison Perry and to Barbara Bannister, Graham Benton and Anna Horsfall for their practical assistance.

I would like to particularly thank the late Fred and Isobella Rhodes for their early encouragement and invaluable overall contribution.

Pat Lancaster

Temperature and Rainfall

Average maximum and minimum daily temperatures and average rainfall for January and July.

	January			July		
	Max	**Min**	**Rainfall**	**Max**	**Min**	**Rainfall**
Bahrain – Manama	20°C	14°C	8mm	37°C	29°C	none
Cyprus – Nicosia	15°C	5°C	76mm	37°C	21°C	slight
Egypt – Alexandria	18°C	10°C	49mm	30°C	23°C	slight
Cairo	18°C	8°C	5mm	35°C	21°C	none
Luxor	23°C	6°C	slight	42°C	23°C	none
Mersa Matruh	18°C	8°C	53mm	28°C	22°C	none
Iran – Abadan	17°C	7°C	38mm	46°C	28°C	none
Bandar Abbas	23°C	13°C	60mm	38°C	30°C	none
Isfahan	8°C	−5°C	16mm	36°C	19°C	slight
Mashad	7°C	−6°C	20mm	34°C	17°C	slight
Tehran	7°C	−3°C	45mm	37°C	22°C	slight
Iraq – Baghdad	16°C	4°C	22mm	43°C	24°C	slight
Basra	18°C	7°C	36mm	40°C	27°C	slight
Mosul	12°C	3°C	72mm	42°C	22°C	slight
Jordan – Amman	12°C	4°C	69mm	33°C	18°C	none
Kuwait – Kuwait City	16°C	10°C	22mm	40°C	30°C	none
Lebanon – Beirut	16°C	10°C	188mm	31°C	23°C	slight
Oman – Muscat	25°C	19°C	28mm	36°C	30°C	slight
Salalah	28°C	18°C	slight	28°C	24°C	28mm
Qatar – Doha	20°C	14°C	8mm	37°C	29°C	none
Saudi Arabia – Jeddah	29°C	19°C	5mm	37°C	26°C	slight
Riyadh	21°C	8°C	slight	41°C	26°C	none
Syria – Damascus	12°C	2°C	43mm	35°C	18°C	slight
Dair al-Zair	11°C	2°C	42mm	41°C	26°C	none
Turkey – Ankara	4°C	−4°C	32mm	30°C	15°C	12mm
Antalya	14°C	8°C	260mm	35°C	23°C	slight
Istanbul	9°C	3°C	108mm	27°C	17°C	45mm
Izmir	13°C	4°C	110mm	33°C	21°C	5mm
Kars	−6°C	−18°C	28mm	25°C	10°C	53mm
Trabzon	10°C	4°C	70mm	25°C	19°C	45mm
Van	1°C	−8°C	56mm	28°C	14°C	5mm
UAE	23°C	18°C	30mm	34°C	28°C	slight
Yemen – Aden	28°C	22°C	5mm	36°C	28°C	5mm

Middle East Currency Table

COUNTRY	CURRENCY	VALUE TO £1.00	VALUE TO $1.00
Bahrain	Dinar	0.6401	0.377
Cyprus	Cyprus Pound	0.8235	0.485
Egypt	Egyptian Pound	3.9275	2.313
Iran	Rial	120.303	70.85
Iraq	Iraqi Dinar	0.5281	0.311
Jordan	Jdn. Dinar	0.6410	0.377
Kuwait	Kuwaiti Dinar	0.4841	0.285
Lebanon	Leb. Pound	670.710	395.00
Oman	Omani Rial	0.6537	0.385
Qatar	Qatar Riyal	6.1807	3.640
Saudi Arabia	Riyal	6.3692	3.751
Syria	Syrian Pound	19.0176	11.20
Turkey	Turkish Lira	2,725.29	1,605.00
UAE	UAE Dirham	6.2368	3.673
Yemen AR	Yemen Riyal	16.7762	9.880
Yemen PDR	Yemen Dinar	0.5824	0.343

Exchange rates as of October 1988.

Religion and Culture

Islam is the religion of most Arabs and is divided into two principal sects, Sunni and Shia. The Sunni are found in Syria, parts of Lebanon, Egypt, all North Africa, and in the original homeland, Saudi Arabia and the Gulf States. The Shia are found in Iraq and southern Lebanon. Turks are Sunni, Iranians mostly Shia. There are also Arab Christians of at least 12 sects chiefly in Lebanon, though minorities exist in Jordan, Syria, Iraq and Egypt. Breakaway sects from Islam have strong links with Zoroastrianism and the ancient mystery religions. These include the Druze in Lebanon, Syria and Palestine, the Alawi in the Syrian mountains and the Yezidi in Iraq.

The five Pillars of Islam, or basic beliefs, common to both Sunni and Shia are:

1) The Profession of Faith, by which a person declares himself a Moslem: 'There is no God but God, and Mohammed is the messenger of God.'
2) The Pilgrimage to Mecca, or Hajj, which all believers should go on, if at all possible, at least once during their lifetime.
3) Giving 10% of one's income to charity, and for the benefit of widows and orphans.
4) Praying five times a day: dawn, mid-morning, noon, sunset, and before sleeping.
5) Fasting during the month of Ramadan, which means abstaining totally from food, drink, and tobacco from dawn until sunset. Ramadan is a lunar month of four weeks, which falls 11 days earlier each year.

Most Moslems observe these at least partially, and the proportion of those who practise all the tenets of the Faith is probably higher than in most other faiths. For Islam is a complete way of life; the social and hygienic habits described in this chapter all stem from Koranic precepts. The position of women is often brought up as a fault in Islam by others; but in Islamic society women have at least always been able to possess and use their own property in their own names. Restrictions upon the role of women in public life have been enforced, but now that education is becoming universal they are gradually becoming eroded. Polygamy does still exist, but is not encouraged. It developed as a social institution at a time when men were frequently killed in battle and left their wives with no protection. The Koran says categorically: 'If you fear that you cannot be equal, then marry only one . . . do not love one to distraction to the prejudice of another whom you keep in suspense,' and elsewhere: 'You may marry two, or three, or four, provided you treat them equally.'

Domestic customs and personal behaviour

Arab manners and social customs are in some ways much more formal and stylised than those found in the West. Hospitality is the chief virtue of the Arab world; respect for others' privacy seems to be more important in the West.

Privacy is not greatly esteemed by Arabs, because it means being alone, and originally being alone in a primitive desert environment meant death. The extended rather than the nuclear family is the custom, and this means that there are very few lonely or neglected old people. Indeed, there is much respect for age, and the old grandfather or grandmother is head of the family until death.

Entertaining guests is far more common than in Western society; a guest is provided with everything except privacy. If he wanted that, why would he come and visit his friends?

However many servants she may have for menial tasks, the lady of the house always attends to its supervision, and often does a good deal of cooking before getting dressed to go out, or to receive guests for lunch. No Arab lady would ever be seen with her hair in curlers, except by female relatives in her bedroom, or at the hairdresser. A great deal of time, money and effort is spent by both sexes on clothes and beauty products, and the results are often spectacular.

Western-style furniture, often of the more ornate variety, is now common in Arab houses, though the traditional reception room, or *Dar*, with hard oblong cushions placed around three sides of a large room with a fountain or brazier in the middle, according to the season, still exists in the Arab countries, and is indeed admired for its picturesque qualities and adherence to tradition. In the same way, some banquets are still offered with the food placed on cloths on the floor, or on low round copper tables, with the guests seated around on cushions. Oriental carpets are usually hung on the walls; of course in a chillier climate fitted plain carpets are appreciated. But it has always been the custom for both kitchens and bathrooms to have stone, tile, or marble floors with a drain in one corner, so that any liquid spilt can be swept away with an ordinary straw brush, or dirt rinsed off with buckets of water.

The noise level is higher, as is natural in a society where outdoor living is possible for much of the year, and where there is competition with other people and the television. Arabs do not object to transistor radios in public, car horns, or loud conversation. They do, on the other hand, regard as highly offensive and ill mannered any sitting posture which places the soles of the feet towards anyone present. It is quite acceptable to sit cross-legged, on a cushion or on the sofa or a chair, though preferable to remove the shoes first. Females should, obviously, wear trousers or long skirts in order to do this decently; indeed any clothes that reveal too much of the female form are to be avoided. It is far more comfortable and cooler to wear long sleeved loose hip-length shirts over trousers, long skirts, or loose kaftan-type dresses.

It may be relevant here to say something about the Arab attitude to drugs, and to informal relationships between the sexes. It is generally believed that the countries of the Levant – Turkey, Syria, Lebanon and Egypt – are ideal places for obtaining and consuming both hashish or marijuana and opium. It is true that the opium poppy is cultivated in Turkey, under strict government supervision, and that occasionally some opium has been known to be diverted to the illegal market, mostly for conversion to heroin in French or Italian underground laboratories, and subsequent smuggling into the USA. It is also true that hashish grows in Morocco, Lebanon and Syria, wild, and that in some remote areas the peasants cultivate it as a cash crop, and sell it to middlemen who then export it. But it is far easier to obtain the hard drugs in London or New York than in Beirut or Cairo, and it is not culturally acceptable to use them. Hashish is obtainable with less difficulty, and young people are sometimes tempted to smoke the odd cigarette. It is, however, strictly illegal in all the Arab countries to use, possess, or trade in any kind of narcotic, and many Americans and Europeans have ended up in prison because they ignored this rule.

Relations between the sexes are also most strictly controlled by custom, and 'dating' in the western sense does not exist. As university education becomes more widespread, students may meet on the campus, study together, and discuss philosophy and politics. But an invitation to a girl from a boy which would involve the two being alone together even briefly is interpreted either as a proposal of marriage or a deadly insult. An Arab proverb says: 'Do not trust a man and woman alone together for any longer than it takes for water to run out of a jar.'

Divorce and re-marriage are quite easy, and carry little social stigma. In Islam marriage is a civil contract, governed by the Shari'a, and the contract may be drawn up with various stipulations which the two parties have agreed upon, including the wife's right (as well as the husband's) to ask for divorce. Children of divorced parents usually go to their father, after the age of five for a boy and eight for a girl. This tends to keep marriages going that might otherwise founder, for often a woman's loyalty is to her children rather than to her husband. Also, in the past, the majority of divorces took place because the wife could not have children, or the husband could not beget them. If a

All smiles in Oman.

couple do split up the woman can remarry far more easily if she is not burdened with children. The tradition of children belonging to the father is so strong that when a young widow wishes to remarry after a decent interval (one to three years) her deceased husband's parents may want to keep the children, and will insist at least on frequent visits. Property distribution is governed by the Shari'a.

In Egypt, and all the Arab countries to the east, parents, from the time that their first son is born, are always known by his name, with the prefix Abu (Father of) or Umm (Mother off) added. This custom seems to have died out, or never existed, in the North African countries; it is an extremely practical one because it does away with the awkwardness of not knowing how to address people for whom a first-name basis would be too familiar and surname too formal. The equivalent of 'Mister' is Sayyid for a Moslem, and Khawaja for a Christian; ladies are Sayida, or Sitt, and girls Anissa (for Miss). After a certain age all ladies are Sitt, the Arabic equivalent of Ms. Indeed, with murmurings of Women's Lib, and the general education and gradual equality of women, it is sometimes observed that parents, instead of being addressed invariably as Umm Fahid or Abu Hassan (both boys' names), may sometimes be Umm Leila or Abu Nala, if their first-born is a girl, or they have only daughters. Other titles have died out; in Egypt there used to be beys and pashas, but both the words and the ranks were Turkish imports. The Arab and Islamic custom holds that no man is better than another (though some may be richer), and the words Amir (Prince) and Malik (King) are purely functional. The Arab kings keep no rigid court protocol and any of their subjects have the right of audience, and of addressing them by their names directly.

On the whole, there is a somewhat ambivalent attitude to older customs; people want the new technological toys and comforts of the West, yet they value the past too, particularly family and religious traditions. Over recent years there has been a rekindling of interest in old buildings and artefacts. After decades of tearing out the old and replacing with new the tide has turned and "old" is no longer necessarily "bad". Indeed, the magnificent museums in Qatar, Kuwait and Saudi Arabia bear witness to a growing interest in the past.

Food

Several large volumes have been written on Middle Eastern food, which, if correctly prepared, is a culinary delight. Arab food is spicier and more strongly flavoured than that of Europe. Most Arabs eat basically Arab food, with European 'extras'. Flat unleavened bread flaps (made and sold in Europe by Greek bakeries as 'pitta' bread) are consumed in large quantities, chiefly for wrapping around pieces of other foods and eating without implements. Rice is the staple cereal, served with stews, or grilled meat on skewers; also used are lentils, cracked wheat (burghul) and chick peas

(hummos). Lamb is the principal meat, beef being scarce, expensive, and tough, and pork forbidden by Koranic injunction. Chickens, turkeys and ducks are popular, so is fish (mostly grilled on charcoal) and game. Any animals or birds must be killed in the Islamic fashion, by cutting the throat so that all the blood drains out, and reciting the invocation *'Bismillah al-rahman al-rahim'* (In the name of God, the Merciful, the Compassionate).

Pork is forbidden in the Islamic, as in the Mosaic, law, because pigs are unclean feeders, and in a hot country it is very easy to get trichinosis from eating pork.

Butter is very little used in Arab cooking; its place is taken by olive oil or *samni* which is clarified sheep or goat butter, much like Indian *ghee*. But this has become less common; vegetable oils such as maize, sunflower, or peanut are now considered healthier. Indeed, some modern ideas have now taken over; fatness is no longer an obligatory sign of prosperity, and fewer middle-class men have large paunches to indicate their wealth.

The usual eating pattern is a substantial breakfast which would consist of tea or sometimes coffee, bread flaps, black olives, goat cheese, cream or cottage cheese called *labneh* which is solidified from *laban* (yoghurt), eggs fried in oil, and fruit juice or fruit. Lunch, served at any time between 1.30 and 3 pm, remembering that in many Arab countries offices close at 2 pm for the day (having begun work at 7.30 am), is the principal meal, with soup, rice with a meat and vegetable stew, another meat dish such as grilled chicken, *kufta* (minced meat on skewers or baked in a round tray in the oven), or kebab. There will be certainly one or two salads, some pickles and sauces, then cheeses and fruits. Depending on the formality of the meal, there might be Arabic cakes (*baklawa, halwa* etc) or an elaborate European-style creamy dessert. Much esteemed, and usually eaten as an afternoon snack, is rice pudding, known as *riz ma haleeb* (rich with milk). It is eaten cold, quite solid, and flavoured with vanilla or orange flower essence. Coffee is always served at the end of a meal; Arabic coffee in tiny cups, un-sweetened, very strong, flavoured with cardamon. In traditional families servants pass around the basin, ewer, and towels, then eau de cologne, and sometimes incense in a brazier to restore agreeable odours that have nothing to do with food. In more modern households people simply make for the nearest bathroom, where a large bottle of eau de cologne will always be provided. Most Arabs use some form of scent.

Tea, whether Indian, Chinese, or mint (in North Africa especially), is normally drunk for breakfast in cups, and throughout the day in small handleless tulip-shaped glasses, as an alternative to Arabic coffee in china cups. It is always drunk very sweet, and tea without sugar is something of an aberration. Milk is not taken in tea, though some people drink it hot and sweet by itself, in the morning.

Fresh vegetables and fruit are important, and no meal is complete without salad. Arabs are not by tradition great meat-eaters, originally for economic reasons, and the commonest types of main dish are peppers or aubergines or tomatoes, baked with a stuffing of rice, minced meat, raisins and pine-nuts: or *yakhni*, a stew with a rich gravy, small pieces of meat, and okra, beans, or peas. On special occasions lambs or young goats might be roasted whole out of doors over a charcoal fire: these are known as *ouzi* or *mechoui*.

The Arabic equivalents of hors d'oeuvres are known as *mezzeh*, and consist of up to 40 small dishes placed on the table at the beginning of a meal, either in a house or restaurant. There will be all kinds of pickled vegetables, and *tabbuleh*, the famous Lebanese salad now eaten everywhere. This is a mixture of parsley, mint, green onions, burghul and tomatoes, dressed with oil, lemon juice, pepper and salt.

Camel herding in Tunisia.

Then there is *hummos*, a dip made of chick peas and *tahineh*, and *mtabbal*, a dip of roasted and pounded aubergines also mixed with *tahineh*. *Tahineh* is thick, creamy sesame oil with a very distinctive smoky flavour. Also included in a mezzeh are small pieces of meat, fish, liver and bone marrow; sometimes raw lamb's liver, which is recommended to those who like steak tartare. All these morsels usually have sharp or spicy sauces. Then there are slices of various smoked meats, cheese, fried bread, various kinds of nuts, and whole tomatoes, hard-boiled eggs, green peppers, lettuce and apples. It is customary for the host or hostess to cut up these whole items and distribute the pieces to the guests: in a restaurant the person who invites, or who wishes to establish his right of paying the bill, does so. He then has a legitimate claim to be the host.

Mezzeh may be served at lunch or dinner, as part of a leisurely meal which may go on for hours. *Arak* (grape spirit flavoured with aniseed, which turns white when water is added), or beer is usually drunk with *mezzeh;* indeed arak is never drunk without some *mezzeh* dishes to accompany it. The Arabs believe that no one should consume alcohol without eating at the same time. However, at everyday meals people drink water when they have finished eating, usually from an *ibriq*, a glass or pottery jug with a narrow spout from which the drinker swallows a stream of water without allowing his lips to touch the spout. Some can swallow the water without spilling a drop, from a distance of two feet; it is a trick that has to be learnt.

Turkey.

Tabbuleh, the salad described earlier, may also be served as a meal, usually in spring or early summer, when vegetables are at their freshest, and sitting out of doors is pleasant. People invite their friends for 'a tabbuleh', or say 'We're making tabbuleh on Wednesday; do you care to join us?' This takes place at tea time, between five and seven in the afternoon, and also served are plates of lettuce leaves, the lettuce being used to convey the tabbuleh to the mouth, as a kind of scoop, open sandwiches with cold meat and cheese, a sweet dish such as *mhalibieh* (much resembling very sugary junket), and fruit. Freshly made lemondade, beer, and sometimes tea, are appropriate drinks.

Particularly in Lebanon, where there is an abundance of fruit, people make their own syrups from fruit juice and sugar, which when diluted make excellent cold drinks. *Tut*, or mulberry, is the most frequently found because there are still many mulberry trees planted at the time when the breeding of silkworms was common in both Syria and Lebanon. Other syrups are lemon, orange, rose, pomegranate and quince. A guest arriving in summer is always offered a cold drink, or Arabic coffee with a glass of cold water.

Various jams and jellies are made, quince jelly being the most popular. Strawberries grow in Lebanon, Egypt, and part of North Africa: they are not indigenous and are regarded as a great luxury, as is their jam. Peaches are common and there are many varieties of citrus fruit; the usual oranges, lemons, grapefruit, tangerines (known commonly as *Yusuf Effendi*, or Mr Joseph), blood oranges, *moghrabeh* (sweet oranges), *uglis* (a cross between orange and grapefruit, bigger than either), sweet lemons, big naval oranges, and bitter Seville oranges for marmalade. Dates grow in Iraq, Saudi Arabia, and North Africa; the harvest is in September and October. Fresh dates are quite different from the preserved kind, and there are many varieties.

Large irregular shaped tomatoes are common everywhere; and most Arabs prepare their own tomato paste, boiling the fresh tomatoes slowly for hours out of doors over wood fires. They are gradually rendered down; the paste is then spread out to dry on wood or metal trays and finally bottled.

Nearly all the common European vegetables are known, though some undergo considerable change in the kitchen. Spinach is used as stuffing, with minced meat, pine-nuts, and onions, for tiny short-crust pasties pinched shut on one side and then fried (*fatayeh*). Pieces of cauliflower are often fried, and then eaten cold with a tahineh sauce. Okra and molokiyeh are two unfamiliar vegetables, both being slightly glutinous: molokiyeh look rather like nettles, green with serrated and pointed leaves, though they do not sting. Instead they serve as the base of a celebrated Egyptian dish, stewed in chicken or lamb stock, with the pieces of meat added, and rice, chopped raw onion, and garlic and coriander sauce served on the side.

Onions, cabbage, and cauliflower are all very popular, but considered to be bad for nursing mothers, because they give the baby indigestion. Cabbage is normally shredded raw for salad, or the whole leaves are used to wrap a mixture of rice and minced meat which is then steamed. This stuffed cabbage is a favourite winter dish, as is *cous-cous*, a semolina dish which is the national food in North Africa, and is known as *mograbieh* in Syria and Lebanon. The North African kind has much smaller grains and is prepared in a special steamer over a sauce of various vegetables (carrots, tomatoes, onions, turnips, leeks, peppers) and lamb, with a fiery chili sauce served alongside. The larger grains of *mograbieh* can be bought in Aleppo and Beirut; they are stewed in meat stock to which small button onions, a few whole chick peas, and lamb or chicken or sometimes both, are added.

The long leaved crisp cos lettuces are the usual variety found in the Arab countries, though other kinds do exist. Radishes are small, round, and red, or long and white, with a strong flavour. There are several salad plants such as rocca and bacli, almost unknown in Europe. Carrots can be black as well as orange. Turnips are mostly made into pickles.

Spices most used are thyme, rosemary, cumin, cardamon, cinnamon, nutmeg, and sumac. A common accompaniment to breakfast is powdered thyme moistened with olive oil into which bread is dipped. *Mana'ish* is also eaten at breakfast; it consists of a pizza-like dough on which a thyme, mint and oil mixture is spread, and the whole put into a baker's oven, then eaten hot. Rosemary flavours lamb, cumin any lentil or pulse dish and cardamon coffee. Cinnamon is powdered on top of rice, and nutmeg put into salads or sweet dishes. Sumac is sprinkled on fried eggs, as are pomegranate molasses (*dibis roumane*). Orange flower essence and rosewater are used to flavour cakes and desserts.

Iran.

Doing business in the Middle East

Once upon a time the Middle East was regarded as a vast, empty desert with little hope of development. The few oases and coastal settlements that dotted an otherwise arid region excited none but the most adventurous. Today we know better – or we think we do.

It is ironic that it was because of a war the Middle East became so prosperous. What followed the conflict of 1973 between the Arab world and Israel has had repercussions far beyond anything that might have been imagined.

When the Arab oil producers increased the price of their crude from an average of $2 to $6 a barrel (35 US gallons) in October that year they signalled, unwittingly, their entry into the 20th century.

Each year revenues from oil grew dramatically and national incomes were being calculated in billions of dollars rather than the millions previously.

And, like a fairly tale, the desert blossomed. Petrodollars, a word that came into existence in the mid-seventies, paid for development on a scale the world had never before seen. This was not reconstruction, as in Europe after the Second World War, but building where none had previously existed.

Tiny aerodromes have become international airports, towns have become cities, desert pistes have become six-lane highways. Wherever you looked something was being built – apartment or office blocks, industrial plants, airports, harbours, hotels, factories and, of course, more refineries. The whole of the Middle East was like a huge construction site.

In the West, meanwhile, with the ever-deepening recession – caused, in part, by rising oil prices – the once devoid Middle East was seen as salvation. The Arabs wanted to buy anything and everything, it seemed, and the West was only too willing to sell – at any price. And this was the West's first mistake.

To put it simply, the West saw the Arab as an immature child with plenty of pocket money which was burning a hole in his *dishdash;* the former helped quell the fire, but frequently swindled the latter in the process.

Admittedly, most companies with contracts in the Middle East traded with honesty and integrity but a few inflated their prices in the full knowledge that the customer would pay without too much argument. Because of these 'fast buck' merchants, most Westerners are now seen by the Arabs as vultures, and not to be trusted; to be used because they have the know-how but to be rid of as soon as a project is finished.

The Arab has learned this the expensive way, but he also learned it quickly. Today, an Arab can beat a Westerner at his own game. And this is rule number one – never underestimate an Arab. He has always been a trader; with the advent of oil riches the rules may have changed but the basics of the game are the same.

Petrodollars paid for development on a scale never before seen.

He may be late for an appointment, give the impression of not listening, may not take an immediate decision and will probably take his time in answering your letters – but be under no illusion. He is totally aware of everything that it going on around him. If you want his business you must do exactly the opposite of what he appears to be doing – or not doing.

Rule number two is an obvious one, but often ignored; observe the simple courtesies of the Middle East. A visitor is expected to be well dressed – irrespective of the outside temperature. In winter, a conservative suit should be worn. During the hot summer months, the jacket may be discarded, unless the meeting is with a government minister, but a tie should always be worn.

Handshaking is mandatory on arrival and departure. And the right hand should always be used for either giving or receiving. During a meeting, you will invariably be offered a drink, normally coffee, and this should be accepted, taken and returned with the right hand. It is customary to drink at least two cups of coffee and if no more is wanted, the returning cup should be shaken slightly, signifying your refusal.

And whenever in the company of a Moslem, you should never make the sole of your foot visible, as this is impolite.

The third rule concerns subjects of conversation to be avoided: domestic and Middle East politics, the Arab-Israeli conflict and international oil politics are all taboo. So too, are discussions regarding national economic relations with the COMECON countries if you happen to be in an Arab state which has ties with the Eastern bloc.

Business is part of the Arab tradition, whether it is the price of oil – or the price of pidgeons.

Rule number four involves respecting Ramadan, the Moslem month of fasting. During this period, Moslems are expected to refrain from eating and drinking from sunrise to sunset. And non-Moslems should not smoke, eat or drink in public places during daylight hours. In the more conservative Arab countries, daylight meals are normally served to a non-Moslem in his hotel room.

Generally speaking, Ramadan is a time to avoid a visit to the Middle East, as business tends to come to a virtual standstill. And many expatriate residents tend to take their annual leave at this time of year.

These are the general social ground rules, which apply to all the countries in the Middle East.

But how do you score at a business meeting?

First, the personal approach is vital. No local entrepreneur likes to discuss business with a commissioned representative or agent, especially if he is based in a neighbouring Arab country. They much prefer to deal direct with a representative sent by the company and capable of making on-the-spot decisions.

And the sales approach should be low-key – the hard sell technique simply does not work in the Middle East.

If a company is about to do business in the Middle East for the first time it is advisable to ask for an irrevocable letter of credit rather than a sight draft. It is also helpful to quote cost, insurance and freight (CIF) prices in the local currency instead of free on board (FOB)

In many Arab countries a local concern may be an importer, wholesaler and retailer. The same company may also have exclusive distribution rights for a variety of competing goods. This does not mean, however, that it will shelve one product in favour of another; all products will be marketed to the best of its ability.

In the more left-wing countries, a large number of products may only be imported by governmental agencies or state appointed companies. (In Libya, for example, no local company may act as an agent for a product which is imported by a government purchasing agency or public sector corporation.)

No matter how well prepared you are to do business in the Middle East, patience and understanding of the area's culture and way of life is required above all else. Occasionally, for example, you may turn up for a business meeting only to find that the person you have an appointment with is entertaining a group of friends or acquaintances in his office. This can be disconcerting, but is it a common practice in the Middle East. You must be adaptable, patient and persevere.

A salesman, who is successful in London, Paris or New York, may be out of his depth in Doha, Amman or Jeddah, if he tries to operate in the same ways as he would at home.

Having mastered the business etiquette of the Middle East, you may well wonder whether the market is still worthwhile commercially.

The whole pattern of trade with the region has changed and will continue to do so. If the tentative peace between Iran and Iraq holds, the international business community will be reaping the benefits of a massive reconstruction effort in the not too distant future. When stability is returned to Lebanon, as surely some day it must be, it is to the west, to American and European conglomerates, that the Lebanese will be looking for the technology to re-establish themselves in the vital world of business, finance and communications.

However, in the main, the big boom years are over. Most countries have almost completed their infrastructure and are now getting on with the day to day business of working and living. Business with the region has entered phase two of industrialisation; the service industries are now taking over from the big plant builders. With hospitals, schools and airports in place, the countries of the Middle East are looking towards the new technology and the acquisition of associated skills to operate them as efficiently and effectively as possible.

The Middle East is still a lucrative market, and will continue to be for some time. The past has seen numerous mistakes made, on both sides. But, as the west has learned more about the Middle East, so have the Arabs learned more about western ways. It would be encouraging to think this knowledge will not be wasted and that the many business relationships forged over the past couple of decades could pave the way for greater understanding between the two camps in the future.

Country
by
Country

BAHRAIN

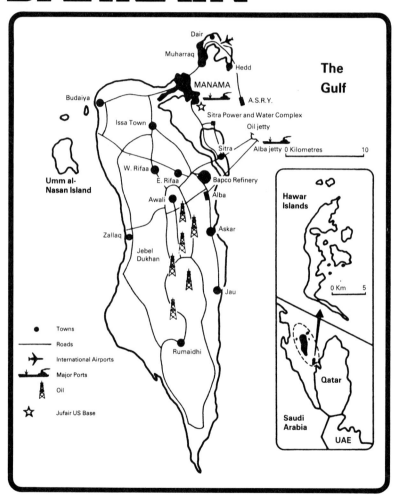

The Gulf

Dair
Muharraq
Hedd
MANAMA
A.S.R.Y.
Budaiya
Sitra Power and Water Complex
Issa Town
Oil jetty
Sitra
Alba jetty
0 Kilometres 10
W. Rifaa
Umm al-Nasan Island
E. Rifaa
Bapco Refinery
Awali
Alba
Zallaq
Askar
Jebel Dukhan
Jau
Rumaidhi

Hawar Islands
0 Km 5
Qatar
Saudi Arabia
UAE

● Towns
— Roads
✈ International Airports
⛴ Major Ports
🗼 Oil
☆ Jufair US Base

Area: 690.8 sq km
Population: 416,275
Capital: Manama

30

Identified as the legendary island of Dilmun mentioned in Babylonian and Sumerian records Bahrain was an important transit port as long ago as the third millenium BC, although its fate and fortune were always tied to the rise and fall of neighbouring dynasties. The island was invaded at the end of the eight century BC by the Assyrians and was later visited by the expeditions of Alexander. Islam came to Bahrain in AD628, and for the next three and a half centuries the country was ruled on behalf of the Caliphs. The Caramathians, Omanis, Portuguese and Persians all fought for control of Bahrain. However, political stability remained illusive until 1782 with the conquest and consolidation of the 35 small islands which now make up the state of Bahrain, by the Al Khalifa family. In the nineteenth century European powers began to show an interest in the Gulf region and in 1861, the first of a series of agreements between the two countries was signed. British interest in the country remained paramount until the Declaration of Independence, signed on 15 August 1971.

A modern state

The Al Khalifas are still the ruling family of Bahrain. The state is currently headed by the Amir, Shaikh Isa bin Salman Al Khalifa, who succeeded his father in 1961, and administered by a Cabinet, first formed in 1971, which includes several members of the Al Khalifa family. In an attempt to further regional co-operation and co-ordination in matters of defence, energy, industry, agriculture and transport, Bahrain joined with Saudi Arabia, Oman, Qatar, Kuwait and the UAE in the Gulf Co-operation Council in 1981. Defence was a major factor in Bahrain's decision to join the group. Although the country is considered to be a "modern" Arab state it has not been without its political concerns over the past decade. With a Shi'ite majority, the revolution in Iran gave rise to considerable concern in Bahrain. This concern gave way to anxiety when in September 1979 a group of Iranian Shi'ites called upon their brothers in Bahrain to demonstrate against the authority of the ruling (Sunni) Amir. And in late 1981 further trouble flared up with the arrest of about 50 people – the majority of whom were Bahrainis – on charges of supporting an Iranian-backed plot to overthrow the government. There were further serious fears of an attempted coup in 1984 and then again in 1985 when Bahrain's security forces actually uncovered a plot. However, since then the country's politics have remained without major incident.

A commercial centre

Oil was first discovered in Bahrain in 1932 and the island was the first of the Gulf oil producers to develop its petroleum industry. However, long before oil was discovered Bahrain's economy was a diverse and well developed one. Trading, pearling and agriculture brought properity to Bahrain from the earliest times. These days oil, along with Bahrain's proximity to international shipping routes and the overlap of its working day with those of some of the world's major money markets, ensures the island's future success as a regional industrial, trading and banking centre.

At the beginning of 1987 Bahrain's oil reserves were estimated at 140 million barrels which, at current rates of extraction, points to total depletion by the mid to late 1990s. Most of the island's crude output is currently gathered from the Abu Saafa field, which it shares with Saudi Arabia. Fortunately, although Bahrain's oil reserves are not expected to last into the next century, natural gas reserves – estimated at 209,000 million cubic metres – look set to extend well beyond the year 2000.

With its oil reserves diminishing Bahrain has had to confront the prospect of economic diversifications as efficiently as possible. Several large-scale industrial projects have already been brought on stream, some of which have been funded in co-operation with Arab states through organisations such as the Gulf Organisation for Industrial Co-operation. There are already a number of large scale industries in operation in Bahrain, among them the Arab Shipbuilding and Repair Yard (ASRY), which was financed by the Organisation of Arab Petroleum Exporting Countries (OAPEC), the aluminium smelter Aluminium Bahrain (ALBA), in which the government has a majority shareholding, and the Gulf Aluminium Rolling Company (GARMCO), established in 1986 in co-operation with GOIC. Smaller operations, such as the projects to revitalise the country's once prosperous

Traditional boat building

fishing and pearling industries, have been launched by the government.

Bahrain's importance as a banking and financial centre rose fairly dramatically during the 1970s, attracted by surplus oil revenues, excellent communication systems, liberal banking regulations and freedom from taxation. OBUs (offshore banking units) expanded rapidly. In 1983 the combined assets of Bahrain-based OBUs were recorded at $62.7 billion. However, in common with other world banking centres Bahrain began to feel the pinch of a depressed world economy in the 1980s. This, together with the growth of domestic banking elsewhere in the Gulf and increased protectionism in neighbouring Saudi Arabia, drastically reduced lending opportunities. A number of OBUs were forced to close down their operations on the island, although there are currently some 68 in operation which, between them, held assets totalling $58 billion at the end of last year. For the future, the government is committed to developing the Bahrain stock market. Legislation is being drawn up to cover the organisation of a new exchange expected to deal in bonds, bills and securities as well as commodities, futures and precious metals.

Popular destination

After a decade of plenty in the 1970s all the oil rich states of the Gulf have had some belt tightening to do during the last few years. Bahrain, although the smallest independent state in the six country Gulf Co-operation Council, started in a better position than most of its neighbours. It began developing its oil before they did and also enjoyed an historic reputation as a trading centre. Its reputation as a "modern" Arab state encouraged businessmen from all parts of the globe to use it as a Gulf base. However, as the world economy settled into the doldrums Bahrain's income from travel and tourism began to show a corresponding decline. The immediate result of the depressed oil market was that less petro-dollars were flowing into the region. As a result, fewer businessmen travelled to the region from abroad to advise on how, where and why the once seemingly endless supply of oil earnings should be spent. Increasing numbers of Bahrain's luxury hotel rooms remained empty. Beaches, bars and restaurants were noticeably less crowded as the expatriate population dwindled and international companies, having completed their contracts, left the island to be replaced in many cases by local firms, in a bid to reduce dependency on a foreign workforce. The prospect of Bahrain's travel and tourism sector was beginning to look distinctly unhealthy until, just in time, the opening of the causeway linking the island with Saudi Arabia turned the entire picture on its head.

The plan to link Bahrain and Saudi Arabia was not a new one. Indeed it had been discussed on many occasions by numerous important officials from both countries. But its timely opening in November 1986 has resulted in an immediate upturn in Bahrain's receipts from trading and tourism. The ambitious 25 kilometer causeway project was wholly funded by Saudi Arabia at a cost of $1.2 million. A major civil engineering feat, the landlink runs from Jasrah in Bahrain to Al Aziziyah in Saudi Arabia and consists of eleven kilometres of embankment supported by 12.5 kilometres of bridging. The idea of a fixed link between Bahrain and Saudi Arabia was first aired in 1953 but it was not until 1980 that the contract on the work was awarded to the Netherlands company Ballast Nedam. Sub-contractors on the scheme included eight Saudi and six Bahraini companies.

The causeway, which is the second longest landlink in the world, enables drivers to drive between Bahrain and Saudi Arabia in 15 minutes, although a further 30 minutes should be added to travelling times because of border formalities.

About 85,000 of Bahrain's population of 420,000 are Bahraini nationals, a high proportion for the Gulf. The remainder are chiefly Palestinians or nationals of North Yemen, Iran, India, Pakistan or other Gulf states. The original inhabitants of the island are thought to be descendents of Arabs taken into Iraq by Nebuchadnezzar, who later fled to the island. The Sunnis, who make up about 40% of the Moslem population in Bahrain, arrived in the country in the 18th century with the ruling Al Khalifa family; the Shia are the original inhabitants and a number of the descendants of African slaves also form part of the indigenous population.

Bahrain is the most liberal of the six Gulf nations. Alcohol is freely available and the top hotels offer a wide range of sophisticated entertainment, including internationally popular entertainers and nightclub acts. Although most western expatriates prefer to base themselves in the liberal atmosphere of Bahrain, the country's hotel industry is actually kept buoyant by visiting Gulf Arabs. Since the opening of the Saudi causeway in November 1986, when traffic into Bahrain reached an all time high, chiefly Saudi Arabians in search of a little western-style nightlife, things have settled down to a reduced but constant and still healthy level.

General Information

Government

The head of State is the Amir or ruler, Sheikh Isa bin Sulman al Khalifa. He governs the country with a Cabinet of appointed ministers.

Language

Arabic is the official language of the country, English is widely spoken and understood in the larger towns.

Religion

Bahrain is a Moslem state. The ruling family is Sunni but the majority of the country's Moslems are Shi'ite (about 60%). There are also Christian, Hindu and other minorities who have their own places of worship.

How to get there

By air: The national carrier of Bahrain is Gulf Air – jointly owned by Oman, Abu Dhabi, Qatar and Bahrain, although a large number of international carriers operate to Bahrain.

By road: The opening of the causeway which links Bahrain with Saudi Arabia has meant Bahrain now has road access to all neighbouring Gulf Co-operation Council states via the Kingdom.

Entry Regulations

Citizens of the UK, Saudi Arabia, Kuwait, Qatar, Oman and the UAE require only valid passports to enter Bahrain. Other nationals must obtain business or tourist visas from their nearest Bahraini embassy. Transit visas for 72 hours are available at the Bahrain Airport Immigration Office. Vaccination against yellow fever is required from visitors travelling from infected areas.

Customs regulations

There are no currency restrictions. A duty free allowance of 400 cigarettes, 50 cigars, half a pound of tobacco and eight ounces of perfume is permitted, plus, for non-Moslems, two bottles of spirits. Personal effects and trade samples are also duty free. It is forbidden to import pearls from outside the Gulf region, arms and ammunition and blacklisted goods on the Arab League boycott list.

Climate

October, November, April and May are pleasant months to visit Bahrain. In the height of summer the climate is hot, humid and uncomfortable. The most uncomfortable months are July to September, when the temperatures can reach 44C from December.

What to wear: Medium light weight clothing is adequate from the end of November to the end of March; a sweater may be needed in the evening. Light weight clothing is necessary for the remainder of the year. Bahrain is more liberal in its attitude to women than most other Gulf states. Sports clothes may be worn in the streets, and short dresses are acceptable. But in summer, protection from, rather than exposure to the sun is, as in most Gulf countries, advisable.

Currency

Bahraini Dinar (BD) BD1 = 1,000 fils.

Business hours

Friday is the weekly holiday when all businesses are closed, although some are open during the morning. The Bahrain Petroleum Co and Aluminium Bahrain are closed on Thursdays and Fridays.
Government: Saturday-Wednesday 0700-1300.
Banks: Saturday-Wednesday 0730-1200; Thursday 0730-1100.
Offices: Saturday-Thursday 0800-1230 and 1530-1830.
Shops: Saturday-Thursday 0830-1300 and 1600-1830.
Bazaars: Saturday-Thursday 0800-1230 and 1530-1830.

Press

In addition to the local Arabic press, Gulf Daily News, POB 5300, Manama, is published daily in English.

Public holidays

New Year's Day, 1 January
First day of Ramadan*, 7 April
Eid al-Fitr*, 7-9 May
Eid al-Adha*, 14-17 July
Hijra*, 4 August
Al-Ashoura*, 13 August
Prophet's Birthday*, 13 October
National Day, 16 December.
The dates of the Muslim holidays, marked with an asterisk, are only approximate as they depend on sightings of the moon.

Transport

By road: Private car, taxi, service taxi, and bus network covering all the islands. Taxis have orange sidewings and black-on-yellow number plates. After midnight all fares are subject to a 50% increase. Taxi fares outside Manama should be agreed upon with the driver before beginning a journey.
Car hire: International Driving Licences are accepted. There are two grades of petrol. Traffic keeps to the right.

Accommodation and food

Hotel accommodation is readily available in Bahrain.

Most of the hotels listed have their own restaurant, but there is also a good selection of restaurants serving all kinds of food including: Arab, European, Indian, Chinese, Russian and American.
Tipping: If a service charge is not included in a hotel or restaurant bill a tip of 10% should be given.

Consulates/Embassies in Manama

Australia: Chamber of Commerce Building, King Faisal Street, Manama. Tel. 255011.
China (trade mission): POB 5806, Sulmaniya Rd, Manama. Tel. 713070.
Denmark: POB 45, Kanoo Tower, Al Khalifa Rd, Manama. Tel. 230363.
France: POB 26134, King Faisal Rd, Diplomatic Area, Manama. Tel. 291734. Telex 9281.
India: POB 26106, Blgd 182, Rd 2608, Qudhaibiya, Manama. Tel. 712785. Telex 9047.
Iran: Sheikh Isa Rd 2709, Manama. Tel. 712151.
Iraq: House 261, Rd 2807, Block 328 Sughaya, Manama. Tel. 250399.
Japan: POB 23720, House 403, Rd 915, Salmaniya, Manama. Tel. 243364.
Jordan: POB 5242, House 1549, Rd 2733, Manama. Tel. 714391.
Korea: POB 5564, King Faisal Rd, Manama. Tel. 291629.
Kuwait: POB 786, Diplomatic Area, 76 Rd 1703, Manama. Tel. 242330. Telex 8830.
Lebanon: POB 752, Al Khaleej Bldg, Government Rd, Manama. Tel. 232120.
Netherlands: POB 350, Sheikh Isa Rd, Manama. Tel. 252986.
New Zealand: POB 5881, Manama Centre, Government Rd, Manama. Tel. 271600. Telex 8748.
Oman: POB 26414, Adiliya, Kuwait Rd,

Manama. Tel. 232606. Telex 9332.
Pakistan: POB 563, House 75, Rd 3403. Mahooz, Manama. Tel. 712470.
Saudi Arabia: POB 1085, Bani Otbah Rd, Qudhaibiya, Manama. Tel. 713406.
Tunisia: Al Mahouz, Manama. Tel. 721431.
United Kingdom: POB 114, 21 Government Rd, Manama. Tel. 254002. Telex 8213.
USA: POB 26431, Off Sheikh Isa Rd, Manama. Tel. 714151. Telex 9398.

Manama

The capital city is at the north end of the island. It has the government buildings, banks, chief hotels, and the *souq* or covered market.

Much land has been reclaimed from the sea in the environs of the capital, and work is continuing. Manama has been a town since the 15th century, when contemporary Portuguese writers mention it, but the ancient capital of Bahrain, Bilad al Qadim, is just outside the modern city. It dates from 900 AD and is now mostly in ruins; the site is of archaeological interest.

The Ruler is responsible for a large residential development called Isa Town, 8km from Manama, which provides housing for some 20,000 Bahrainis. The centre is forbidden to car traffic, and is decorated with fountains and climbing plants. There are two elegant mosques with tall minarets and blue domes; also a sports stadium, swimming pool, cinema, library, children's playground and clinic.
Entertainments: There are several cinemas in Manama showing Arabic and English films. The better nightclubs and lounge bars are located in Manama's principal hotels.
Sports: Many sports are available in Manama including sailing (through the Manama Sailing Club). fishing, riding, horse racing, swimming and tennis.
Shopping: There is a wide range of shops in Manama with all kinds of imported goods but few local products except for pearls. There are some small shops specialising in curios and antiques from the Gulf.

Other towns

The village of **A'ali** is just south of the date gardens, on the edge of the ancient Dilmun tumuli. It is famous for its pottery, and the kilns can be seen smoking from far away; some are actually inside the burial mounds. Red clay is shaped into traditional pots, bowls, water-jars and dishes.

The oil company town, **Awali,** justifies the somewhat unkind nick-name of 'Surbiton-in-the-sand'. It could be any English or American suburb, set in a hot climate. It was built by the Bahrain Petroleum Company (BAPCO) to provide housing, shops, and separate leisure facilities for its expatriate staff.

The Ruler's country residence is by the sea and fronts what is known as the Sheikh's Beach, a pleasant spot for tourists, with sandy beaches, a tea and soft drinks shop and separate swimming pool. Near the Palace at **Rifaa** is the Saafra racecourse where horse and camel races take place on Fridays. A new racecourse was completed in early 1979 and opened by the visiting British Queen.

Zellaq on the west coast has several beaches and a sailing club; some Bahrainis have villas here. The southern part of the island contains the oil and gas deposits, and is otherwise barren, with rocks and sand dunes. It is now used as a hunting and hawking area; the industry that the Ruler is encouraging will creep slowly into the area as the oil recedes. The highest part of the island, **Jebel Dukhan,** 122m, is in the middle of the oil fields; the entire island can be seen from its summit.

The other islands of the archipelago include **Halat al Suluta** and **Halat al Khulaifat,** which are off Muhaaraq and have some fine old Bahraini merchants' houses. **Nabih Salih** is much favoured by swimmers and water skiers. It is just south of Jufair and is covered with date palms. **Sitra** contains the power stations and desalination plant, as well as the oil terminal.

Only 50 years ago Sitra was completely isolated from Bahrain by the sea. When oil was discovered in 1932, a deep water harbour and anchorage for sea-going tankers was required. Because of the potential dangers of shallow waters and coral reefs around the Bahrain islands, the choice of a suitable site was restricted. Eventually Sitra was selected as the most appropriate site for the new industrial area.

Hotels

NAME	ADDRESS	TELEPHONE	TELEX
MANAMA			
Aradous	PO Box 5878	41011	8900
Al Jazira Hotel	PO Box 5898	258810	8999
Bahrain Hilton	PO Box 1090	250000	8288
Bristol Hotel	PO Box 832	258989	8504
Delmon Hotel	PO Box 26	234000	8224
Diplomat Hotel	PO Box 5243	531666	
Grundy Hotel	PO Box 5324	59979	8970
Gulf Hotel	PO Box 580	233000	8241
Holiday Inn	PO Box 5831	531122	9000
Le Vendome	PO Box 5368	257777	8888
Middle East Hotel	PO Box 838	54733	8296
Moon Plaza Hotel	PO Box 247	728263	8308
Omar Khayyam	PO Box 771	713941	8401
Ramada	PO Box 5750	714921	8855
Regency Inter-Continental	PO Box 777	231777	9400
Sheraton	PO Box 30	233233	9440

CYPRUS

Mediterranean Sea

Rikarpaso
Yialousa
Kyrenia
Nicosia
Xeros Lefka
Famagusta
Polis
Pedhoulas Ayia Napa
Troodos
Platres Larnaca
Paphos
Kouklia
Limassol

0 Kilometres 40

- Towns
— Roads
✈ International Airports
⚓ Major Ports

De-facto
partition line

Akrotiri (British Sovereign Base Areas)
Dhekelia (BSBA)

Area: 9,251 sq km
Population: 673,100 (1987 provisional estimate)
Capital: Nicosia

Cyprus has sun, sea, snow and rich unspoiled scenery for all to enjoy, together with 8,000 years of archaeology, history, art, theatre and unique festivals. The visitor can swim, sail, horse-ride and explore the numerous fishing villages and historical relics of Greek, Roman and Egyptian civilisations.

Although the country is still in a state of truce, supervised by United Nations' forces, tourist arrivals have continued their upward trend. Most of the island's hotels were formerly in the northern and north eastern section of the island. This has led to an enormous demand for tourist accommodation elsewhere. The building boom is on again in the Greek sector, many new hotels have been built in the resort areas and more are under construction.

There is no freedom of movement between the two sections of the island and although tourism is promoted in the Turkish-occupied sector, it has only resulted in local travel from Turkey itself.

Beaches and mountain scenery

The third largest island in the Mediterranean, Cyprus has an area of 9,251 sq km. Its maximum length is 240 km east to west, and greatest north-south width is 96 km. The nearest country is Turkey, a mere 64 km away, and Cyprus is only 100 km from the coast of Syria. The Greek mainland is some 800 km to the west, although Rhodes is only 380 km away.

The coastline is rocky and indented, with numerous sandy coves and beaches. The north coast is backed by a steep range of limestone hills rising to 1,000 m, but the highest ground is in the mountain massif of Troodos, covered with pine, cypress and cedar trees, reaching nearly 2,000 m at Mount Olympus. Between the two hill and mountain ranges are the fertile Messaoria plain in the east and the more fertile Morphou basin to the west.

Nearly 18% of the land is covered with forest. Another 50% is arable, and used for wheat, barley, potatoes, vegetables and the ubiquitous olive tree. There are vineyards on the southern and western slopes of the Troodos mountains, and the valleys support fruit.

The history of Cyprus, as a vulnerable prize for successive conquerors of the eastern Mediterranean, has left its people tragically divided. The Ottoman Turks who occupied the island in the 16th century came in large numbers, and today their descendants comprise one-fifth of the population, divided by religion, class and social customs from the Greek Cypriot majority.

Early history

According to the evidence of neolithic monuments that still stand near Larnaca, Cyprus has a pre-history dating back to 6000 BC. By 2000 BC the Achaean Greeks had established city-kingdoms on the Mycenaean model and introduced the Greek language and way of life.

Cyprus (the Greek word for copper) has long been known for its copper and its forests, and was constantly fought for by the Assyrians, Egyptians and Persians.

Alexander the Great removed the Persians, but the division of his empire after his death meant that Cyprus came under the rule of the Greek Ptolemies who had become rulers of Egypt, and then under the Romans from 58 BC to 330 AD, when it became an important part of the Byzantine empire.

In the Middle Ages Cyprus was conquered by Richard I of England, it then passed to the Knights Templar. The Lusignans from France established a feudal kingdom from 1192 to 1489. The Republic of Venice was in control between 1489 and 1571, when the Turks conquered the island and settled much of it.

Turkish control lasted until 1878 when the island was ceded to Britain by the Treaty of Berlin. British rule lasted until 1960.

Recent history

A Greek Cypriot campaign for *Enosis,* or union with Greece, gathered momentum in the late 1950's although an international agreement, guaranteed by Greece, Turkey and Britain, gave Cyprus an independence constitution that temporarily shelved the basic inter-communal problems.

Under the presidency of Archbishop Makarios, Cyprus managed to avoid full-scale civil war, but in 1963 Turkish Cypriots rebelled and were forced to evacuate mixed villages, and in 1967 there was an even greater separation of the two communities.

In Greece itself the military junta were getting impatient with Makarios's reluctance to bring about *Enosis,* and in July 1974 they staged a coup to overthrow the Archbishop. This caused bitter fighting between Greeks and provoked a Turkish military invasion in the same week. Moreover the Greek junta in Athens failed to fight the Turks and itself collapsed.

The Turkish forces moved in massively and eventually occupied 40% of Cyprus. The reluctance of the Turkish community to negotiate realistically for another power-sharing formula is based on the bitter experiences of the 1960s, when their position and influence (favoured under British rule) had been steadily eroded.

The Turkish invasion displaced an enormous number of Greek Cypriots – over 200,000 according to the United Nations. There are also problems for the Turks still in the south and for Greeks unable to leave the north. Significant numbers of Greeks have left for Greece, or other countries, and in the north there has been an influx of mainland Turks. Attempts at reconciliation have all failed, and in December 1983 the Turkish half of Cyprus declared itself independent. Since then peace proposals have achieved little success despite efforts by the UN to help find an acceptable settlement.

Economy

The 1974 war left the Cypriot economy in ruins. Agriculture, industry, trade, tourism and communications were all badly hit. Agriculture has long been the single most important economic activity in Cyprus but the division of the country to the north and south of the 'Attila line' had devastating effects on the sector. The Turkish Cypriot north inherited about 80% of the island's citrus groves, all the tobacco fields, 40% of the carobs, 80% of carrots and about 15% of potatoes. The Greek Cypriot government launched a series of emergency development plans covering agriculture and irrigation schemes. Substantial loans were given to farmers and agriculture in the Greek sector began to respond favourably.

The construction sector enjoyed a boom after the 1974 division, particularly in house building, which was necessary to fulfil the needs of the refugee population. The massive blow to tourism was one of the major economic set backs the Greek Cypriot government had to face after the Turkish invasion, since some 90% of the island's hotels were situated north of the 'Attila line' and came under Turkish Cypriot control. The best hotels still exist in the Turkish Cypriot sector but most remain unused. However, tourist receipts continue to increase in the Greek Cypriot sector.

The inter-factional fighting which continues in Beirut has boosted the economy of Cyprus in a number of ways. Many of the businessmen and entrepreneurs forced out of Lebanon by the escalating violence chose to relocate in Cyprus, as did a number of newspapers, press agencies and journalists. The entire ambience of the major towns has changed over the past few years to become increasingly more sophisticated and cosmopolitan. Port development schemes are underway at Larnaca and Limassol, and a new port is planned for Paphos, in order that Cyprus can efficiently manage a larger portion of the freight trade previously handled by Beirut.

Ultimately, the economic future of Cyprus will depend on the island being able to solve its political problems. The round of meetings between Greek Prime Minister Andreas Papandraou and his Turkish counterpart Turgut Ozal in 1988, is generally considered to be a hopeful sign by Cyprus watchers but it is noteworthy that as negotiations continue, two seperate blueprints for development are under consideration, north and south of the Attila line.

General Information

Government

The President is a Greek Cypriot elected every five years. The constitution allows for a Turkish Vice-President and minority Turkish participation in the House of Representatives, but this arrangement has not functioned since 1964. A separate government has been set up in the Turkish occupied area, but it has not been recognised – except in Turkey.

Languages

Greek, Turkish, English and Arabic. Virtually all Cypriots speak some English.

Religion

Greek Orthodox (78%) and Moslem (18%).

How to get there

By air: Cyprus Airways is the national carrier on the island republic.
By sea: The main ports in the Government-administered region are Larnaca and Limassol. A car-ferry service operates from Athens and Rhodes.

Famagusta is in the Turkish-occupied zone.

Entry regulations

Passports are required by all visitors, but visas are not needed by citizens of Austria, Belgium, Britain and Commonwealth countries, Denmark, Finland, France, West Germany, Greece, Iceland, Ireland, Italy, Japan, Luxembourg, Netherlands, Norway, Spain, Sweden, Switzerland, USA and Yugoslavia. Other citizens should apply for visas at Cypriot diplomatic missions abroad.

Custom regulations

The import and export of Cyprus currency is forbidden beyond the value of £C10. Traveller's cheques and foreign currency may be cashed at any bank.

Import allowances are 200 cigarettes or 250 grams tobacco; 0.75 litres of wine and half-litre spirits; lotion and perfume up to 1 litre.

Climate

The sun shines 340 days a year in Cyprus. Temperatures can vary between 60°F in January and 92°F in July. The climate is healthy with long, dry summers; hotter on the coast and bracing in the mountains.

Winter is mild, and the sea is usually warm enough for swimming at any time of year. Snow falls in the mountains between December and March.
What to wear: light-weight clothing is suitable for most of the year, warmer clothing may be needed for the winter evenings.

Currency

Cyprus Pound (£C) divided into 1,000 mils.

Business Hours

Banks: Monday-Saturday 0830-1200
Offices: *Winter* Monday-Friday 0830-1300 and 1430-1730; Saturday 0830-1300. *Summer* Monday-Friday 0830-1300 and 1600-1830; Saturday 0800-1300. Most shops close on a Saturday afternoon.

Press

The Cyprus Mail, P.O. Box 1144, 24 Vassilious Voulgaroktonos St., Nicosia, is published in English daily.

Public holidays

New Year's Day, 1 January
Epiphany Day, 6 January
Greek Independence Day, 25 March
Labour Day, 1 May
Greek *Oxi* Day, 28 October
Christmas Day, 25 December
Boxing Day, 26 December
The dates of the following holidays are changeable.
Good Friday (Greek Orthodox)
Saturday following Good Friday (Greek Orthodox)
Easter Monday (Greek Orthodox)

Transport

Buses connect all the towns and villages of the government-controlled area. Efficient taxi services also connect the main towns.

There are car hire services, including Avis, Budget and Hertz; information available from Tourist Information Offices. Driving is on the left side of the road. Roads in Cyprus are either paved, earth or gravel. There are no railways in Cyprus.

Accommodation and food

Cyprus' 1,000 km of coastline are studded with attractive beaches and resort hotels. Many of the hotels are new and range from large de-luxe to modest small hotels. The hill resorts, too, have a similar but lesser variety.

The main accommodation centres are Nicosia, Limassol, Larnaca, Paphos and the hill resorts. The inclusive hotel rates are very reasonable by modern standards. Several tour operators offer holiday flats and villas. There are guest houses in the main centres.

Most of the better hotels have good dining facilities where you can taste local specialities or eat continental fare. The local tavernas are fun to visit. Try them for freshly caught, simply broiled, fish, goat cheese, doughnuts and stuffed vine leaves; don't miss trying a glyko – a mixture of lemons, oranges and whole green walnuts in a sugary syrup.

Tourist information

Cyprus Tourism Organisation: 18 Th. Theodotou Street, Tel: (021) 43374, Telex: 2165, P.O. Box 4535, Nicosia, or **Tourist Information Bureaux in Cyprus**
Nicosia: Laiki Yitonia, Tel: (021) 44264
Limassol: 15 Spyrou Araouzou St, Tel: (051) 62756
Larnaca: Democratias Square, Tel: (041) 54322; Larnaca International Airport, Tel: (041) 54389
Paphos: 3 Gladstone St, Tel: (061) 32841; Paphos Airport, Tel: (061) 36833
Ayia Napa: Tel: (037) 21796
Platres: Tel: (054) 21316.

Embassies and High Commissions in Cyprus

Australia: 4 Annis Komninis St, 2nd Floor, Nicosia. Tel: (02) 473001. Telex: 2097.
Bulgaria: 15 St Paul St, Nicosia. Tel: (02) 472486. Telex: 2188.
China, People's Republic: 27 Clementos St, POB 4531, Nicosia. Tel: (02) 473041.
Cuba: 39 Regas Phereos St, Acropolis, Nicosia. Tel: (02) 427211. Telex: 2306.
Czechoslovakia: POB 1165, 7 Kastorias St, Nicosia. Tel: (02) 311683. Telex: 2490.
Egypt: 3 Egypt Ave, POB 1752, Nicosia. Tel: (02) 465144.
France: 6 Ploutarchou St, Engomi, POB 1671, Nicosia. Tel: (02) 465258. Telex: 2389.
German Democratic Republic: 115 Prodromos St, Nicosia. Tel: (02) 444193. Telex 2291.

Germany, Federal Republic: 10 Nikitaras St, POB 1795, Nicosia. Tel: (02) 444362. Telex: 2460.

Greece: 8/10 Byron Ave, POB 1799, Nicosia. Tel: (02) 441880. Telex: 2286.

Holy See: POB 1964, Paphos Gate, Paphos St, Nicosia. Tel: (02) 462132.

Hungary: 6 Vas. Tefkrou St, Ayios Dhometios, Nicosia.

India: 4th Floor, Anemomylos Bldg, POB 5544, 8 Michael Karaolis St, Nicosia. Tel: (02) 461741. Telex: 4146.

Israel: 4th Floor, 44 Archbishop Makarios III Ave, POB 1049, Nicosia. Tel: (02) 445195. Telex: 2238.

Italy: Margarita House, 15 Themistoclis Dervis St, POB 1452, Nicosia. Tel: (02) 473183. Telex: 3847.

Lebanon: 1 Vasilissis Olga St, POB 1924, Nicosia. Tel: (02) 442216. Telex: 3056.

Libya: 9A Kypranoros St, POB 3669, Nicosia. Tel: (02) 49363.

Romania: 37 Tombazis St, Nicosia. Tel: (02) 445845. Telex: 2431.

Syria: Corner Androcleous and Thoukidides Sts, POB 1891, Nicosia. Tel: (02) 474481. Telex: 2030.

USSR: 4 Gladstone St, POB 1845, Nicosia. Tel: (02) 472141.

United Kingdom: Alexander Pallis St, POB 1978, Nicosia. Tel: (02) 473131. Telex: 2208.

USA: Dositheon St, and Therissos St, Lykavitos, Nicosia. Tel: (02) 465151. Telex: 4160.

Yemen, People's Democratic Republic: Nicosia.

Yugoslavia: 2 Vasilissis Olga St, Nicosia. Tel: (02) 445511.

Nicosia

Capital of Cyprus since the 12th century AD, when the coastal cities were being heavily raided, Nicosia is the only inland town on the island. Its palaces, residences and cathedral of St. Sophia date from the medieval rule of the Frankish Lusignan kings. Worth seeing are: Cyprus Museum, Folk Art Museum, the Venetian walls, the Archiepiscopal Palace and the Cathedral of St John.

Modern Nicosia has modern shops, hotels, cinemas, theatres and night clubs, and is well placed for visiting more of the island's regions. There is also an international conference centre.

Tourist Information: Cyprus Tourism Organisation, 5 Princess de Tyras St, tel: 44264.

Larnaca

A few minutes from the international airport and only half an hour's drive from Nicosia, Larnaca is a pleasant seaside town, of great historical interest. It is on the site of the Mycenean city of Kition, which was the home of Zeno, founder of the Stoic school of philosophy in Athens.

One of the most interesting monuments is the Church of St. Lazarus. Also worth seeing are the Phaneromeni megalithic monument, the ancient castle, the Pierides Museum and the Tekke of Umm Haram (foster mother of the Prophet Muhammad).

In the region of Larnaca is the Khirokitia neolithic site dating back 8,000 years, Stavrovouni Monastery and the interesting villages of Lefkara and Pyrga. Of scenic interest is the Salt Lake near Larnaca, with its flamingoes and surrounding woods.

There is a public beach, 7 km east of Larnaca. Among the facilities offered are changing rooms and showers, modern restaurant and bar, parking and water sports.

Tourist Information: Cyprus Tourism Organisation, Democratias Sq, tel: 54322.

Larnaca International Airport, tel: 54389.

Ayia Napa

Ayia Napa is only accessible from Larnaca, although Turkish-occupied Famagusta is the nearest town. It is a picturesque, unspoilt fishing village with sea caves, windmills, fine sandy beaches and clear water. The village with its attractive harbour and 16th century monastery is also a choice spot for walks in delightful scenery.

Limassol

A festive and busy town with a history going back to the ancient kingdoms of Curium and Amathus, and to the Crusade. Richard Coeur de Lion married Berengaria of Navarre here and the Knights of St. John of Jerusalem established their headquarters here in 1291.

There is much to see and do in Limassol. You can visit the historic Episkopi Museum, explore Kolossi Castle, the gardens and the zoo. There are Roman floors and mosaics at Curium. A tour of Keo's, the wine producer, can be arranged. The September wine festival is held here annually.

15 km inland from Limassol is Lefkara, the home of producers of unique and unusually beautiful handmade lace.

Tourist Information: Cyprus Tourism Organisation, 15 Spyrou Araouzou St, tel: 62756.

Hill resorts

The main hill resorts are Platres, Prodromos, Troodos, Pedhoulas, Kakopetria, Kalopanayiotis, Moutoullas (with medicinal springs), Perapedhi, Omodos, Galata and Agros.

With snow from December to March, there is a popular winter season with skiing on the heights of Mount Olympus, legendary home of the Gods.

The area is endowed with interesting monuments and churches. Among the monasteries is the Trooditissa monastery. The main appeal is the natural beauty of the well-forested mountains. Visitors can ride horseback through the pines, hike along mountain trails. Cedar Valley and the look-out point are spectacular.

Paphos

Paphos is a pleasant seaside resort with a combination of beautiful landscapes and historic interest. The archaeological sites include those of the ancient Greeks, the

The legendary birthplace of Aphrodite, Goddess of Love.

Romans, the Byzantines and the medieval period.

The town itself (formerly known as Ktima) is colourful and attractively set on a rocky cliff overlooking the sea and the harbour of New Paphos. Seafood is served fresh in harbourside restaurants. An annual wine festival is held in September.

In the town are: the fourth century St. Paul's Basilica, brilliant Roman mosaic floors in the houses of Dionysus and Thesus are worth viewing. Also the fourth century St. Paul's Basilica and the Byzantine Castle of 40 pillars. Other ancient sights include the Curmin Temple of Apollo, with theatre and baths; the Kolossi Castle, once a Medieval strong-hold, now a shell with magnificent views.

Carved out of cliffs are the 'Tombs of the Kings'. Some contain impressive Doric pillars. At a distance of 15 km east is Old Paphos (known as Koukalia) with the remains of the Temple of Aphrodite, a centre of pilgrimage in the ancient world. Further in the same direction is the legendary birthplace of Aphrodite.

St. Neophytos monastery with Byzantine frescoes and icons is 11 km north of modern Paphos. Further inland, through Paphos forest, are the two ancient monasteries of Chryorroyiattiss and Ayia Moni. Also worth visiting are the Cedar Valley and the Spring of Love, near Polis, as well as the monastery of Kykko and the spectacularly-sited tomb of Archbishop Makarios.

A new archaeological monument, the house of Folk Architecture at Yeroskipou, has been opened to the public. This shelters an important collection of folk art from the Paphos district.

Hotels

NAME	ADDRESS	TELEPHONE	TELEX
NICOSIA			
Cyprus Hilton	Archbishop Makarios Ave	(02) 464040	2388
Ledra	Grivas Dhigenis Ave	(02) 441086	3355
Cleopatra	8 Florina St	(02) 445254	2316
Kennedy	70 Regaena St	(02) 475131	2202
Nicosia Palace	4 C. Pantelides Ave	(02) 463718	–
Alexandria	17 Trikoupi St	(02) 462160	–
Carlton	13 Princess de Tyras St	(02) 442001	–
LIMASSOL			
Amathus Beach	PO Box 513, Amathus	(051) 21152	2683
Churchill Limassol	28th October Ave	(051) 24444	3447

[Hotels]

Curium Palace	Byron St	(051) 63121	3150
Adonia Beach	PO Box 4434, Amathus	(051) 21111	4230
Golden Arches	PO Box 4104, Amathus	(051) 22433	4142
Eastland	23 A. Dhroushioti St	(051) 77000	3415
Limassol Palace	99 Spyros Araouzos Ave	(051) 52131	–

LARNACA

Golden Bay	Larnaca-Dhekelia Rd	(041) 23444	4570
Flamingo Beach	Piale Pasha St	(041) 21621	3777
Four Lanterns	19 Athens Ave	(041) 52011	2491
Baronet	Makarios Ave	(041) 57111	3913
Cactus	8 Shakespeare St	(041) 27400	5391

AYIA NAPA

Grecian Bay	PO Box 6, Famagusta	(037) 21301	2980
Dome	PO Box 198, Famagusta	(037) 21006	3212
Florida	PO Box 105, Famagusta	(037) 21821	4499
Bella Napa Bay	PO Box 192, Famagusta	(037) 21601	5177
Chrysland	PO Box 50, Famagusta	(037) 21311	3952
Leros	PO Box 162, Famagusta	(037) 21126	–

PAPHOS

Annabelle	Posidonos St	(061) 38333	5481
Alexander the Great	Posidonos St	(061) 44000	4652
Paphos Beach	Posidonos St	(061) 33091	3202
Dionysos	1 Dionysou St	(061) 33414	2849
King's	Tombs of the King's Rd	(061) 33497	–

TAKE A GUIDE ROUND AFRICA

You can explore Africa with IC's four regional travel guides. Each pocket-sized paperback guide contains over 200 pages of comprehensive, up-to-date information on the travel and tourist facilities, handicrafts, customs regulations, hotels, currencies, climate, health, economy, culture, people and political history of the countries of each region. Each guide is fully illustrated with maps and photographs.

EGYPT

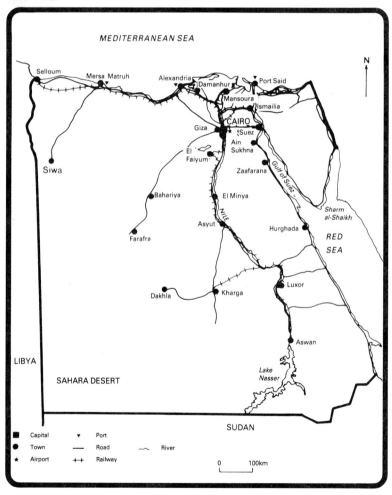

Map of Egypt showing major cities, roads, railways, rivers, airports and ports.

Area: 997,738 sq km
Population: 50 million (official estimate)
Capital: Cairo

Everybody wants to visit Egypt. Well over a million and a half tourists flock into the country every year to experience the unique attractions of this ancient nation and the number is increasing every year. It is not difficult to see why Egypt attracts so many visitors. The country's legacy of historical sites is unparalleled in its magnificence. The pyramids, the sphinx, the temples of Luxor and Karnak, the Valleys of the Kings and Queens, Philae and Abu Simbel all inspire an almost religious fervour in tourists from every part of the world. But there are other attractions, as in Cairo itself with its sky-scrapers and expresso bars side by side with ancient mosques and camel markets, or in Aswan where the healthy warm winter climate offers an escape for Europeans from the rigours of their native rains and snows. Visitors in search of sea bathing and beaches can find them in Alexandria, along the Mediterranean coast, or at Red Sea resorts like Hurghada. And there is the magnificent natural spectacle of the Nile, threading its path through the desert and between the densely cultivated irrigated fields that have been the basis of Egyptian civilization for millennia.

The Land and the People

Most of Egypt's million square kilometres is flat, barren desert. Almost 50 million people are crammed into the fertile areas, with the main concentrations at the base of the Nile Delta in Cairo, in the Delta itself and along the length of the Nile Valley. Vegetation is confined to these areas, the Mediterranean coast and the oases. There is little rainfall outside the northern coastal region, which can be quite wet in winter. Summer temperatures are normally very high, almost unbearably so in the extreme south. Without the blessing of the Nile, Egypt would be almost wholly uncultivable and largely uninhabited.

To the west of the Nile lies the Western Desert, a vast expanse of rock and sand broken by densely palmed oases, stretching away to the Libyan border. East of the Nile the land rises to rocky uplands, often hard to penetrate and cross, falling to a narrow coastal strip on the Red Sea shore. The Red Sea coast has fine beaches and offers excellent opportunities for deep-sea diving in its waters rich with marine life. On the other side of the Suez Canal lies the Sinai Desert, which was returned to Egypt as part of the Camp David agreement with Israel.

As might be expected in a largely agricultural country, the *fellahin* or peasant farmers make up the bulk of the population. They live mainly in the Delta and Nile Valley, often in circumstances little changed from their traditional ways of life. Their farming systems have remained the same for centuries; they continue to use the *saqia*, a wooden water-wheel pulled by oxen and the *shadoof*, the Archimedes screw-technique for pumping water – old fashioned but still effective. New mechanisation is being introduced gradually but overall progress is slow in rural areas.

The population is expanding rapidly and there is a continual drift of people from the countryside to the towns. Since 1952 when the monarchy was over-thrown by the Free Officers, government policies have stimulated a radical modernisation of many aspects of Egyptian life. Industrialisation and the expansion of administration have created a new breed of Egyptian with an outlook and lifestyle very different from the peasantry. Older traditions such as polygamy have been curbed, and women's influence has been brought increasingly into everyday life. Signs of middle-class consumerism are clearly visible in the stores of the larger towns. In common with other Middle Eastern countries, Egypt has recently experienced a resurgence of Islamic traditionalism, particularly in the south, to which the Government has been forced to respond, but the visitor will still encounter few of the restrictions on behaviour to be found in the stricter Islamic states such as Saudi Arabia.

The poverty in the countryside and the huge city of Cairo has not yet been diminished either by Nasser's revolution or by Sadat's, and now Mubarak's, economic policies. Many of the urban poor live on squatted land without the essential amenities of power, water or sewage. Until such general living conditions begin to improve Egypt's development remains insecure. However, the lessons of history have taught Egyptians the art of patience and tolerance.

Culture

Egyptians have a hybrid background, reflecting the number of people who have crossed and occupied the country. The majority stem from the Arab tribes who settled as a result of the Moslem conquests of the seventh century. More recently Italian, Greek and Armenian communities have settled. These, however, have been seriously reduced in size since 1952, as a result of President Nasser's policies, and this has had the effect of changing the cosmopolitan nature of the major cities, Cairo and Alexandria. The Christian Copts who number about four million claim to be the descendants of the original inhabitants of the country, who were an Hamitic people living along the banks of the Nile. Copts have traditionally been subjected to harassment by extremists, a situation aggravated by the new spirit of Islamic revival in the country.

Egypt's 5,000 years of history and culture are apparent everywhere. There are the well-known Egyptological sites centred in the Cairo area and up and down the Nile, *Graeco-Roman* remains in Alexandria, Coptic churches in Cairo and Alexandria, and Moslem mosques and houses dating from the earliest period of the Arab invasion to the present day.

The cultural carry-over can be seen reflected in the jewellery, glassware, and other articles which can be bought in *Khan al Khalili* in Cairo and other tourist centres. The Egyptian government is, of course, aware that it is the historic and cultural aspect of the country which draws the tourists. Over the last few years great effort has gone into ensuring that foreign visitors are

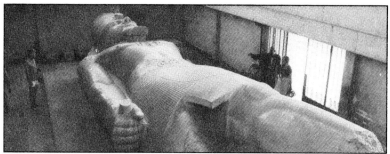

Statue of Ramses II at Memphis.

adequately catered for. Hotel building continues apace, official tourist guides are obliged to undergo specialist instruction before being allowed to take visitors to Egypt's many monuments and historic sites and tourist police in holiday centres such as Luxor are usually in evidence to ensure that tourist rip-offs remain at an 'acceptable' level. Culture, in the form of traditional craftsmanship, is apparent all around. Carpets, brassware, gold and silverware, perfumes, leatherware and the ubiquitous replicas of ancient artefacts abound. However, beware of "authentic" items from archaeological digs. These will almost always be fakes. Although the illicit antiques trade still flourishes in Egypt, it is conducted via a highly organised international network. However, visitors will find that the Egyptian authorities are particularly eagle-eyed when it comes to spotting anything resembling an ancient artefact being taken out of the country. On a recent departure from Luxor airport I was unlucky enough to be one of more than a dozen travellers who, after having proceeded to the departure lounge, was called back to open up items of luggage containing nothing more than fairly poor quality soapstone replicas of Ramses II, because the shape of the item – as revealed by the airport X-ray machine – was suspicious. The Egyptians – with a great deal of their ancient heritage currently housed in museums all over the world – are understandably anxious that those antiques which remain in the country should continue to do so.

History

The Old Kingdom: The uniting of the two kingdoms of Egypt – one in Lower Egypt in the Delta, and the other in Upper Egypt along the River Nile – by Menes in about 3188 BC is generally taken to mark the formal beginning of Egyptian history. Government had expanded, particularly under the Pharaoh Zoser, at the beginning of the III Dynasty, to cover the area from Aswan to the Mediterranean. He had the step pyramid built at Saqqara. His successors, especially in the IV Dynasty with their capital at Memphis on the apex of the Delta, were responsible for such technical achievements as the Great Pyramid at Giza.

Tutankhamun.

The Middle Kingdom: After a period of internal troubles, during which the south rebelled, union was restored under Mentuhotep I, and the city of Thebes (present-day Luxor) was founded. The Pharaohs of the XI and XII Dynasties extended their kingdom eastwards and southwards to the Second Cataract in Nubia, reaching their zenith of power in about 2000 BC. From 1788 BC and the beginning of the XIII Dynasty confusion set in, and the Hyksos conquered the land from the Sinai desert.

The New Kingdom: After expelling the Hyksos, the Amenhoteps and Tuthmosis Pharaohs of the XVIII Dynasty, between 1570 and 1320 BC, were able to expand the kingdom into an empire extending to the Orontes, the Euphrates and the Third Cataract of the Nile, 400 km south of the present frontier. This dynasty left its mark up and down the land, especially around Thebes and through such figures as Amenhotep III, Nefertiti, his queen, and his son-in-law, Tutankhamun.

A subsequent decline was offset by Ramses III of the XX Dynasty who defeated the Hittites, but thereafter the empire began to disintegrate. In succession Egypt suffered invasion by the Libyans, Nubians, Ethiopians and Assyrians. Under the Saite rulers of the XXVI Dynasty, between 663 and 525 BC, there was some revival of trade and former influence but, in the latter year, the Persian Emperor Cambyses overran the country. The Pharaonic era ended in 332 BC with the arrival of Alexander the Great.

Hellenic and Roman Period: The foundation of the new capital bearing Alexander's name marked the beginning of a period of renewed sophistication, and the line of the Ptolemies. But while Alexandria retained a pre-eminence, law and order declined under these rulers, as Egyptians, now second-class citizens in their own country, revolted. The famed Cleopatra gave herself and her country to Julius Caesar, and then to Mark Antony. After the deaths of Antony and Cleopatra, Augustus took possession of Egypt in the name of Rome in 30 BC. For six and a half centuries the Romans used Egypt as their empire's granary and ruled with forceful efficiency.

In time the provincial authority broke down, and about AD 300 the Emperor Diocletian arrived to restore order and reform the administrative system. After his abdication in AD 305 Egypt again fell into confusion, with the land being taken over by landlords forming huge feudal estates.

Christian Period: Christianity had come to Egypt during the First Century AD, and during the Fourth Century Byzantium replaced Rome as ruler. The Coptic Church was acknowledged during the Fifth Century as being separately established.

Arab invasion: (640–969): An Arab army under Amr Ibn al-Aas invaded Egypt in 640, just eight years after the death of the Prophet Muhammad, and in April 641 Alexandria surrendered. Al-Fustat was established as the capital in part of what is now Cairo. For two centuries Egypt was administered first as part of the Omayyad Caliphate and then as part of the Abbasid empire. Two locally-based dynasties – the Tulunids and the Ikhshidids – ruled between 868 and 969 in near independence from the Caliphate.

Fatimids and Ayyubids: (969–1250): The Ikhshidid rule was overthrown in 969 by an invasion from Tunisia. The General Jawhar laid out a new capital beside Al-Fustat, which became the basis for modern Cairo. He also founded the university of Al-Azhar. A familiar pattern ensued, following an initial period of prosperity and fine administration the Fatimid empire began to break up. Its power in Egypt became nominal, and passed to the Arab rulers in Syria who were fighting the Crusaders. The last Fatimid was deposed in 1171, and Egypt formed part of Saladin's empire. On Saladin's death in 1193, his empire was divided among his heirs, and the Ayyubid branch ruled in Cairo.

The Mamluks: (1250–1517): These were the slave bodyguards of the rulers originally, but their power increased as that of their masters declined. It was from the ranks of the Mamluks that new rulers eventually emerged. Although an alien element largely exploiting the land for their own ends, they protected Egypt from the Mongols and Crusaders. The numerous mosques and public works of this era indicate Egypt's wealth, but the overall condition of the country declined from the middle of the 14th century.

The Colossi of Memnon near Luxor.

Ottoman Egypt: (1517–1798): Selim I overthrew the last Mamluk sultan in a battle outside Cairo in 1517. In the following period, only Al-Azhar retained its prominence as Egypt sank into obscurity as a province and a backwater too far removed from the main trade routes. The Mamluks succeeded in reasserting their autonomy later, however.

The European Era: Napolean Bonaparte's arrival in Alexandria and the defeat of the Mamluks in July 1798 brought Egypt rudely into contact with Europe. The enforced withdrawal of the French was followed by a struggle for power which resulted in a triumph by Muhammed Ali, an Albanian, recognised as sultan in 1805. A passionate believer in the benefits of European sophistication, he encouraged its influences – a trend followed by his successors. Under the rule of Ismail, Muhammad Ali's grandson, the Suez Canal was opened in 1869.

Creeping financial commitments and the consequences of Egypt's first modern nationalist revolt under Ahmed Orabi led, in 1882, to the British occupation. Egypt now passed under another set of alien rulers. Men like Lord Cromer and Sir Eldon Gorst may have built Egypt up materially, but they did nothing for its national pride. There was an unsuccessful revolt in 1919, and between 1922 and 1939 – the former date marking Britain's acknowledgement of Egypt as an 'independent' State – the Wafd Party, the King and Britain competed for control.

The Anglo-Egyptian Treaty of 1936 ended the occupation, but gave Britain the right to station troops in the Suez Canal area. The build-up of dissatisfaction with Egypt's status and with King Farouk, and the 1948 defeat by Israel contributed to the formation of the Free Officers led by Gamal Abdel-Nasser. They siezed power on 23 July 1952 and overthrew the monarchy.

Revolution: (1952–70): The nationalist aspirations of this group ran through all their policies. But it was not until 1954 that Nasser was able to emerge fully as leader, having outmanoeuvred General Neguib, who was President and the Free Officers' front man. Political parties were banned and land holdings limited. The British military presence was ended in 1954.

Nasser's standing in Egypt and the Arab world was consolidated by his leadership during the tripartite attack on Egypt by Israel, France and Britain in 1956, ostensibly in reaction to the nationalisation of the Suez Canal.

Between 1958 and 1961, Egypt became known as the United Arab Republic (UAR) as it entered an unsuccessful union with Syria. This undertaking was only slightly less unproductive than the Egyptian military development in Yemen between 1962 and 1967.

During the 1960s Nasser inaugurated sweeping nationalisation to bring the country's economy under state control. The Soviet Union acquired its first major economic foothold in 1958 by agreeing to finance the building of the Aswan Dam, after a Western withdrawal. The dam was built between 1960 and 1970. Egypt's involvement in war with Israel, in June 1967, ended disastrously and transformed the Middle East scene.

The period after the 1967 war was spent trying to keep the economy expanding, while building up the armed forces, and looking for settlement through the UN resolution of the Security Council of November 1967. An artillery and aircraft war was brought to an end by a US-proposed ceasefire in August 1970. President Nasser died in September after mediating in the civil war between King Hussein's forces and the Palestinian guerrillas in Jordan. Many of the latter had been forced out of the West Bank and Gaza when the Israeli forces took up occupation in June 1967.

Sadat the President: Nasser was succeeded by his Vice-President, Anwar Sadat, who in May 1971 defeated a challenge to his authority led by a former Vice-President, Ali Sabri. Sadat found the strains of a 'no war, no peace' situation increasingly difficult to control. But in 1972 he expelled the Soviet military personnel and in October 1973 he staged the military action that is now officially known as the 'Victory'. The Israeli's were driven from the Suez Canal. With this achievement Sadat set about opening up the country to the West. Commercial and travel restrictions were lifted. Huge loans flooded in, principally from the US and the Gulf states. However, there were severe economic strains in a country where the majority of the people remain poor, dependent on a largely agricultural base, and where there are few prospects of oil wealth on the scale of Saudi Arabia's or Libya's.

In November 1977 President Sadat launched negotiations with Israel by dramatically flying to Jerusalem for talks with the then Prime Minister Menachem Begin. Although the momentum for an agreement with Israel flagged temporarily in 1978, President Carter of the US wielded his influence to bring Sadat and Begin together at Camp David in September 1978. This led to the final signing of a treaty on 26 March 1979. By this time Egypt was being ostracised by the rest of the Arab world, which now found unprecedented unity in its opposition to Sadat's move – because of the treaty's failure to restore the rights of Palestinians. President Sadat was assassinated on 6 October 1981. Hosni Mubarak was sworn in as his successor on 14 October. During his term of office President Mubarak has pursued generally pragmatic and moderate policies. A general election in April 1987 returned the President to office for a second, six year term.

Economy

Although 90% of Egypt's land area is desert, the country is heavily dependent on its agriculture – an activity that is only possible on the banks of the Nile and in the river's sprawling delta. Half the country's population is involved in the growing of food, cotton and other crops. But the harsh conditions of life in the agricultural sector have prompted many families to move to the cities – there to face often equally bad conditions.

In the past 25 years land reforms have reduced the enormous disparities of wealth among the rural people and have helped to increase production of cotton and food crops. Larger farmers have been able to acquire modern machinery, but only a minority are able to benefit significantly in the present system. There remains an enormous rural peasantry without much hope of improvement in its living standard.

The main crops for export are cotton and rice, but there is also production of fruits, vegetables, wheat, barley, maize, millet and sugar. Attempts to reclaim land, in the Nile Valley area as well as in the Aswan High Dam area, have met great difficulties. As a result, Egypt has failed to produce enough of its own food and is now heavily dependent on food imports.

Industry has become an expanding economic sector in the past 25 years, with food processing and textiles in a prominent position. There are iron and steel works (established by the USSR), fertiliser, cement and paper plants. The continual expansion of this sector has been possible since the Aswan High Dam increased electric power supplies. However, the expansion of industry is not sufficient to reduce Egypt's unemployment problems.

Since 1974 Egypt has adopted an 'Open Door' economic policy, offering generous incentives to foreign investors and foreign banks. In return the government hopes that the country will begin to earn hard currency from its expanding tourist industry, Suez Canal revenues and oil export revenues.

Egypt's chief hard currency earners are workers' remittances – from Egyptians employed outside their homeland – the Suez Canal and tourism. Although oil revenues have fallen as a result of declining international markets, oil earnings still contribute about one-fifth of GDP and some two thirds of annual export earnings. The oil price fall has put Egypt under severe pressure but with the support of an agreement with the International Monetary Fund (IMF) a long term economic reform programme has been implemented. Ultimately, however, much of Egypt's future economic recovery hinges on a recovery in oil market prices, further broadening of the economic base and the successful development of alternative export opportunities.

Nile cruises are a popular tourist option.

General Information

Government

President Hosni Mubarak has extensive powers, but government is carried out by the Cabinet of Ministers and legislation must be passed by the People's Assembly. The largest party in the Assembly is the National Democratic Party.

Languages

Arabic is the language used everywhere, although French and English are also widely spoken.

Religions

Islam is dominant, but all shades of Christianity are represented, particularly the Coptic Church. There is a small Jewish community.

How to Get There

By air: There are frequent direct flights to Cairo operated by the national carrier, Egypt Air, and other major international airlines. Cairo Airport is situated 22.5 km from the city centre. Transport into the city is available. Many international airlines now also fly direct to Luxor airport, which is particularly popular in the tourist season.

By road: The only feasible access for motorists from Europe is by sea to Alexandria from a Mediterranean port.

By sea: There are sailings from many European ports to Alexandria. There are twice-weekly ferries from Piraeus in Greece and a three-times-weekly service from Venice. Three ferries a week ply between Jeddah and Suez.

Entry Regulations

Tourist visas should be applied for in advance from any Egyptian consulate or embassy. They can be issued for any period up to one month and should take only 48 hours to be issued. Applications from writers or journalists can take longer, so be prepared.

Visitors should register with the police or Ministry of the Interior within one week of arrival in Egypt. Hotels usually arrange this.

Visitors coming from areas infected by cholera or yellow fever must have certificates of inoculation. Inoculation against typhoid and paratyphoid is recommended.

Customs Regulations

All personal effects, used or unused, are exempt from customs duties and other taxes and dues. Also exempt, though they must be declared, are such items for private use as cameras, radios, recorders, binoculars and jewellery. A copy of the declaration is left with the customs office, and the original kept for submission on departure. The first £20 worth of foods, alcoholic drinks, cigarettes, cigars and medicines, bought for personal consumption are not dutiable.

On departure everything bought by visitors holding entry or transit visas may be exported, provided the total cost of the new articles does not exceed the amount declared by the visitor to be in his possession on entry, and provided the articles are in the nature of gifts or for personal use. Receipts for such purchases should be kept.

Egyptian currency and banknotes may not be taken in or out of the country by tourists, who may exchange unused Egyptian currency into the original foreign currency at the official rate.

There is no limit to the amount of foreign currency that tourists may bring with them in banknotes, travellers cheques, money orders, bank drafts or letters of credit.

Climate

Egypt lies between the Mediterranean and the 23rd parallel north of the equator and is sunny for all but a few days in the year. Rain does not fall on more than 40 days a year, and then only in a few places. Within Egypt there is the contrast between the coastal Mediterranean climate and the hot dryness of the interior. In the desert areas there is a sharp contrast between day and night temperatures.

The winter months of January and February can be quite cool. In April and May the *Khamsin* wind raises dust storms.

What to wear: Egypt is an informal country where open-necked shirts are acceptable for business and entertainment – except in predictably self-important establishments. For the summer, the lightest cotton wear is recommended and for winter ordinary woollens and light raincoats. Be prepared for a fall in temperature after sundown. A light cotton jacket, woollen cardigan or wrap will usually compensate adequately.

Health Precautions

Egypt is free from diseases that would not be met with in normal circumstances anywhere in the world but the chance of stomach upset – especially at the beginning of a visit – is always present.

Drinking water in Cairo and Alexandria is safe. Care should be taken in selecting salads, fruit, mineral waters and iced drinks.

Swimming is best confined to pools or the sea, because of the risk of contracting bilharzia through swimming elsewhere. Fly and insect repellent is advisable, particularly in summer. Hospitals, clinics, and chemists are open to tourists and the

public every day in most areas. Hotels will usually arrange for a doctor to visit you in your room should this be necessary. Most of these practitioners are fluent in English and/or French.

Business Hours

Banks: open daily (except Fridays) from 0830-1230 and 1000-1200 on Sundays.
Shops: open from 0900-1330 and from 1700-2100.
Government offices: open from 0900-1400 every day except Friday and national holidays.
Commercial offices are open from 0830-1400 in summer daily except Fridays, and in winter 0900-1300 and 1600-1900 except on Thursday afternoons and Fridays.
Post Offices are open daily except on Friday. The Central Post Office in Ataba Square in Cairo provides a 24-hour service.

Press

The English language Egyptian Gazette, 24-26 Sharia Zakaria Ahmad, Cairo, is published daily in the capital.

Public Holidays

First day of Ramadan*, 7 April 1989
Evacuation Day, 18 June
Eid al-Fitr*, 7-9 May 1989
Revolution Day, 23 July
Eid al-Adha*, 14-17 July 1989
Hijra*, 4 August 1989
Al-Ashoura*, 13 August 1989
Prophet's Birthday*, 13 October 1989
Victory Day, 6 October
Banks are closed on 1 January and Coptic Christian festival days. The Nile Festival is held in December each year at Luxor and Cairo.

*The dates of the Moslem holidays marked with an asterisk are only approximate as they depend on sightings of the moon.

Embassies/Consulates in Cairo

Afghanistan: *Interests served by India.*

Albania: 29 Sharia Ismail Muhammad, Cairo (Zamalek). Tel: (02) 3415651.

Algeria: *Interests served by India.*

Angola: 12 Midan en-Nasr, Cairo (Dokki). Tel: (02) 707602.

Argentina: 8 Sharia as-Saleh Ayoub, Cairo (Zamalek). Tel: (02) 650862.

Australia: 5th Floor, Cairo Plaza Annexe, Corniche en-Nil, Cairo. Tel: (02) 717022. Telex: 92257.

Austria: Riyadh Tower, Cnr 5 Sharia Wissa Wassef, Cairo (Giza). Tel: (02) 651898. Telex: 92258.

Bahrain: *Interests served by Pakistan.*

Bangladesh: 18 Sharia Souris, Madinet el-Mohandessin, Cairo (Dokki). Tel: (02) 706294.

Belgium: 20 Sharia Kamel esh-Shennawi, Cairo (Garden City). Tel: (02) 3547494. Telex: 92264.

Bolivia: El-Misr Bldg, Midan ar-Rimaha, Cairo (Giza).

Brazil: 1125 Corniche en-Nil, 11561 Cairo (Maspiro). Tel: (02) 756938. Telex: 92044.

Brunei: Room 401, Nile Hilton, Tahrir Sq., Cairo. Tel: (02) 750666.

Bulgaria: 36 Sharia el-Missaha, Cairo (Dokki).

Burkina Faso: 50 Sharia Ahmad Orabi, Madinet es-Sahafeyin, Cairo. Tel: (02) 3440301. Telex: 93871.

Burma: 24 Sharia Muhammad Mazhar, Cairo (Zamalek). Tel: (02) 3404176.

Burundi: 13 Sharia el-Israa, Madinet el-Mohandessin, Cairo (Dokki). Tel: (02) 3462173. Telex: 20091.

Cameroon: POB 2061, 42 Sharia Babel, Cairo (Dokki). Tel: (02) 704843.

Canada: 6 Sharia Muhammad Fahmy es-Sayed, Cairo (Garden City). Tel: (02) 3543110. Telex: 92677.

Central African Republic: 13 Sharia Chehab, Madinet el-Mohandessin, Cairo (Dokki). Tel: (02) 713291.

Chad: POB 1869, 31 Sharia Adnan Oumar Sedki, Cairo (Dokki). Tel: (02) 703232. Telex: 92285.

Chile: 5 Sharia Chagaret ed-Dorr, Cairo (Zamalek). Tel: (02) 3408711. Telex: 92519.

China, People's Republic: 14 Sharia Bahgat Aly, Cairo (Zamalek). Tel: (02) 809459.

Colombia: Apt 141, 1 Sharia Sad el-Ali, Cairo (Dokki). Tel: (02) 717278.

Côte d'Ivoire: 39 Sharia el-Kods esh-Sherif, Madinet el-Mohandessin, Cairo (Dokki). Tel: (02) 699009. Telex: 2334.

Cuba: 9 Sharia Hussein Ahmad Rashad, Cairo (Dokki). Tel: (02) 381704. Telex: 93966.

Cyprus: 23A Sharia Ismail Muhammad , Cairo (Zamalek). Tel: (02) 3411288. Telex: 92059.

Czechoslovakia: 4 Sharia Dokki, Cairo (Giza). Tel: (02) 3485531.

Denmark: 12 Sharia Hassan Sabri, Cairo (Zamalek). Tel: (02) 3407411. Telex: 92254.

Djibouti: 157 Sharia Mohandessin, Sharia Sudan, Cairo. Tel: (02) 709787. Telex: 93143.

Ecuador: 8 Sharia Abd ar-Rahman Fahmy, Cairo (Garden City). Tel: (02) 26372.

Ethiopia: 12 Midan Bahlawi, Cairo (Dokki). Tel: (02) 705133.

Finland: 10 Sharia el-Kamel Muhammad, Cairo (Zamalek). Tel: (02) 3411487.

France: 29 Sharia Giza, Cairo. Tel: (02) 728033. Telex: 92032.

Gabon: 15 Sharia Mossadek, Cairo (Dokki). Tel: (02) 702963. Telex: 92323.

German Democratic Republic: 13 Sharia Hussein Wassef, Cairo (Dokki). Tel: (02) 3484500. Telex: 22354.

Germany, Federal Republic: 8 Sharia Hassan Sabri, Cairo (Zamalek). Tel: (02) 3410015. Telex: 92023.

Ghana: 24 Sharia el-Batal Ahmad Abd al-Aziz, Cairo (Dokki). Tel: (02) 704275.

Greece: 18 Sharia Aicha et-Taimouria, Cairo (Garden City). Tel: (02) 30443.

Guatemala: 29 Sharia Dr Muhammad

Mandour Madinet Nasr, Cairo. Tel: (02) 600371. Telex: 93242.

Guinea: 46 Sharia Muhammad Mazhar, Cairo (Zamalek). Tel: (02) 699088.

Guinea-Bissau: 37 Sharia Lebanon, Madinet el-Mohandessin, Cairo.

Holy See: Apostolic Nunciature, Safarat al-Vatican, 5 Sharia Muhammad Mazhar, Cairo (Zamalek). Tel: (02) 3406152.

Hungary: 55 Sharia Kods esh-Sherif, Cairo (Mohandessin). Tel: (02) 805091.

India: 5 Sharia Aziz Abaza, Cairo (Zamalek). Tel: (02) 3413051. Telex: 92081.

Indonesia: 13 Sharia Aicha et-Taimouria, Cairo (Garden City). Tel: (02) 27200.

Iran: *Interests section at Swiss Embassy closed, by order of Egyptian Government, May 1987.*

Iraq: *Interests served by Yugoslavia.*

Ireland: POB 2681, 3 Sharia Abu el-Feda, Cairo (Zamalek). Tel: (02) 3408264. Telex: 92778.

Israel: 6 Ibn el-Malek, Cairo (Giza). Tel: (02) 726000. Telex: 93363.

Italy: 15 Sharia Abd ar-Rahman Fahmi, Cairo (Garden City). Tel: (02) 3543195. Telex: 94229.

Japan: Immeuble Cairo Centre, 3rd Floor, 2 Sharia Abd al-Kader Hamza, 106 Kasr el-Eini. Tel: (02) 3553962. Telex: 92226.

Jordan: 6 Sharia Juhaini, Cairo. Tel: (02) 982766.

Kampuchea: 2 Sharia Tahawia, Cairo (Giza). Tel: (02) 3489966.

Kenya: 8 Sharia Medina Mounawara, POB 362, Cairo (Dokki). Tel: (02) 704455. Telex: 92021.

Korea, Democratic People's Republic: 6 Sharia es-Saleh Ayoub, Cairo (Zamalek). Tel: (02) 699532.

Kuwait: 4 Sharia al-Montazeh, Cairo (Zamalek). Tel: (02) 816252.

Lebanon: *Interests served by France.*

Liberia: 11 Sharia Brasil, Cairo (Zamalek). Tel: (02) 819864. Telex: 92293.

Malaysia: 7 Sharia Wadi en-Nil, Mohandessin, Cairo (Agouza). Tel: (02) 699162.

Mali: 3 Sharia al-Kawsar, Cairo (Dokki). Tel: (02) 701641.

Mauritania: 31 Sharia Syria, Cairo (Dokki). Tel: (02) 707229. Telex: 92274.

Mauritius: 72 Sharia Abd el-Moneim Riad, Cairo (Agouza). Tel: (02) 3470929. Telex: 93631.

Mexico: 5 Dar es-Shifa, Cairo. Tel: (02) 28622.

Mongolia: 3 Midan en-Nasr, Cairo (Dokki). Tel: (02) 650060.

Morocco: *Interests served by Senegal.*

Nepal: 9 Sharia Tiba, Cairo (Dokki). Tel: (02) 704541.

Netherlands: 18 Sharia Hassan Sabri, Cairo (Zamalek). Tel: (02) 3408744. Telex: 92028.

Niger: 28 Sharia Pahlaw, Cairo (Dokki). Tel: (02) 987740. Telex: 2880.

Nigeria: 13 Sharia Gabalaya, Cairo (Zamalek). Tel: (02) 3406042. Telex: 92038.

Norway: 8 Sharia el-Gezireh, Cairo (Zamalek). Tel: (02) 3403340. Telex: 92259.

Oman: 30 Sharia Montazah, Cairo (Zamalek). Tel: (02) 698073. Telex: 92272.

Pakistan: 8 Sharia es-Salouli, Cairo (Dokki). Tel: (02) 988977.

Panama: Apt 9, 97 Sharia Mirghani, Cairo (Heliopolis). Tel: (02) 662547. Telex: 92776.

Peru: 11 Sharia Brasil, Cairo (Zamalek). Tel: (02) 301971. Telex: 93663.

Philippines: 5 Sharia ibn el-Walid, Cairo (Dokki). Tel: (02) 3480396. Telex: 92446.

Poland: 5 Sharia Aziz Osman, Cairo (Zamalek). Tel: (02) 3409583.

Portugal: 15A Sharia Muhammad, Cairo (Zamalek). Tel: (02) 3405583. Telex: 20325.

Qatar: 10 Sharia ath-Thamar, Midan an-Nasr, Madinet al-Mohandessin, Cairo. Tel: (02) 704537. Telex: 92287.

Romania: 6 Sharia Kamel Muhammad, Cairo (Zamalek). Tel: (02) 698107. Telex: 93807.

Rwanda: 9 Sharia Ibrahim Osman,

Mohandessin, Cairo, PB 485. Tel: (02) 361079. Telex: 92552.

Saudi Arabia: 12 Sharia al-Kamel Muhammad, Cairo (Zamalek). Tel: (02) 819111.

Senegal: 46 Sharia Abd al-Moneim Riad, Mohandessin, Cairo (Dokki). Tel: (02) 815647. Telex: 92047.

Sierra Leone: 6 Sharia Hindawi, Midan Finny, Cairo (Dokki). Tel: (02) 700699.

Singapore: POB 356, 40 Sharia Babel, Cairo (Dokki). Tel: (02) 704744. Telex: 21353.

Somalia: 38 Sharia esh-Shahid Abd el-Moneim Riad, Cairo (Dokki). Tel: (02) 704038.

Spain: 9 Hod el-Laban, Cairo (Garden City). Tel: (02) 3547069. Telex: 92255.

Sri Lanka: POB 1157, 8 Sharia Yehia Ibrahim, Cairo (Zamalek). Tel: (02) 699138. Telex: 23575.

Sudan: 4 Sharia el-Ibrahimi, Cairo (Garden City). Tel: (02) 25043.

Sweden: POB 131, 13 Sharia Muhammad Mazhar, Cairo (Zamalek). Tel: (02) 3414132. Telex: 92256.

Switzerland: 10 Sharia Abd al-Khalek Saroit, POB 633, Cairo. Tel: (02) 758133. Telex: 92267.

Tanzania: 9 Sharia Abd al-Hamid Lofti, Cairo (Dokki). Tel: (02) 704155. Telex: 23537.

Thailand: 2 Sharia al-Malek el-Afdal, Cairo (Zamalek). Tel: (02) 3408356. Telex: 94231.

Tunisia: *Interests served by Senegal.*

Turkey: Ave en-Nil, Cairo (Giza). Tel: (02) 726115.

Uganda: 9 Midan el-Missaha, Cairo (Dokki). Tel: (02) 3485544. Telex: 92087.

USSR: 95 Sharia Giza, Cairo (Giza). Tel: (02) 731416.

United Arab Emirates: *Interests served by Turkey.*

United Kingdom: Sharia Ahmad Raghab, Cairo (Garden City). Tel: (02) 3540852. Telex: 94188.

USA: 5 Sharia Latin America, Cairo (Garden City). Tel: (02) 28219. Telex: 93773.

Uruguay: 6 Sharia Loutfallah, Cairo (Zamalek). Tel: (02) 3415137. Telex: 92435.

Venezuela: 15A, Sharia Mansour Muhammad, Cairo (Zamalek). Tel: (02) 813517. Telex: 93638.

Viet-Nam: 47 Sharia Ahmad Hishmat, Cairo (Zamalek). Tel: (02) 3402401.

Yemen Arab Republic: *Interests served by India.*

Yugoslavia: 33 Sharia Mansour Muhammad, Cairo (Zamalek). Tel: (02) 3404061.

Zaire: 5 Sharia Mansour Muhammad, Cairo (Zamalek). Tel: (02) 3403662. Telex: 92294.

Zambia: POB 1464, 22 Sharia en-Nakhil, Cairo (Dokki). Tel: (02) 709620. Telex: 92262.

Transport

By air: Egypt Air operates frequent flights between Cairo and Luxor (80 minutes) and Cairo and Aswan (1 hour and 45 minutes). There are day return flights from Aswan to Abu Simbel. A less frequent service connects Cairo and Hurghada on the Red Sea coast.

By road: Taxis are available in all cities and towns and accommodate up to five people. Fares are reasonable but, as always, it is preferable to arrange a mutually agreeable fee at the outset. Day or long-distance trips can be negotiated at rates which more than compensate for the lack of a formal car hire service. Cars can, however, be hired from the large hotels. Tourists bringing their own cars are required to have a carnet de passage and an international driving licence.

By rail: Good inexpensive and comfortable rail services are available between Cairo and the major cities and towns. Sleeper trains are comfortable, inexpensive and popular with long distance travellers.

By river: Apart from the Lake Nasser steamer running between Aswan and Wadi Halfa in Sudan, there are boats plying different sections of the Egyptian Nile. *Feluccas*, the traditional Nile river craft, can be hired in most towns.

Nile cruises, either between Cairo and Aswan or Luxor and Aswan, are a very popular tourist option.

Accommodation and Food

All classes of hotels exist in Cairo and at the prominent tourism centres. Elsewhere there are plenty of hotels, but in the lower quality bracket. In our listing we have omitted these for reasons of space. There are many such hotels in the city and they are listed in pamphlets

available from the Egyptian State Tourist Office.

Demand for high-standard hotel accommodation is heavy and all intending visitors should book in advance of their visit.

Egyptian cuisine is excellent, a combining of many of the best traditions of Middle Eastern cooking. All international standard hotels have their own restaurants. The major tourist destinations such as Cairo, Alexandria and Luxor also boasts an impressive selection of large and small restaurants offering international cuisine. Cafés and snack bars are to be found in abundance in the cities.

The Sphinx.

[Hotels]
ASWAN

Amoun Village	P.O. Box 118	24826	24407
Isis	–	24905	23459
Kalabsha	–	323222	92720
New Cataract	–	323434	–
Oberoi	–	23455	92120
Pullman Cataract	–	323434	92720

ARISH

Oberoi	–	778033	63453
Fayoum	–	324924	93095

HURGHADA

Magawish Club Med	–	–	–
Sheraton	P.O. Box 125	3488410	93355

LUXOR

Akhenaton Club Med	–	9577575	091000
Etap/PLM Azur	–	82011	92080
Isis	–	82750	92078
Luxor	–	2400	92160
Movenpick Jolie Ville	–	383400	93825
New Winter Palace	–	774116	92160
Sheraton	–	84544	24437

MINIA

Etap Nefertiti/PLM Azur	–	326282	23608

PORT SAID

Etap	P.O. Box 1110	20892	63175

Hotels

NAME	ADDRESS	TELEPHONE	TELEX
CAIRO			
Concorde	P.O. Box 2741	693737	93402
El Salam Hyatt	P.O. Box 5614	2455155	92184
Heliopolis Movenpick	–	2470077	93402
Heliopolis Meridien	–	2905055	23064
Marriott	P.O. Box 33	650840	93464
Mena House Oberoi	–	855444	93096
Meridien	P.O. Box 2288	845444	22325
Nile Hilton	–	740777	92222
Novotel Airport	–	661330	20953
Ramada Renaissance	P.O. Box 70	538111	93595
Ramses Hilton	–	74400	94260
Safir	–	3482828	92531
Semiramis InterContinental	–	3557171	942257
Shepheards	P.O. Box 553800	21379	92726
Sheraton Cairo	P.O. Box 11	3488600	488600
Sheraton/El Gezira	P.O. Box 264	411333	21812
Sheraton Heliopolis	P.O. Box 466	667700	93300
Siag Pyramids	–	856007	93522
Sonesta	–	611066	93242
ALEXANDRIA			
Montazeh Sheraton	–	969220	54706
Palestine	–	968662	54027
Ramada Renaissance	P.O. Box 85	867444	866111

Cairo

With a population of over 12 million, Cairo is the largest city in Africa. Brash modern architecture and traditional buildings jostle in an untidy mixture of styles; broad avenues and squares contrast with the narrow, winding streets of the poorer districts. The centre of the city is the east bank and the two islands of Gezira and Roda. Central Cairo around Tahrir Square is not for the faint-hearted, with its chaotic traffic, endless queues, and busy throng of street vendors and pedestrians. The frantic overcrowded scene will either excite the visitor by its intensity and vigour, or awaken a desperate longing for tranquility. There is peace to be had along the Corniche on the river bank and a fine view of the city can be obtained by mounting the 180 metres tall Tower of Cairo on Gezira island.

The most famous sights in the Cairo area are the ancient Egyptian monuments which spread along the west bank of the Nile south of the city. The Giza pyramids rise up where the city meets the desert. The site at Giza affords a panoramic view over the Nile Valley. The largest monument is the Great Pyramid of Cheops, a mighty structure of almost two and a half million stone blocks. There are guided tours to the funerary chambers (not recommended for claustrophobics). The Pyramids of Chephren and Menkure, also 4th Dynasty, stand nearby. The famous Sphinx keeps guard over Pharaoh Chephren's tomb. Smaller temples and tombs, called mastabs, lie all around the major monuments. South of Giza is Saqqara, site of the 3rd Dynasty Step Pyramid of Zoser, the earliest of the great pyramids. Other tombs and pyramids abound, including the elaborately decorated Tomb of Ti. Still further southward, the ruins of the city of Memphis, the capital of the Old Kingdom, will attract the historically-minded, although little remains to be seen except a recumbent colossus representing Ramses the Second.

Returning to Cairo itself, most of the main Islamic buildings are to be found in the eastern part of the city. Saladin's Citadel, on the Mokattam Hills, offers a fine view across the city to the Giza pyramids in the distance. Inside the Citadel stands the 19th century Mosque of Mohammed Ali. Other Islamic monuments in the area worth visiting include: Al-Azhar University and Mosque, built partly in the 10th century; Al-Hussein Mosque in the square opposite; Sultan Hassan Mosque at the foot of the citadel with its ceramics and twin minarets; the old-style Ibn Tulun Mosque with its rare minaret mounted by an outside staircase; and the Museum of Islamic Art, among whose rare objects are notable Koranic manuscripts and Arab ceramics. It is easy to see how the Egyptian capital became known as the city of a thousand minarets.

In the southern part of the city on the east bank of the Nile lies Old Cairo, site of the country's most ancient mosque, attributed to the first Arab conqueror Amr Ibn Al-Aas. But Old Cairo is most renowned for its Coptic churches and monastries. Chief among them are El-Moallaqah (the Hanging Church) which dates from the 7th century, the even older Abu Serga Church, and the Church of Saint Barbara. Well worth a visit is the Coptic Museum with its fine collection of early Christian craftsmanship in glass and wood.

No tourist should miss the Egyptian Museum, just north of busy Tahrir Square. The vast collection of ancient artefacts includes the fabulous treasure of Tutankhamun. The museum is a paradise for Egyptologists, but it is easy for the layman to be overwhelmed by the sheer quantity of exhibits.

Tourists to Cairo will find no shortage of events to amuse and entertain. The *Son et Lumiere* show at the Pyramids is well worth a visit (check which language

CAIRO

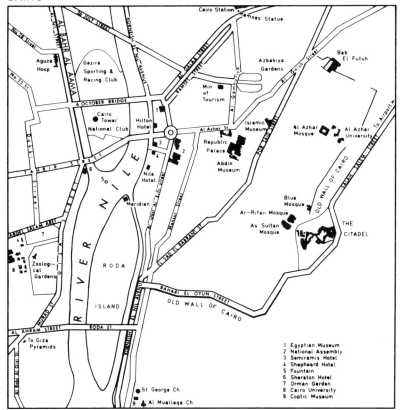

1 Egyptian Museum
2 National Assembly
3 Semiramis Hotel
4 Shepheard Hotel
5 Fountain
6 Sheraton Hotel
7 Orman Garden
8 Cairo University
9 Coptic Museum

is playing before booking). In addition to numerous cultural events – usually listed at the city's new Opera House – Cairo boasts a wide selection of nightclubs and restaurants. Floor shows and oriental dancing can be seen at the larger hotels, at such places as *Auberge des Pyramides*, *Covert Garden* and *Arizona* on the road to the Pyramids, and beside the Nile at *Kasr el-Nil* and *Al-Shagara*, and *Fontana* on Roda island.

There is also dancing and a floor show at *Sahara City*, 12 km from the Pyramids. There are several theatres, mainly for Arab works, and many cinemas specialising in western films. *Son et Lumiere* can be seen at the Pyramids (tel: 852880), and the Citadel (tel: 53260).

Sports: At the Pyramids there are two riding schools, and another on Gezira Island. At sporting clubs in Gezira, Maadi and Heliopolis visiting membership can be arranged and swimming, tennis, golf, squash and basketball enjoyed. There are swimming pools at most of the city's luxury hotels although few smaller hotels offer this facility.

Shopping: For tourists, the main area is

69

Khan el-Khalili where modern reproductions of antiquities are readily available. Of special value are jewellery, spices and copper, ivory and mother-of-pearl inlaid work. For the keen bargainer with the practised eye genuine antiquities, old Coptic cloth and Moslem relics may be found.

Tourist Information: Ministry of Tourism, 5 Adly St, Cairo, tel: 923657.

Alexandria

If Cairo is Arab Africa, Alexandria is the Mediterranean. The corniche and buildings stretch along the shore, and their layout and the cooler temperatures make Alexandria the natural focus for a mass summer exodus from Cairo. Situated between the sea and Lake Maryut it is Egypt's second-largest city and its main port. In the early days of Christianity it was one of that religion's main centres.

For a glimpse into the monarchical age the museum of the former royal palace of al-Montazah should be visited. For those in search of the past there is the *Gràeco-Roman* museum and Pompey's pillar standing among the ruins of the Serapium Temple. Near the port are the catacombs of Kom al-Shuqafa, dating back to about AD 100. At the northern tip of the harbour entrance, where the Pharos used to stand, is the Fort of Qait Bey. The mosque of Abu al-Abbas al-Mursi, with its high minaret and four domes, dates from 1767 and is the chief Islamic monument.

Alexandria's chief glory is its beaches. Among the best known and most crowded are, from east to west, Al-Maamoura, Al-Montazah, Al-Mandara, Al-Assafra, Miami, Sidi Bishr, San Stefano, Glym and Shatby. These all lie along the corniche but on the western boundaries of the city are the beaches of Agami and Hanoville.

Restaurants: The top hotels all have high-class Oriental and Western cuisine.

However, the quality of food in even the city's humblest establishments, is generally very good.

Sports: Beside swimming and water-skiing facilities, the visitor can without difficulty become a temporary member at the **Smouha** and **Sporting** clubs. Both have a golf course, horse racing, tennis and squash. Membership can also be arranged for yachting, rowing and automobile clubs.

Tourist Information: Main tourist office: Saad Zaghlul Square, Ramleh Station (tel: 807985). Tourists can also obtain information from the Sea terminal office (tel: 37090).

Mersa Matruh

Some 290 km west of Alexandria is the small but expanding port of **Mersa Matruh,** with a seven-km beach, boasted as being one of the best in the world. It can be reached by rail, by air, and by road from Alexandria.

From Mersa Matruh it is also possible to travel 300 km south-west to the Siwa Oasis near the Libyan border. In this oasis, where dates, olives and grapes are grown, the village has moved down from a craggy outcrop of rocks to leave a remarkable shell of tall uninhabited buildings on the heights. The remains of the temple of Amun, whose oracle was once consulted by Alexander, can still be seen.

The Red Sea

One of Egypt's most spectacular tourist regions for those who prefer swimming and sunbathing to sightseeing.

From **Suez** to **Halayib** on the border with Sudan is a 1,000-km coastal strip, between craggy hills and blue waters, rich in fish and coral for the underwater swimmer. In winter it is warm and sunny, and in summer cooling breezes make the heat tolerable.

Two centres have been established. At

Travelling light in Luxor.

Ain Sukhna, 55 km from Suez, there is a first-class hotel of the same name. **Hurghada,** 375 km south of Suez, is the area's best site for underwater photography and fishing.

On the road between Suez and Ain Sukhna is **Zaafarana,** the starting point for visits to the monasteries of St Anthony and St Paul.

El Faiyum

The nearest Egypt has to a national park is the El Faiyum area. This is the country's most fertile oasis, situated 125 km south west of Cairo and occupying a huge area surrounded by desert. It can be reached by car or frequent bus services.

The area is striking for its abundance of greenery, fruits and vegetables, set among streams with waterwheels. Sportsmen are drawn by Lake Qarun, whose waters are full of fish. Between autumn and spring there is duck shooting. Also in the area is Syllin village with its amphi-theatres and mineral water, the Queen's Pyramid and the historic pyramids of Amenemhat III and Senusert II.

The Nile Southwards

Travelling up the Nile by steamer is by far the most pleasant way to grasp the significance of this river for Egypt. After the noise and bustle of modern Cairo, the river cruise is not only peaceful but gives a better idea of Egypt's variety as it passes towns, small villages and sights of traditional life.

El Minya

This should be a priority stopping-off point, whether reached by car, train or steamer. It is situated 247 km south of Cairo on the west bank. El Minya is a suitable centre for visiting sites in the area. **Beni Hassan** is 20 km south of El Minya on the east bank. It is best to travel by steamer or car to Abu Korkas and then cross by sailing boat to see a Middle Kingdom cemetery and rock tombs decorated with remarkable paintings of hunting, sporting events, agricultural and military activities.

From Mallawi, 45 km south of El Minya and within a 20-km radius on the same western bank are **Al-Ashmunein,** with temples and statues from the XIX Dynasty to Christian times, and **Tuna Al-Gabal** with attactively decorated tombs. Some 16 km away, on the east bank, is **Tel El-Amarna,** which was the capital city established by Amenhotep IV (Akhenaten) after renouncing Amun. It contains the tombs of the royal family and nobles carved in rock.

Luxor

Luxor is a beautifully situated site 670 km south of Cairo on the east bank of the Nile. It was known in ancient times as Thebes and was for a long time the capital of Pharaonic Egypt.

In the middle of town is the magnificent temple of Luxor with its court of lotus-bud columns. A brief drive along the river bank brings the visitor to the massive, magnificent temple of **Karnak,** the Great Temple of Amon-Ra.

Luxor has long been a popular tourist destination, although a new airport just a few kilometres outside the town has meant an increase in direct flights from most international locations.

A short journey across the river by ferry opens the way through fertile fields of sugar-cane, cotton and wheat, to Egypt's most spectacular ancient relics. These include the **Valley of the Kings** and **Valley of the Queens,** containing the frescoed tombs of Tutankhamun, Sety I, Amenhotep II, Ramses II, Ramses III, Ramses VI and Queen Nefertari, as well as the tombs of nobles.

Other sites include the funeral temples of the kings, the Ramasseum of Ramses II, the temple of Medinet Habu, and the ramps and terraces of Queen Hatshep-sut's Funerary temple of Deir el-Bahari. To the north and south of Luxor on the same side of the river as the Valley of the Kings, the temples of Dendera, Esna and Edfu should be visited.

Tourist Information: Ministry of Tourism Office, tel: Luxor 2215.

Aswan

This town is a winter resort of considerable attraction, but unbearably hot in summer, with the temperature rising to 40°C. It stands on the First Cataract on the border between Egypt and Nubia.

From the granite quarries of the area the Pharaohs of ancient Thebes obtained stone for their statues and monuments. The famous **Aswan High Dam** is situated about 8 km south of the town along with its earlier counterpart, built in 1902.

There are several important sites to be visited from Aswan. Two km to the south is the classically laid out temple of **Philae,** saved from the waters of the dam under an arrangement similar to that which saved the Abu Simbel temples. Just 45 km to the north, situated on a hill overlooking the Nile, is the temple of **Kom Ombo.** Some 123 km north of Aswan stands the temple of **Edfu** on the west bank. Dedicated to Horus, it is one of the best preserved temples in Egypt. The town is accessible by road and has a good hotel.

Southwards from Aswan are the temples of **Abu Simbel,** hewn out of sandstone cliff, then raised above the dam waters and replaced under a Unesco-backed project between 1963 and 1968. The temples were built between 1300 and 1233 BC by Ramses II, four seated statues of the Pharoah mark the entrance to one of the temples. The other is dedicated to Nefertari. It is preferable to fly to Abu Simble rather than travel by hydrofoil since the Nile waters have swallowed up the villages and vegetation, leaving a largely featureless landscape.

Also saved from the waters of the dam is the temple of Kalabsha, dating from the time of the Roman Emperor Augustus. The temple was removed from a site 55 km south of the dam and now occupies a new position just beside it.

Tourist Information: Ministry of Tourism Office, tel: Aswan 3297.

IRAN

Area: 1,648,000 sq km
Population: 49.7 million (1986 census)
Capital: Tehran

Under the Shah's regime, Iran was one of the most frequently visited Middle East countries. A large number of Western businessmen and technicians were resident there, and the country was marked for tourist development. But the events of winter 1978/79, in which demonstrators repeatedly expressed their hostility not only to the Shah but also to foreigners and foreign influence, led to an exodus of foreign residents and the cessation of tourism. After the establishment of the Islamic Republic, fears of a hostile attitude to foreigners remained. Many hotels had been damaged or closed down; others stood empty. The strict Islamic code of the ruling regime does not encourage tourism but some business visitors are returning to the country. Iran's declaration, in July 1988, that it was prepared to accept a UN sponsored ceasefire, has given rise to much optimism. However, although the guns may have fallen silent, the conflict is far from over. An arduous and uncertain road lies ahead, bedevilled by the antagonisms which years of bitter warfare have exacerbated. However, with a little luck and a lot of forbearance, Iran and Iraq could be edging towards peace – and an era of new prosperity.

The Land and The People

Iran's 1,648,000 sq km, extending from the Caspian Sea to the Sea of Oman, are a complete geography lesson in land-use and associated activities.

North of Tehran, the Elburz Mountains form an imposing barrier between the high plateau and the Caspian. The highest peak, Mount Damavand, is 5,671 metres high (higher than Mount Blanc).

In the intensely farmed Caspian basin, autumn is the most picturesque season. Babolsar is the centre of Iran's caviar industry. Sturgeon are caught during spawning time: March-May.

In the west, the Zagros Mountains border Turkey and Iraq, and further barren ranges rise inland from the Sea of Oman.

Central Iran is largely desert, punctured by *qanats*, or irrigation canals, The Dasht-e Kevir, a desert of stones, and the Dasht-e Lut, an ocean of sand, cover an area the size of France.

Contrasts are everywhere: rivers lined with golden poplars, the sudden green of a desert oasis, and, in winter, the snow-capped Elburz Mountains whose ski-fields are a short drive from Tehran.

Iran's population of 50 million comprises many ethnic backgrounds, but the majority is of Aryan stock. There is variety in costumes, folklore and building styles.

The Aryans were the first Indo-European peoples to settle in Persia from the north-east; the name Iran stems from Aryana. Fars (when Persia) was the heart of Aryan country. The Achaemenian empire resulted from the fusion between the Persians and the Medes, who settled further north. This essentially Persian nucleus remained little affected by the numerous invasions.

Today there is still an enormous variety among Iran's tribes: Turcoman shepherds wrapped in felt cloaks, smock-wearing Kurds and nomadic Qashqai women in eye-catching scarlet robes. Many of these minority groups speak their own langugage.

The several million Kurds and Lurs who live in the north-west Zagros Mountain region and the Baluch, in south-eastern Iran, lead a way of life quite removed from the majority. This also applies to the Qashqai of Fars, today slowly settling to sedentary lives, but once numbering some 150,000 – constituting the biggest tribe of nomads in the world.

The Bakhtiari nomads pitch their triangular black tents in remote valleys in the Zagros range. Each winter they migrate south to the fertile Khuzestan and Lurestan plains, but as modernisation in the form of houses, clinics and schools reaches outlying villages, more and more tend to settle into new agricultural development areas.

Persia was largely a rural society when, in the 10th and 11th centuries, it was invaded by Turkish and Mongol nomads from the steppe country. Large-scale nomadism, which prevailed in much of Iran, was mainly caused by the invasions and not, as is generally thought, by climatic conditions. However in southern Iran, where rainfall is scanty, life was always founded on a nomadic society.

Later the steppe nomads settled in the cooler mountain areas and on the fertile plains. The return to sedentary life has been slow, but as the tribes formed huge nomadic alliances and demanded political representation the process has speeded up.

There are enormous gaps between the urban elite and poor rural families, drawn into the city hoping for a better life. Many rich Iranians left during the last days of the Shah's regime but even for those who remain the pattern of life under the strictly Islamic regime is much changed.

Some of Isfahan's mosques date back as far as the early 1700s AD

History

The Achaemenian dynasty was founded by King Achaemenus, who ruled the Aryan tribes who had settled in the area south of Parsa, in the ninth century BC. Other Achaemenian groups, among them the Medes, had settled in the high plateau even earlier. In 722 their capital was Hamadan and their evolution can be traced to the fourth millenium BC.

Cyrus II, who reigned from 559 to 529 BC, was the first to unify and shape the country. He captured Tintyr (Babylon) in 538 BC. The Persian Empire then stretched from Asia Minor and India as far as the Nile. Persepolis was built and a new capital, Pasargade, was founded in the region of Fars.

The next prominent emperor was Darius, who developed the heritage of Cyrus. His famous army of 10,000 men, the 'Immortals', conquered western India, the Black Sea and the Danube coast. They crossed the Red Sea and dug a canal on the present site of Suez, thus linking the extreme frontiers of the Achaemenian empire.

Darius's dream of capturing the Hellenistic capital, Athens, failed when the Persian forces suffered defeat at Marathon in 490. His son, Xerxes, also attempted to conquer Athens but was defeated at Salamis, in 480 BC.

Alexander shared the common dream of a unified world and his aim was to engender Persian participation in the new, still essentially Greek, civilisation. When he died, in 323, an officer, Seleucus, reaped the rewards of this cultural fusion sought by the great conquerer. But although the 'Hellenised' Persian aristrocracy supported the Seleucids, the dynasty survived less than a century.

In 247 BC, the Parthians rose to power, reigning during the rise of the Roman empire. Gradually rejecting Greek influence, they restored Zoroastrianism as the traditional religion, and during this period Persia began to recover its personality.

AD 224 saw the rise to power of the Sassanids from Fars who ruled for four centuries, until the Arab conquest of Persia. While the Sassanids were busy rebuilding Persia, Mohammad was preaching Islam in Arabia. A Persian, Sulman, became one of his prophets and the people gradually became influenced by his teachings, adopting the Shi'ite branch of Islam.

The Arabs finally vanquished the Sassanid forces in the battle of Al-Qadisiyah and Persia was absorbed into the new Arab empire with many Moslem converts chosen as local governors.

The ninth century AD saw a new awakening when the governor of Khorasan, on the Caspian coast, founded a new Persian dynasty. Now, however, began a series of Turkish invasions which continued until the 15th century. Mahmoud el-Ghazhri founded a vast empire, promoting the combined Islamic-Persian civilisation in those countries captured. The Seljuks, his successors, ruled over an area from China to the Bosphorus.

The beginning of the 13th century saw the start of devastating raids by Mongol hordes led by Genghis Khan. They were inefficient rulers and entrusted much local power to the feudal Persians.

In the closing years of the 14th century, Persia was again invaded, this time by Tamerlane, who split it into several kingdoms. Tamerlane brought the same evils as the Mongols had done over a century previously. Agriculture declined as people fled to the mountains to escape heavy taxes and barbarous treatment, town life atrophied and the country was generally depressed. Yet the kingdom, although administered by the Turks, retained its deep-seated Persian culture.

The 16th century saw the initially glorious rule of the Safavid shahs, but Persia began a decline which was not arrested until Shah Abbas assumed power in 1587. Shah Abbas set up his capital in Qazvin, but moved the court to Isfahan, which he built into a most beautiful city – *Isfahan nis-i-jhan*.

The Turks withdrew to Tabriz, which Shah Abbas occupied in 1602, going on to reconquer Baghdad in 1623. Under Shah Abbas Persia developed diplomatic and commercial links with Europe. But after two centuries of rule, the Safavid dynasty weakened and Afghan invaders captured Isfahan in 1722.

Persia found a new strength in a non-commissioned army officer, Nadr, a Turcoman who drove the Afghans out in a series of successful campaigns. Uzbekestan and Iraq were seized, Delhi was taken in 1739 and Nadr was proclaimed Shah.

After Nadr's death, in 1747, Afghanistan and Persia were soon separated and a new dynasty was founded by the Zands, who chose Shiraz as their capital.

In Turkey the Qajars had become very strong, and in 1779 they took over Persia, electing to rule from Tehran.

European countries were by now experiencing the process of industrialisation and Persia, still a feudal state, became involved in the power struggle, largely Anglo-Russian. In 1907, both powers signed a Persian trusteeship agreement, and on the outbreak of World War 1 Persia was divided into British and Russian zones.

When the last Qajar ruler was deposed another army man, Reza Khan, founded the Pahlavi dynasty in 1924. The Shah abdicated when the allies occupied Iran in 1941 and he was succeeded by his son, Mohammed Reza Shah Pahlavi. Surviving unrest in the early 1950's the Shah ruled for 37 years. With the backing of Britain and the United States he pressed for modernisation and intensive economic development along Western lines. His rule was autocratic and opposition was rigorously suppressed.

In 1978, protests against the trend of Iranian development by left-wing and Islamic groups provoked a brutal response from the Shah's forces. Demonstrations and strikes multiplied, drawing strength from each fresh act of repression. In January 1979, the Shah fled the country and an Islamic Republic was declared under the leadership of Ayatollah Khomeini, who continues to play a vital role in Iranian politics despite his advanced years.

Culture

Iran has one of the richest cultures in the Middle East, a deep-rooted civilisation which has survived repeated invasions and occupation by foreign societies.

Certain art forms are wholly Persian, but art has also been influenced by surrounding civilisations. The 13 centuries of Arab occupation saw a fusion with Islamic art.

Elamite art, dating to 2000 BC, testifies to great development in architecture. Bronze reliefs and skilfully worked varnished brick panels were probably used inside the megalithic-type tombs. The first Persian invaders lavishly decorated these tombs. Amlash in particular has yielded splendid vases embellished with domestic animals.

The Sakiz treasure throws valuable light on the origins of Achaemenian art. Gold accoutrements and inlaid ivory-work were discovered in a bronze sarcophagus.

During the Achaemenian period (530-331 BC) art was influenced by countries under Persian sovereignty: Assyria and Babylonia with a certain diffusion of Greek and Egyptian styles. Achaemenian art was primarily directed towards the adulation of the king, seen in splendid bas-reliefs at Persepolis. Achaemenian artists were also skilled in depicting animals, including lions and unicorns.

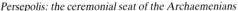

Persepolis: the ceremonial seat of the Archaemenians

Hellenistic influence is apparent in Parthian sculpture, bas-reliefs depicting hunting scenes and the usual vassals bearing gifts to the emperor.

Early Persian art, by now diluted with various Oriental trends, saw a renaissance under the Sassanid shahs, who were great builders of palaces, bridges and other monuments. Palace walls were decorated with lavish frescoes and stucco, and floors were covered in mosaic paving featuring Eastern, Greek and Roman motifs.

The Moslem occupation of Persia contributed fresh ideas and even experts find difficulty in distinguishing Persian from Islamic art of this period. This fusion of styles is reflected in arabesques and geometric patterns, especially in tile decoration, frequently found on the cupolas of mosques. Mausoleums were also sumptuously decorated.

No better example exists of Islamic-Persian architecture and associated arts than the city of Isfahan, the richest repository of Persian art. Its lofty 'Friday Mosque' is a veritable museum of nine centuries of work by sculptors and craftsmen. It was built under the Sejuk shahs, but every successive dynasty contributed something. The work of the ornamentalists is most evident in the rich mosaic faience adorning the side walls of the south porch.

Craftsmen excelled in pottery, weaving, sculpture and mosaic work, but it was probably in miniature paintings that Persian art reached a peak. The style developed in the 14-15th centuries, attained its zenith during Mongol rule and maintained a high creative level under the Safavid shahs.

Persian literature has its beginnings in antiquity in poems attributed to the prophet Zoroaster himself. Again, literature was influenced by Islam. In the ninth century, Persian poetry was enjoyed far beyond the limits of the empire. In poetry the epic was most popular, and in its most classic form Persian poetry was characterised by refinement of expression.

After the centuries of Arab rule, literature experienced a revival. The vast heritage of epic legends is combined in the famous *Book of Kings* by Firdausi. A 50,000-couplet masterpiece, it relates the dawn of civilisation and the history of Persia until the end of the Sassanid empire.

Persia has produced some great names in the arts and sciences, including Omar Khayyam, an astronomer and mathematician as well as a poet, and Sadi and Hafiz, two most cherished poets.

Today, the *naqqal*, or professional narrator, keeps the riches of Persian poetry alive in recitations to the illiterate. Indeed poetry reading is still much practised in cheaper Persian cafés.

Wildlife

Iran has a wide range of wildlife, mainly found in the mountainous north.

Lynx, leopard and Persian cheetahs still exist, but the Persian lion is believed extinct. Red and roe deer, wild sheep, goats and ibex abound in the mountain ranges and, in the forests, there are bears, wild pigs, porcupines, badgers and squirrels.

Though mainly preferring forest cover, rabbits, hares, jackals, foxes and wolves are distributed through the country. In the deserts wild asses are found. Iran also boasts a variety of bird life.

The Caspian Sea is noted for many varieties of sturgeon, white fish, pike, catfish, perch and salmon. Northern streams abound in brown trout and some 200 species of fish inhabit the Persian Gulf, plus shrimp, lobster and turtles.

Iran has strict conservation laws governing not only unlawful hunting and fishing in protected areas, but also pollution of rivers and lakes and mutilation of trees.

Economy

Oil is the unquestioned key to Iranian economic development. No matter how drastically the new Islamic regime seeks to rebuild the country in every sphere of its economic, political and social life, the oil basis is firmly established until the crude runs out. However, the exorbitant cost of fuelling the war with Iraq, which started in 1979, has undoubtedly deprived Iran's economic sector of the large scale investment the country's oil producing neighbours have enjoyed over the past decade.

The Shah sought to wrench Iran into the developed world through oil revenues and oil-related industrialisation – and in the process brought about his own downfall. The upheavals of land reform and rapid economic expansion, and the disappointed expectations of poorer Iranians, all provided the grievances which provoked the crisis. Iran had already embarked on a major industrial and agricultural growth programme when oil prices quadrupled in 1973 leading to a frenzy of economic activity. By 1977 Iran was able to register a 14% growth in GDP, with industrial production leaping ahead in the 1973-6 period by 17%. Great hopes were vested in petrochemical and steel output using domestic oil and gas, and in a host of assembly line projects using imported foreign parts. Major foreign companies were lured into the country to marry Iranian capital with Western technology. And to supplement oil earnings, large investment was made in natural gas exploitation which, it was hoped, could eventually produce a quarter of the income currently supplied by oil exports.

But the Islamic Republic inherited an economy badly strained by the Shah's ambitions and reforms. Attempts at industrialisation often proved costly and unprofitable. Poor communications, power shortages, rampant inflation and shortages of skilled labour made the road to industrial development a rough one. The war with Iraq inevitably put back all development plans. Private Iranian money was never attracted to the long-term risks of major projects, preferring safe but unproductive investment in property and trading. Far from becoming a new Japan, Iran was faced with the prospect of building a succession of loss-making industries which had to be protected from outside competition.

Iran has enormous potential. In addition to its oil, the country also boasts rich mineral deposits, fertile agricultural regions, an emergent steel industry and vast manpower reserves. However, while the war with Iraq continued none of these sectors could make significant economic progress. If the proposed peace with Iraq is successful Iran will be faced with an enormous rebuilding programme if it is to repair the devastation wrought by almost a decade of war. But until there is a settlement of the conflict, which has cost so much in money, resources and life, Iran cannot sensibly begin to put its house – or its economy – back in order.

The pattern of life under the strictly Islamic regime is much changed

General Information

Government

Islamic Republic

Languages

About 50% of the population speak Persian (Farsi), the official language. Other languages include Turkic tongues, Kurdi, Baluchi and Arabic. English and French are widely spoken amongst the educated classes.

Religion

98% Moslem (90% Shia) with minorities of Christians, Jews and Zoroastrians.

Business Hours

Banks: *Winter* Saturday-Wednesday 0800-1300 and 1600-1800. *Summer* Saturday-Wednesday 0730-1300 and 1700-1900; Thursday 0730-1130.

Shops: *Winter* Saturday-Thursday 0800-2000 and Friday 0800-1200. *Summer* Saturday-Thursday 0800-1300 and 1700-2100; Friday 0800-1200.

Government offices: Saturday-Wednesday 0800-1400 and Thursday 0800-1200.

Offices: *Winter* 0800-1700; *Summer* 0800-1300 and 1800-2000.

Many offices are closed on Thursday afternoon and all day Friday. The bazaars close at sunset.

Customs Regulations

Visitors should check on the customs currency regulations before going to Iran, as these are liable to change at short notice.

Climate

The temperature in Tehran ranges from a maximum of over 38°C (100°F) to a minimum of −14°C (7°F) with January temperature averaging 3°C (38°F) and July-August temperature averaging 29°C (84°F). Humidity is low, but the nights stay hot and dry in summer. There is usually a short rainy season in the spring and early winter, but no rain between the end of April and the beginning of October. In winter there are heavy snowfalls. In mountain regions there are extreme changes of temperature. The Gulf and Caspian areas are extremely hot and humid and the winters are mild.

What to wear: In summer extremely light clothing is necessary – made of cotton, linen or silk. In winter very warm clothes are needed. Coats, hats and warm shoes should be taken.

Health Precautions

Drinking water is quite safe in most large towns, but it should be asked for specifically at hotels, as the tap water may taste unpleasant. In rural areas it is wise to drink only tea and soft drinks. Public baths are a great Iranian institution.

Public Holidays

With the new Islamic rigour of the Republic, the Moslem holidays will be strictly observed. April 1st is Islamic Republic Day.

Embassies/consulates in Iran

Afghanistan: Abbas Abad Ave, Pompe Benzine, Corner of 4th St, Teheran. Tel: 627531.

Algeria: Vali Asr Ave, Ofogh St, No. 26, Teheran. Tel: 293482. Telex: 212393.

Argentina: POB 98-164, Ave Mossadegh, Blvd Nahid, No. 35. Tajrish, Teheran.

Australia: 123 Khaled al-Islambuli Ave, POB 11365-8643, Teheran 15138. Tel 626202. Telex: 212459.

Austria: Taleghani Ave, Corner Forsat Ave No. 140, Teheran. Tel: 828431. Telex: 212872.

Bahrain: Park Ave, 31st St, No. 16, Teheran.

Bangladesh: Gandhi Ave, 5th St, Building No. 14, POB 11365-3711, Teheran. Tel: 682979. Telex: 212303.

Belgium: Fereshteh Ave, Shabdiz Lane, 3 Babak St, POB 11365-115, Teheran 19659. Tel: 294574. Telex: 212446.

Brazil: 58 Vanak Sq., Vanak Ave, Teheran 19964. Tel: 683498. Telex: 212392.

Bulgaria: Vali Asr Ave, Tavanir St, Nezami Ganjavi St No. 82, POB 11365-7451, Teheran. Tel: 685662. Telex: 212789.

China, People's Republic: Pasdaran Ave, Golestan Ave 1 No. 53, Teheran.

Colombia: Bihaghi Ave, 14th St, No. 15, POB 41-3315, Teheran.

Cuba: Africa Ave, Amir Parviz St No. 1/28, Teheran. Tel: 632953.

Czechoslovakia: Enghelab Ave, Sarshar St No. 61, POB 1500, Teheran. Tel: 828168.

Denmark: Intersection Africa and Modaress Expressway, Bidar St No. 40, POB 11365-158, Teheran. Tel: 297371. Telex: 212784.

Finland: Gandhi Ave, 19th St, No. 26, POB 15875-4734, Teheran. Tel: 684985. Telex: 212930.

France: ave de France No. 85, Teheran (diplomatic relations broken off by France 1987).

Gabon: POB 337, Teheran. Tel: 823828. Telex: 215038.

German Democratic Republic: Mirza-ye Shirazi Ave, Ali Mirza Hassani St 15, Teheran. Tel: 627858. Telex: 212453.

Germany, Federal Republic: 324 Ferdowsi Ave, POB 11365-179, Teheran. Tel: 212488. Telex: 2488.

Ghana: Ghaem Magham Farahani Ave, Varahram St No. 12, Teheran.

Greece: Park Ave, 35th St No. 20, Teheran. Tel: 686096.

Holy See: Razi Ave, No. 97, ave de France Crossroad, POB 11365-178, Teheran (Apostolic Nunciature). Tel: 643574.

Hungary: Abbas Abad Park Ave, 13th St, No. 18, Teheran. Tel: 622800.

India: Saba Shomali Ave, No. 166, POB 11365-6573, Teheran. Tel: 894554. Telex: 212858.

Indonesia: Ghaem Magham Farahani Ave, No. 210, POB 11365-4564, Teheran. Tel: 626865. Telex: 212049.

Ireland: 8 Mirdamad Ave, North Razan St, Teheran. Tel: 222731. Telex: 213865.

Italy: 81 ave de France, Teheran. Tel: 672107. Telex: 214171.

Japan: Bucharest Ave, N.W. Corner of 5th Av, POB 11365-814, Teheran. Tel: 623396. Telex: 212757.

Korea, Democratic People's Republic: Fereshteh Ave, Sarvestan Ave, No. 11, Teheran.

Korea, Republic: 37 Bucharest Ave, Teheran. Tel: 621125.

Kuwait: Dehkadeh Ave, 3-38 Sazman-Ab St, Teheran. Tel: 636712.

Lebanon: Bucharest Ave, 16th St, No. 43, Teheran.

Libya: Motahhari Ave, No. 163, Teheran.

Malaysia: Bucharest Ave, No. 8, Teheran. Tel: 629523.

Mauritania: Africa Ave, Sayeh St, No. 78, Teheran. Tel: 623655. Telex: 213524.

Netherlands: Vali Asr Ave, Ostad Motahari Ave, Sarbederan St, Jahansouz Alley No. 36, Teheran. Tel: 896012. Telex: 212788.

New Zealand: Mirza-ye-Shirazi Ave, Kucheh Mirza Hassani, No. 29, POB 11365-436, Teheran. Tel: 625061. Telex: 212078.

Nicaragua: Teheran.

Nigeria: Jomhoori Islami Ave, 31st St, No. 9, POB 11365-7148, Teheran. Tel: 684934.

Norway: Bucharest Ave, 6th St, No. 23, POB 15875-4891, Teheran 15146. Tel: 624644. Telex: 213009.

Oman: Pasdaran Ave, Golestan 9, No. 5 and 7, POB 41-1586, Teheran. Tel: 243199. Telex: 212835.

Pakistan: Dr Fatemi Ave, Jamshidabad Shomali, Mashal St No. 1, Teheran. Tel: 934331.

Philippines: Bucharest Ave, No. 6, POB 14155-5337, Teheran. Tel 625392.

Poland: Africa Expressway, Piruz St No. 1/3, Teheran. Tel: 227262.

Portugal: Mossadegh Ave, Tavanir Ave, Nezami Ghanjavi Ave, No. 30, Teheran. Tel: 681380. Telex: 212588.

Qatar: Africa Expressway, Golazin Ave, Parke Davar No. 4, Teheran. Tel: 221255. Telex: 212375.

Romania: Fakhrabad Ave 22-28, Teheran. Tel: 759841. Telex: 212791.

Saudi Arabia: Bucharest Ave, No. 59, POB 2903, Teheran. Tel: 624297. (Diplomatic relations broken off by Saudi Arabia in 1988).

Senegal: Vozara Ave, 48th St, BP 3217, Teheran. Tel: 624142.

Somalia: Shariati Ave, Soheyl Ave No. 20, Teheran.

Spain: Ghaem Magham Farahani Ave, Varahram St No. 14, Teheran. Tel: 624575. Telex: 212980.

Sudan: Gandhi Ave, 21st St, No. 5, Teheran.

Sweden: Taleghani Ave, Forsat Ave, Teheran. Tel: 828305. Telex: 212822. British interests section at Royal Swedish Embassy, 143 Ferdowsi Ave, POB 11365-4474, Teheran 11344. Tel: 675011. Telex: 212493.

Switzerland: Boustan Ave, POB 11365-176, Teheran. Tel: 268226. Telex: 212851.

Syria: Bucharest Ave, 10th St, No. 42, Teheran.

Thailand: Baharestan Ave, Parc Amin ed-Doleh No. 4, POB 11495-111, Teheran. Tel: 301433. Telex: 214140.

Turkey: Ferdowsi Ave No. 314, Teheran. Tel: 315299.

USSR: Neauphle-le-Château Ave, Teheran.

United Arab Emirates: Zafar Ave, No. 355-7, Teheran. Tel: 221333. Telex: 212697.

Venezuela: Bucharest Ave, 9th St, No. 31, Teheran. Tel: 625185. Telex: 213790.

Yemen Arab Republic: Bucharest Ave, No. 26, Teheran.

Yemen, People's Democratic Republic: Bucharest Ave, 10th St, No. 41, Teheran.

Yugoslavia: Vali Asr Ave, Fereshteh Ave, Amir Teymour Alley, No. 12, Teheran. Tel: 294127. Telex: 214235.

Zaire: Vali Asr Ave, Chehrazi St, No. 68, POB 11365-3167, Teheran. Tel: 222199.

Tehran

The capital is a modern city in nearly every sense of the word, with up-to-date shops, traffic fumes, noise, impersonal high buildings and extensive suburbs. But there are places of architectural interest. The Sepahsalar Mosque, completed in 1830, has eight minarets from which the city can be viewed. Museums include the Archaeological Museums, the Decorative Arts Museum and the National Arts Museum, and there are several cooling parks and gardens. Visitors to the capital were greatly reduced following the revolution and the war. All the leading hotel chains pulled out. It is advisable to seek advice on the availability of accommodation from the Iranian embassy.

Outside Tehran there is some fine scenery. Only 8 km south is **Rev** with early monuments. West of Tehran is **Qazvin** (150 km) on the Asian Highway, an ancient city full of mosques.

Azarbaijan – The Western Gateway

This province borders Turkey, Iraq, and the Soviet Union and for most overland travellers to pre-Republican Iran represented the first taste of the country. It has mountains and fertile valleys and the great salt lake of Rezaiyeh.

The first town on the Highway is **Maku** from which various ancient sites, including Armenian churches, can be explored.

Rezaiyeh town, about 20 km from the western lake shore, claims to be the birth place of Zoroaster and its mosque was built on the site of an important fire-temple. The bazaars contain beautiful hand-carved inlaid woodwork.

Tabriz, is the second-largest city in Iran and is linked with Tehran (640 km) by rail, air and bus services. It has a number of reasonable hotels around the town centre. The covered Qaisariyeh bazaar dates back to the 15th century and offers carpets, rugs, silks, leather goods and jewellery. There is some fine cooking in Tabriz too.

Tabriz has the once-ruined but now restored Blue Mosque, completed in 1465 in the reign of Jahan Shah, when the city was the capital of Iran. There are two museums. From Tabriz there is a 218 km journey to **Ardebil,** skirting Mount Sabalen (4,800 m) associated with Zoroaster's vision of the holy scriptures. Ardebil has the mausoleum of Shaikh Safieddin, buried there in AD 1334.

The tomb of Cyrus the Great, near Shiraz

The 'Golden Triangle'

The ancient cities of **Hamadan, Kermanshah** and **Khorramabad** form the corners of the Golden Triangle of Ancient Persia, in the west of modern Iran, near the Iraqi border. This 'Triangle' contains the city of **Hamadan** itself – the summer capital of Cyrus the Great; the treasure mounds of Nush-e Jan, Baba Jan, Godin, Giyan, Ganj Dareh; Harsin, site of the 'Lorestan Brozes', the ancient potters' village of Lalajin; the temple of Artemis; the grottoes of Taghe Bostan and the bas-reliefs of Bisotun.

The Silk Route to China and the Royal Road of the Achaemenians also passed through the Triangle. There is pleasant rolling hill scenery in this part of Iran, interspersed with the enigmatic mounds (or *tappeh*) that house ancient treasures. **Hamadan** does not reveal much of its ancient history, except the 'Stone Lion' dating from the time of Alexander, the 'Mausoleum of Esther and Mordecai' which is now in fact thought to contain the remains of a different Jewish queen, Shushan Dokht, wife of a Sassanian king, Yazdegerd (around AD 400). The village of **Lalajin** is 24 km from Hamadin: it is famous for its pottery production.

Kermanshah is a good base for visiting **Taghe Bostan,** 9 km to the north, with its grottoes and bas-reliefs on the cliffs. **Bisotun,** 'The Mountain of the Gods', with a bas-relief 60 metres above the ground showing the deeds of Darius, is 32 km from Kermanshah. Unfortunately for the average visitor it is only visible from a distance, but there are several other extraordinary reliefs on the mountainsides in this region.

The Seleucid temple of Artemis at **Kangavar,** 31 km from **Sahneh,** consists of massive fallen columns, which are being reassembled. They are thought to have been damaged by an earthquake. The **Kangavar Valley,** 10 km east of Kangavar, is also rich in remains.

Isfahan

A former capital city of Persia (in the 11th or 13th and 16th to 18th centuries) Isfahan is still a central feature of the country, located midway between Tehran and Shiraz. It has a moderate climate, with an altitude of 1,500 m on the Zayan-dehrud river plain; it is protected from southern winds by the Zagros mountains and it receives cool northern breezes in spring and summer.

Isfahan has a central square unmatched in elegance and spaciousness anywhere in the world. It is seven times the size of the Piazza San Marco in Venice, and puts the grandeur of the surrounding palaces and mosques into appropriate proportions.

Among the most rewarding features of Isfahan are its mosques, palaces, bridges, gardens and trees. The Friday Mosque – Masjid-e Jomeh – is one of Iran's finest buildings, with something from every era of Persian architecture. The Shaikh Lotfullah Mosque has an exquisite dome, and the 17th century King's Mosque – Masjid-e Shah – is famous for the stalactite effect of its northern entrance. Other sights are the Ali Qapu Palace, the Seosepol Bridge with its 33 arches, the Chehel Soton (columned palace) and the Kiaban-e Chadar Bagh (four gardens' avenue).

The bazaars of Isfahan take travellers completely from the outside world and immerse them in an age-old rhythm of life, an atmosphere full of the market-cries of vendors, the hammering of the coppersmiths, the activities of carpet-weavers, silversmiths and cloth printers, the grilling of kebabs and the preparation of spices. The distinctive artefacts include carpets, rugs, pottery, embroidery, hand-printed cloth, jewellery, silver, brass and copper.

Shiraz (Fars Province)

One of the great ancient cities of Iran. Craftsmen from Shiraz helped the building of ancient Persepolis in 550 BC. The city was always prosperous and grew to fame in the 18th century when Karim Khan Zand made it his capital. Among the historic buildings are Jasjid-e Jame (Friday Mosque, begun in AD 894), Masjid-e Now (New Mosque, begun the 12th century), Shah Cheragh (King of Light Shrine, a pilgrimage centre with fine mirror work) and Narenjestan-e Qavam (the Orange Grove). There are

beautiful gardens. Shiraz artefacts on sale in its many bazaars and shopping arcades include Qashqai tribal carpets, mats, tablecloths, inlaid woodwork, gold, silver, glass and ceramic work.

Flying to Shiraz takes less than two hours from Tehran. The bus takes about nine hours.

Persepolis, 50 km from Shiraz, is the ceremonial seat for the Achaemenians, built on an enormous platform carved out

Isfahan: the richest repository of Persian art

of the Kuhe Rahmat. Darius the Great began the project in 521 BC. His son Xerxes and successors added to its palaces and halls. This was the setting of the 2,500th Persian Empire Anniversary celebrations in October 1971. Nearby is Naqshe Rustam, with rock-cut tombs and a Zoroastrian temple. **Pasargade,** 80 km north of Persepolis, is in the plain of Morghab, capital of Cyrus the Great.

Khuzistan

The scene of early Persian civilisations dating back to 8000 BC, Khuzistan has several archaeological sites of great interest. **Haft Tappeh,** north of Ahwaz, includes more than a dozen burial mounds and the remains of the Elamite city of Tikni (1500 BC). **Choga Zanbil** has the remains of an important religious centre dating back 3,000 years. **Shush** (Susa) has a museum that has gathered impressive samples of architecture and remains from several eras. It is also the site of Daniel the Prophet's tomb.

Caspian Coast

The coast has a lush sub-tropical climate and vegetation and is popular with Iran's own holidaymakers. The main resorts are **Ramsar, Babolsar, Nowshahr** and **Bandar Enzeli.**

Khorasan

A huge province in the east of Iran, stretching between the Elburz mountains and the Great Kevir desert, Khorasan means 'the land of the rising sun'. It was from here that Persian culture spread to central Asia and here also occurred the great revival of learning in the Islamic era. The cities of Toos and Neishabur became centres of calligraphy, poetry, philosophy and science.

Mashad is today the most populous city in Khorasan. It used to be a crossroads of caravan traffic on the Silk Route to China, but it was modernised earlier this century, with avenues and parks. The Sacred Precincts and the old bazaar now exist separately from the modern city. The bazaar became famous for its hidden alleyways, backstreet turquoise workshops and carpet factories. In the days of the Shah up to four million pilgrims and tourists visited the city and shrine each year.

The courtyards, mosques, libraries and colleges surrounding the holy shrine in Mashad were built under successive rulers over an immense expanse of time. For non-Moslems entrance to the 'Sacred Threshold' itself is prohibited.

About 130 km west of Mashad is the ancient town of **Neishabur,** home of Omar Khayyam, poet, mathematician and astronomer. His tomb there was once a principal tourist attraction.

Toos, 30 km north-east of Mashad, is where Persia's 11th century poet Ferdowsi was born and died.

The main roads to Khorasan province are the northern route, through Gorgan and the Caspian region, and the southern route, which follows the ancient Silk Route, passing many historic ruins, shrines and mosques.

Kerman

In the southern desert region, the city of Kerman was founded by the Sassanid King Ardashir I. Turks and Mongols occupied it successively until the Safarid dynasty, when it became prosperous for a while, though it was subsequently destroyed in the 18th century. However the most exquisite architecture of the Friday Mosque, built in 1348 and restored by the Safarids in the 16th century, has survived to display its stunning beauty, proportions and decoration. The city of Kerman is full of beautiful mosques and worth a visit. It also has a fine shady garden and a ruined citadel said to have been built by Ardashir.

IRAQ

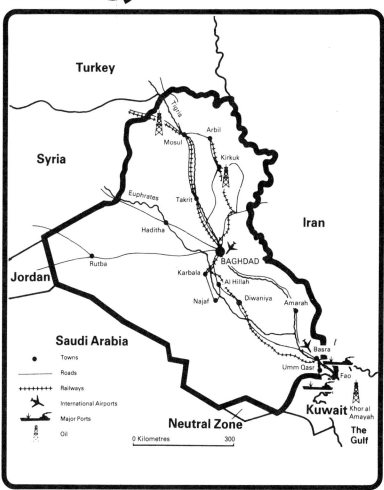

Area: 438,466 sq km
Population: 14,110,425 (latest official estimate)
Capital: Baghdad

Before the outbreak of war with Iran in 1980, Iraq had plans to launch an extensive development programme, funded by oil revenue, which would have boosted tourism at both public and private sector levels. Had the scheme gone ahead it is likely that Iraq would today be reaping the benefits of being a major Middle East tourist destination. However, the war with Iran put paid to those plans. Hopes for tourism and other revenue earning projects are largely dependent on the success of the truce agreed with Iran in July 1988.

Cradle of civilisation

Iraq is a country of contrasts, both in its landscape – with hills, mountains, deserts and marshes – and its people, who are ethnically and religiously diverse. A relatively rich country with a long, chequered history, Iraq is, with justification, often called the cradle of civilisation.

Iraq's present Islamic culture is the latest in a long series of influences which have dominated the region, in fact the country still boasts the remains of the great cities that ruled past civilisations like Ur, Babylon and Nineveh. Considerable trouble is taken to preserve and display to advantage the historical remains of these past cultures, most of which are accessible by road or rail.

The central feature of Iraq is its two major rivers, the Tigris and the Euphrates – its ancient name of Mesopotamia is Greek for 'land between the two rivers'. Yet although these rivers traverse the length of Iraq, from the Turkish and Syrian borders in the north to the Gulf in the South, it is a country of contrasting scenery with distinctly different regions.

The north-east is a mountainous region – the highest peak, the Hasarost, being 4000 m. This is almost a temperate zone with abundant rainfall and snow in winter. The lower slopes of the mountains are cultivated to grow fruit, vegetables and tobacco.

This area is inhabited predominantly by Kurds who constitute about 15% of the population of Iraq. They have preserved their own distinctive way of life. The area also includes small numbers of Assyrians (about 40,000) who speak a form of Syriac, Yazidis (65,000) who also have their own language and Turkomans (about 100,000) who speak a Turkish dialect. The Assyrians live mainly in the foothills of the mountains where the rainfall is less. With the help of irrigation, however, they produce cereals as well as vegetables.

The west of Iraq is a sparsely populated desert and semi-desert zone where nomadic tribes roam, living off their herds of camels, goats and sheep. Rainfall is minimal here and summers are very hot. In places the underlying rock protrudes through the sand and scrub and it is from this that present-day Iraq – meaning cliff – gets its name. The people of this area are essentially the same Arab tribes that inhabit the eastern parts of Jordan and the north-eastern parts of Saudi Arabia.

The majority of Iraq's population, however, is concentrated along the two

The marsh Arabs of southern Iraq

rivers. This area is relatively fertile, although rainfall is slight, falling mainly in winter. The rivers flood regularly in spring, especially in the south where they flow several feet above the surrounding plain, raised on the levels of silt which they deposit.

The central plains north of Baghdad are well irrigated, sometimes on the basis of systems which are thousands of years old, and many crops are produced, including cereals, vegetables and cotton. South of Baghdad the severe flooding has resulted in areas of both marshland and desert. Yet in the areas which have been drained and irrigated, dates, citrus fruits, cereals (including rice) and cotton are grown. Date cultivation is concentrated mainly in the area of Basra. Winters in the plains are mild but summers are hot and very humid.

It is in the southern marshlands that the much-photographed 'Marsh Arabs' live. They are concentrated mainly in the area of Al-Chebayish just before the Tigris and the Euphrates join together in the Shatt al-Arab waterway which takes them to the Gulf. The area was once well cultivated, but in the seventh century it was flooded, leaving only the higher areas above water. There are now more than 1,000 islands, each supporting a few houses, and the only form of transport is the *mashhouf* – a small boat made of reeds. The 12,000 inhabitants of this area have constructed artificial islands of papyrus and mud, and bridges now connect some of the islands.

In general, however, the people of the central plains are Arabs but of very mixed ancestry. They are mostly Moslem, but are divided between the two main sects of Islam – the Sunni and Shi'a. The Sunni are mainly in the northern areas and are from the wealthier sections of society, while the Shi'a are concentrated in the south. There are in addition some 400,000 Christians of various sects scattered throughout Iraq.

Iraq society therefore has not only substantial ethnic minorities, but also religious minorities. The Kurds and Turkomans, for example, although distinct ethnic groups, are Sunni Moslems, while the Assyrians are Christian. The Yazidis, on the other hand, have a religion of their own which includes pagan as well as Islamic and Christian elements. Although this adds to the diversity of Iraq it also causes problems.

History and culture

The history of civilisation in what is now Iraq is at least 6,000 years old. Legend would suggest that it is even older, for it locates the site of the Garden of Eden at Al-Qurna, where the Tigris and Euphrates rivers join to form the Shatt al-Arab, and 120 km north-west of Baghdad excavations have revealed signs of a settlement dating back to 7000 BC.

The first well-known settlers, however, were the Sumerians, whose city states, based on a sophisticated agricultural economy, were flourishing around 3500 BC. The sites of two of these cities, Ur and Uruk, can be seen near Nasiriya, which is between Baghdad and Basra.

By 2300 BC the empire began to collapse with the entry into the area of various Semitic tribes. Ur flourished briefly again in 2100 BC but was finally sacked by the Amorites, another Semitic tribe from Arabia. After several centuries of disunity, a new empire was forged by the Semitic King Hammurabi, whose capital was Babylon. The city, however, was sacked by the Hittites in the 17th century and the focus of power moved northwards.

The Assyrian empire based on the northern city of Nineveh lasted from about 1400 BC until about 600 BC and at its height extended as far south as Egypt. The remains of the great Assyrian cities of Nineveh, Nimrud and Ashur can still be seen in the hills some 400 km north of Baghdad.

Nineveh was sacked in 612 BC by a combined revolt of the peoples subjected to the Assyrians' harsh rule and Babylon came into its own again. King Nebuchadnezzar reconstructed the city and built the famous hanging gardens, and his Chaldean Empire reached its peak in about 570 BC. Babylon subsequently fell to the Achaemenian Persians and then to Alexander the Great, after whose death in 323 BC it ceased to be an important political centre, but the ruins of its former glory are still standing some 59 miles south of Baghdad.

Subsequently Iraq fell under the sway of the Seleucids and the Parthians. The Parthian Persians and then the Sassanids held the area against the Romans and then the Byzantine Empire until 637 AD when the Arabs, fired with the new religion of Islam, invaded the region.

The first centre of Islamic civilisation was Damascus under the Umayyad dynasty, but in 750 AD the Abbasids became dominant with the support of the Shi'a in Iraq and the centre of Islamic power was transferred to Baghdad – a new city built for the purpose. This was the era of Caliph Haround al-Rashid of the *Thousand and One Nights* who encouraged the flowering of Arabic cultures. Most of the beautiful mosques built during this period are still standing, many of them with gold domes and minarets. But perhaps the most renowned of Iraq's Islamic attractions are the Shi'a shrines at Karabala and Najaf.

Gradually areas at a distance from Baghdad began to break away from the Abbaside Empire and it became weaker until the final blow was struck by the Mongol invasions of the 13th century. Iraq then ceased to be of any

Baghdad's Martyr's Mosque and the Tomb of the Unknown Soldier

importance and was conquered by the Turks in the 16th century. As the Ottoman Empire began to decline the various areas of present-day Iraq enjoyed considerable local autonomy and by the early 19th century the Western European powers were showing an interest in the region.

Arab nationalism began to have some influence by the end of that century and during the First World War the British used this to persuade the Arabs to fight against the Turks who had ruled them for so long. The promised independence never came, however, and Iraq found itself a British mandated territory. A series of Anglo-Iraqi treaties followed under which Britain safeguarded its interests while giving Iraq more and more nominal independence. But there were recurring problems over borders and with the various ethnic minorities.

Modern Iraq began in 1958 with the overthrow of the monarchy which Britain had imposed on the country. There followed a series of fairly bloody *coups d'etat* ultimately bringing to power the Baath Party which rules today.

Because of its long and varied history, Iraq is a culturally rich country. There is much to see dating from as far back as the Sumerian civilisation through the succeeding civilisations to the Islamic culture which predominates today. The people vary from the Marsh Arabs of the south to the nomads of the west and the Kurds in the north with their brightly coloured and distinctive clothes. Crafts which are still followed include copper work and the weaving of carpets.

Naturally the war with Iran has had devastating effects on some of Iraq's major towns and cities but reports suggest that most of the country's ancient sites escaped missile attack.

Economy

Iraq's economy is based on oil and agriculture. Oil is the principal source of wealth and all the country's oil resources are in government hands. The war with Iran has been an enormous drain on the economy. All the countries of the Gulf Cooperation Council – Saudi Arabia, Kuwait, Oman, Qatar, Bahrain and the UAE – have contributed to the Iraqi war effort but even their help was not able to secure a swift end to the bloody conflict. Conscription of able bodied men into the armed forces also had its effect; with all available men at the front, women were left to keep things ticking over at home. Agriculture, always a mainstay of the Iraqi economy, still employs more people than any other sector of the economy (about 30%) and is the most important economic sector after oil.

The government realised at an early stage of the war with Iran that agricultural production would be a crucial factor in supplying the troops and, with that in mind, various programmes to encourage greater private initiative were implemented. A wide variety of crops are grown but the most important are barley and wheat. Other crops are rice, vegetables, maize and millet, sugar cane, oilseeds, pulses and dates, Iraq's main export after oil. Self sufficiency in food production is still a priority but realistically this is unlikely to be achieved until vast domestic reconstruction goals have been achieved. River control and irrigation remain important areas of attention, however, as part of the general drive towards agricultural development.

Before the outbreak of war with Iran, Iraq was the second largest Middle East oil producer after Saudi Arabia with an average export rate of 3.2 million barrels of oil daily (b/d). In order to sustain these levels of throughput, Iraq utilised a network of pipelines running through Turkey, Syria and Lebanon. This arrangement was not without its problems and export capacity decreased. War damage to refineries, such as Basra which was bombed early in the war effectively closing down operations, and Dawra also had economically devastating effects. Iraq has been heavily dependent on foreign borrowing, the country's total foreign debt in 1986 was estimated at $50bn. However, an encouraging plus point is the identification of five major oilfields for future development. Exploitation of these fields could increase production capacity by 2m barrels a day. But until the July 1988 ceasefire all Iraq's available funding was chanelled to helping the war effort, effectively depriving all other economic sectors of the opportunity to develop and prosper.

General Information

Government

The Revolutionary Command Council (RCC) has supreme power; it is made up of members of the Regional Command of the Arab Socialist Baath Party led by President Saddam Hussain.

Languages

Arabic is the official language. Minority groups in the north speak Turkish and Kurdish. French and English are taught in schools. Many businessmen speak English.

Religion

Over 90% of the population is Moslem more than 50% of whom are Shi'ite. There are small communities of Christians in many towns and a small Jewish community in Baghdad.

How to get there

The national carrier of Iraq is Iraqi Airways.

Entry regulations

A passport is required by all travellers. Nationals of Iraq, Egypt, Jordan and Palestinians holding Jordanian passports do not require entry visas, otherwise all travellers require visas. Visas are obtainable from Iraqi embassies abroad. Visas will not be issued to holders of Israeli visas. Usually a written invitation to visit Iraq from a government organisation is demanded before a visa is issued. Applications should be made well in advance as delays sometimes occur in obtaining visas.

Visitors need a valid international certificate of vaccination against small-pox. If arriving from endemic areas visitors should be vaccinated against cholera, yellow fever and typhoid.

Custom regulations

It is forbidden to export more than ID5 in local currency. Foreign currency has to be declared on entry and it is not allowed to export sums in excess of the amount declared on entry.

Visitors are allowed to take into Iraq, free of duty, one litre of spirits and 200 cigarettes or 50 cigars or 250 gms of tobacco and one litre of wine or spirits. Travellers' personal effects are not subject to customs duty.

Climate

The central and southern areas of the country are characterised by a cold winter and long, dry summer. From May till the end of September it is excessively hot with no rainfall and temperatures are between 38°C and 49°C. In Basra the humidity is high throughout the summer and the nights are hot. From October to April the weather is usually dry and warm during the day, while from December to March the nights are cold. Rain falls normally between October and April.
What to wear: In summer, lightweight clothes are essential and headgear and sunglasses are advisable. From the end of October to mid-April medium-weight clothing is required.

Currency

Iraqi Dinar (ID); ID1 = 1,000 fils.

Business hours

Government offices: *Summer* Saturday-Wednesday 0800-1400 and Thursday 0800-1300. *Winter* Saturday-Wednesday 0830-1330 and Thursday 0830-1330.

Shops: *Summer* Saturday-Wednesday 0800-1400 and 1700-1900; Thursday 0800-1300. *Winter* Saturday-Wednesday 0830-1430 and 1700-1900; Thursday 0830-1330.

Banks: Saturday-Wednesday 0800-1200 and Thursday 0800-1100. *Winter* Thursday 0900-1200.

Press

The Baghdad Observer, POB 624, Karantina, Baghdad is published daily in English.

Public holidays

New Year's Day, 1 January
Army Day, 6 January
Anniversary of Revolution, 8 February
Nairuz, 21 March
First day of Ramadan*, 7 April 1989
Labour Day, 1 May
Eid al-Fitr*, 7-9 May 1989
Baath Revolution Day, 17 July
Eid al-Adha*, 14-17 July 1989
Hijra*, 4 August 1989
Al-Ashoura*, 13 August 1989
Prophet's birthday*, 13 October 1989
The dates of the Muslim holidays, marked with an asterisk, are only approximate as they depend on sightings of the moon.

Transport

Subject to drastic alteration because of war.

By air: Iraq Airways operates regular air services between Baghdad, Basra and Mosul.

By road: Major towns are connected by a road network, and there are regular bus services from Baghdad and other main cities. Taxis are plentiful but it is advisable to negotiate the fare before the start of the journey. Self-drive facilities are available.

By rail: The Iraqi Republican Railways aim to run regular passenger and goods services but much of Iraq's railway system was destroyed by Iranian bombs.

Accommodation and food

Hotel prices are government-controlled. It is advisable to arrange for advance booking.

The prices of restaurant meals are also government-controlled. Restaurants serve both oriental and European dishes. Popular Iraqi dishes are *Kubba;* a special preparation of wheat known as *Borghul* is mixed with minced meat, flattened, and pieces stuffed with meat and filled with nuts, sultanas, spices, parsley and onion. They are formed in the shape of flat platters or round balls, then boiled and ready to serve; *Dolma,* made from stuffed vine leaves, cabbage, lettuce, onions, egg-plants, marrow or cucumbers. The stuffing is made of rice mixed with minced meat and spices; *Tikka,* small chunks of mutton on skewers grilled on a charcoal fire; *Quozi,* a small lamb boiled whole and then grilled. It is usually stuffed with rice, minced meat and spices, and served on a large tray heaped with rice; *Masgoug,* this is fish from the Tigris, which is cooked right on the river bank, fresh from the river.

Consulates/Embassies in Baghdad

Afghanistan: Maghrib St, Ad-Difa'ie, 27/1/12 Waziriyah, Baghdad. Tel: 422-9986.

Algeria: Ash-Shawaf Sq., Karradat Mariam, Baghdad. Tel: 537-2181.

Argentina: Hay al-Jamia District 915, St 24, No. 142, POB 2443, Baghdad. Tel: 776-8140. Telex: 3500.

Australia: Al-Karada ash-Sharqiya Masba 39B/35, POB 661, Baghdad. Tel: 719-3423. Telex: 212148.

Austria: POB 294, Hay Babel 929/2/5 Aqaba bin Nafi's Sq., Masbah, Baghdad. Tel: 719-9033. Telex: 212383.
Bahrain: 44/7/605 Hay al-Mutanabi, Al-Mansour, Baghdad. Tel: 542-8945. Telex: 213304.
Bangladesh: 75/17/929 Hay Babel, Baghdad. Tel: 718-4143. Telex: 2370.
Belgium: Hay Babel 929/27/25, Baghdad. Tel: 719-8297. Telex: 212450.
Brazil: 609/16 Al-Mansour, Houses 62/62-1, Baghdad. Tel: 551-1365. Telex: 2240.
Bulgaria: 9/12 Harthiya, Baghdad. Tel: 542-0049.
Canada: 47/1/7 Al-Mansour, Baghdad. Tel: 542-1459. Telex: 212486.
Central Africa Republic: 208/406 Az-Zawra, Harthiya, Baghdad. Tel: 551-6520.
Chad: 97/4/4 Karradat Mariam, POB 8037, Baghdad. Tel: 537-6160.
China, People's Republic: New Embassy Area, International Airport Rd, Baghdad. Tel: 556-2740. Telex: 212195.
Cuba: St 7, District 929 Hay Babel, Al-Masba Arrasat al-Hindi. Tel: 719-5177. Telex: 212389.
Czechoslovakia: Dijlaschool St, No. 37, Mansour, Baghdad. Tel: 541-7136.
Denmark: Zukak No. 34, Mahallat 902, Hay al-Wahda, House No. 18/1, POB 2001, Alwiyah, Baghdad. Tel: 719-3058. Telex: 212490.
Djibouti: POB 6223, Al-Mansour, Baghdad. Tel: 551-3805.
Egypt: Baghdad.
Finland: POB 2041, Alwiya, Baghdad. Tel: 719-6174. Telex: 212454.
France: 102/55/7 Abu Nawas, Baghdad. Tel: 719-6061. Telex: 212160.
German Democratic Republic: 12/10/929 Hay Babel, Baghdad. Tel: 719-0071.
Germany, Federal Republic: Zukak 2, Mahala 929 Hay Babel (Masbah Square), Baghdad. Tel: 719-2037. Telex: 212262.
Greece: 63/3/913 Hay al-Jamia, al-Jadiriya, Baghdad. Tel: 776-9511. Telex: 212479.
Holy See: As-Sa'adoun St 904/2/46, POB

2090, Baghdad. Tel: 719-5183.
Hungary: Abu Nuwas St, Az-Zuwiya, POB 2065, Baghdad. Tel: 776-5000. Telex: 212293.
India: Taha St, Najib Pasha, Adhamiya, Baghdad. Tel: 422-2014.
Indonesia: 906/2/77 Hay al-Wadha, Baghdad. Tel: 719-8677. Telex: 2517.
Italy: 1 Zukak, 73 Mahalla, 913 Hay al-Jamia (University Circle), Jadiriya, Baghdad. Tel: 776-5058. Telex: 212242.
Japan: 929/17/70 Hay Babel, Masba, Baghdad. Tel: 719-3840. Telex: 212241.
Jordan: House 200/406, St 11, Area 213, Hay al-Hindi, Baghdad. Tel: 541-2892. Telex: 2805.
Kuwait: 35/5/915 Hay al-Jamia, Baghdad. Tel: 776-3151. Telex: 212108.
Lebanon: Iwadia Askary St, House 5, Baghdad. Tel: 416-8092. Telex: 2263.
Malaysia: 6/14/929 Hay Babel, Baghdad. Tel: 719-2048. Telex: 2452.
Mauritania: Al-Mansour, Baghdad. Tel: 551-8261.
Mexico: 601/11/45 Al-Mansour, Baghdad. Tel: 719-8039. Telex: 2582.
Morocco: Hay al-Mansour, POB 6039, Baghdad. Tel: 552-1779.
Netherlands: 29/35/915 Jadiriya, POB 2064, Baghdad. Tel: 776-7616. Telex: 212276.
New Zealand: 2D/19 Az-Zuwiya, Jadiriya, Baghdad. Tel: 776-8177. Telex: 212433.
Nigeria: 2/3/603 Al-Mansour, Baghdad. Tel: 542-1750.
Norway: 20/3/609 Hay al-Mansour, Baghdad. Tel: 541-0097. Telex: 212715.
Oman: POB 6180, 213/36/15 Al-Harthiya, Baghdad. Tel: 551-8198. Telex: 212480.
Pakistan: 14/7/609 Al-Mansour, Baghdad. Tel: 541-5120.
Philippines: Hay Babel, Baghdad. Tel: 719-3228. Telex: 3463.
Poland: 30/13/931 Hay Babel, Baghdad. Tel: 719-0296.
Portugal: 66/11 Al-Karada ash-Sharqiya, Hay Babel, Sector 925, St 25, No. 79, POB 2123, Alwiya, Baghdad. Tel:

776-4953. Telex: 212716.

Qatar: 152/406 Harthiya, Hay al-Hindi, Baghdad. Tel: 551-2186. Telex: 2391.

Romania: Arassat al-Hindia, Hay Babel, Mahalla 929, Zukak 31, No 452/A, Baghdad. Tel: 776-2860. Telex: 2268.

Saudi Arabia: 48A/1/7, 609 Al-Mansour, Baghdad. Tel: 551-3566.

Senegal: Jadiriya 75G 31/15, POB 565, Baghdad. Tel: 776-7636.

Somalia: 603/1/5 Al-Mansour, Baghdad. Tel: 551-0088.

Spain: Ar-Riad Quarter, District 929, Street No. 1, No. 21, POB 2072, Alwiya, Baghdad. Tel: 719-0176. Telex: 2239.

Sri Lanka: 07/80/904 Hay al-Wahda, POB 1094, Baghdad. Tel: 719-3040.

Sudan: 38/15/601 Al-Imarat, Baghdad. Tel: 542-4889.

Sweden: 15/41/103 Hay an-Nidhal, Baghdad. Tel: 719-5361. Telex: 212352.

Switzerland: Al-Karada Sharqiya Masbah, House No. 41/5/929, POB 2107, Baghdad. Tel: 719-3091. Telex: 212243.

Thailand: 1/4/609, POB 6062, Al-Mansour, Baghdad. Tel: 541-8798. Telex: 213345.

Tunisia: Mansour 34/2/4, POB 6057, Baghdad. Tel: 551-7786.

Turkey: 2/8 Waziriya, POB 14001, Baghdad. Tel: 422-2768. Telex: 214145.

Uganda: 41/1/609, Al-Mansour, Baghdad. Tel: 551-3594.

USSR: 4/5/605 Al-Mutanabi, Baghdad. Tel: 541-4749.

United Arab Emirates: Al-Mansour, 50 Al-Mansour Main St, Baghdad. Tel: 551-7026. Telex: 2285.

United Kingdom: Zukak 12, Mahala 218, Hay al-Khelood, Baghdad. Tel: 537-2121. Telex: 213414.

USA: 929/7/57 Hay Babel, Masba, POB 2447, Alwiyah, Baghdad. Tel: 719-6138. Telex: 212287.

Venezuela: Al-Mansour, House No. 12/79/601, Baghdad. Tel: 552-0965. Telex: 2173.

Viet-Nam: 29/611 Hay al-Andalus, Baghdad. Tel: 551-1388.

Yemen Arab Republic: Jadiriya 923/28/

29, Baghdad. Tel: 776-0647.

Yemen, People's Democratic Republic: 906/16/8, Hay Al-Wahda, Baghdad. Tel: 719-6027.

Yugoslavia: 16/35/923 Babel Area, Jadiriya, POB 2061, Baghdad. Tel: 776-7887. Telex: 213521.

Baghdad

Baghdad, the capital of Iraq, houses almost a fifth of the population. It was originally built on the western bank of the Tigris but has gradually spilled over onto both banks, connected by a number of bridges. The contrast between the many impressive new buildings in the city and the older, shabbier backstreets is striking, but will gradually lessen if the master plan for urban development is put into action. The plan gives priority to adequate housing, parks and recreation areas and is designed to preserve the character of the old architecture and the ruins of certain historic buildings, such as the Abbasid palace or Mustansiriya college (possibly the oldest university in the world).

Basra

Basra is the biggest city of the south and is situated on the banks of the Shatt al-Arab about 60 km from the Gulf and about 600 km south of the Baghdad, to which it enjoyed links by rail, road and air before the war. It is the centre of date production and is on the edge of the desert. It has been called the Venice of the east because of its numerous canals, but is of primary importance as Iraq's only direct link with the sea. Nearby is **Al Qurna,** said to be the site of the Garden of Eden where there is a famous old tree called Adam's Tree. Basra, which has several shrines dating back to the early days of Islam suffered extensive bomb damage during the war with Iran.

Mosul

Mosul is the main town of the north and is situated on the eastern bank of the Tigris some 500 km north of Baghdad. It is an important centre of trade and communications. The distinctive building material used in Mosul is limestone set in a gypsum cement and alabaster. In the past it was famous for making muslin which is derived from the town's name. Its museum houses some Assyrian and early Islamic items, and there is also the 13th century palace of Qara Sarai as well as the old mosque of Nabi Jirjis.

Kirkuk

The other important northern town is Kirkuk which assumed greater import-ance after oil was found in 1927. One of the strangest sights near the town is the Eternal Fires – the endless burning of natural gas seepages which are believed to be the burning furnace of the Old Testament which Daniel had to face. Kirkuk also boasts a castle dating from Ottoman days.

Arbil

Arbil, also in the north, is believed to be the oldest, constantly inhabited city in the world. It is first mentioned in 2000 BC, as Arbileam and later became famous as Arbella in the fourth century BC. It shows various stages of habitation throughout history and before the war had become a tourist holiday centre.

Hotels

NAME	ADDRESS	TELEPHONE	TELEX
BAGHDAD			
Al Mansour Melia	P.O. Box 6153	5470041	212976
Al Rasheed Oberoi	P.O. Box 8070	7766127	213204
Babylon Oberoi	P.O. Box 5273	7761964	213530
Ishtar Sheraton	P.O. Box 510	8863336	213147
Palestine Meridien	P.O. Box 3100	8875641	213151
BASRA			
Sheraton	(Non-operational)		
MOSUL			
Nineveh Oberoi	P.O. Box 1014	811933	8023

JORDAN

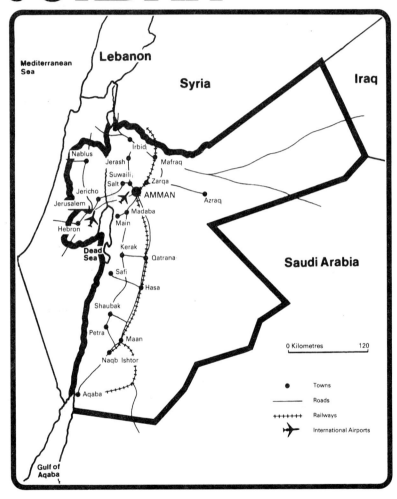

Area: 95,394 sq km
Population: 3,515,000 (official estimate).
Capital: Amman

Jordan is one of the smallest Middle East states, but it is extremely rich in historical remains, which cover 10,000 years. The country is frequently and aptly described as 'an open museum'. The dry climate has helped to preserve these ancient crusader castles and sacred shrines and visitors pour into the country to see them, making tourism one of the major resources. The ancient cities and relics – notably Petra, Jerash and Madaba – are easily visited from the capital, Amman, which itself embodies historic superlatives such as the second century AD Roman amphitheatre.

Jordan's scenery is striking, the climate and food good and the visitor warmly welcomed. Moreover, there has been a great improvement in tourist facilities generally. Visitors are, therefore, staying longer, not only to see the antiquities but to enjoy the beautiful beaches and splendid coral reefs of the Red Sea at Aqaba and the fascination of the desert, which covers 80% of Jordan's surface area.

The land

The capital, Amman, is situated at a height of 800m on a high plateau extending 324 kms from Syria to Ras en Naqb in the south.

The country is linked north-south by two parallel roads, the Kings Highway and the Desert Highway. The former descends from Amman, south through spectacular Wadi Mujib, to Petra. The Desert Highway, 324 kms long, is the main thoroughfare from Amman to Aqaba on the Red Sea.

North-west of Amman are undulating hills, some forested, others under cultivation. South-west is the Dead Sea depression, at 400m below sea-level the lowest level on earth. The River Jordan flows through this valley which is the agricultural heart of Jordan.

Trans-Jordan was a sparsely populated, primarily Bedouin patriarchy, ruled from its creation in 1921 by the Amir Abdullah, second son of the Sherif Hussein of Makkah – a Hashemite descendant of the Prophet.

The total population is an estimated 3.5 million, including the West Bank. 76% is urban and 29% rural, with nomadic tribes accounting for about 4%. About half a million of the population of East Jordan are classified as Palestinian refugees and are supported by the United Nations Relief and Works Agency. A further quarter of a million people were displaced by the events of 1967.

The majority of people are Moslem, but a relatively large Christian minority has settled in Amman.

Cultural interest

Apart from its rare antiquities and religious artefacts, Jordan is notable for mother of pearl *objets d'art*, olive wood, striking examples of weaving and embroidery and ethnic music. It is a land which has preserved not only rich archaeological mementos from the beginning of time but also a sanctuary for the principal bird migration route in an historic Middle East oasis. In Amman, on Citadel Hill, stands an outstanding museum with the chronological review of Jordan's history in relics from the past. The country's rich archaeological heritage can be seen at sites such as Petra, Jerash and Madaba.

Since time immemorial, Jordan has been the camping-ground of Bedouin tribesmen. A rugged desert life often precludes creative activities, but the Jordanian Bedouin women are famous for their beautifully woven robes – usually black and embroidered in colourful geometric designs around the neck, sleeves and hem. The traditional styles are displayed in the Folklore and Costume Museum in Amman.

Ethnic music resembles Middle Eastern music elsewhere. The main instruments in the *takht*, or orchestra, are the three-stringed *rababa*, or violin, the *qanun* which resembles a small harpsichord, the *oud*, or Islamic lute usually made from gazelle horn, and percussion implements such as the *riq tablah* and *daff.*

Jordanian art can be seen on permanent display at the Art Gallery of the Ministry of Culture and Youth. The Gallery, intended mainly for local art, is situated in the basement of the Ministry near the Haya Centre in Amman.

History

The Jordan Valley is considered by many historians to be the original site where man began a sedentary life.

Positioned between the Arabian deserts and the Mediterranean, with this fertile valley belt, it was natural that Jordan saw the passage of both travellers and invaders.

Canaanites, Egyptians, Babylonians, Persians, Greeks, Romans, Byzantines, Crusaders and ultimately European powers have occupied and quarrelled over Jordan.

Severe desert conditions forced the original settlers, the Canaanites, onto the eastern Mediterranean littoral. Migrations from the Arabian peninsula continued throughout the Bronze Age. Some historians maintain that famine in the Land of Canaan drove the descendants of Abraham into Egypt, about 1700 BC, but that in 1560 BC the Egyptians expelled their Hyksos, shepherd overlords and enslaved the Israelites who were later led back to Canaan by Moses.

Amid the ruggedly beautiful scenery of Mount Nebo, Moses indicated the rich River Jordan valley. Obeying, the Jews moved to Jericho and into Palestine. In 1000 BC King David moved his capital from Hebron to Jerusalem.

In 578 BC the Babylonians occupied Jerusalem until routed by Cyrus the Great in 538 BC; under Persian rule, the Jews were allowed to return. Alexander the Great imposed Hellenistic civilisation on the region but it was not conquered by another until the Roman imperial expansion, which sacked

Jerusalem in 70 AD. Thereafter Roman civilisation was forced upon the people. The last to fall under Roman domination were the industrious Nabataeans in their rocky stronghold of Petra, in south-west Jordan.

Roman rule continued in Jordan until the fourth century when the Emperor Constantine adopted the Christian faith and Jordan became a province of Byzantium.

Jerusalem was again conquered by the Persians in the seventh century. This time Christians were massacred and their churches destroyed. However, the occupation lasted only two decades. By now the Arabs had grown powerful, defeating the Byzantine rulers and introducing Islam.

In 1099, the Crusaders attacked Jerusalem, capturing the city and building their famous fortresses along the profitable caravan route from Arabia.

The Christian knights suffered defeat by Saladdin in 1187, but shortly after, Ayyubite rule ended when the Mamluks invaded Jordan and Syria, remaining until 1516.

It was then the Ottoman Turks who invaded the Holy Land, imposing a harsh regime which lasted until the Arab revolt of 1916.

Under command of the Hashemite Sherif of Hejaz, in co-operation with Colonel Lawrence, the Arabs laid siege to Turkish troops, driving them out of the region.

Allied victory over the Germans and Turks was declared in 1918 and the Arab world was split into British and French mandates.

In 1917, the Balfour Declaration declared the country, which had been Arab for centuries, a home for the Jews who, at that time, constituted only 7% of the population.

Palestine was made a British mandate, Trans-Jordan was devised and the son of the Sherif, Abdullah, made first head of state.

Petra: inhabited by the Nabateans from about 3000 BC

After the 1948 war with Israel, Trans-Jordan occupied part of Palestine and the holy sites of Jerusalem. In 1951, parliamentary representatives from both West and East Banks formed a constitution for a united Jordan.

In 1967, Israel conquered the West Bank and Jerusalem which are considered by Jordan as occupied territory.

Economy

Jordan lost its best-known assets and 80% of its hotel accommodation in the Six Day War. This loss of the West Bank in 1967 created acute economic problems for Jordan. Its major agricultural area was gone and it suddenly found itself host to 400,000 refugees, factors which severely curtailed normal development.

Growth was further inhibited by Israeli raids which saw Jordan directing large sums into military spending. Confidence further weakened following the 1971 confrontation with local Palestinian organisations.

Other factors contributed to the depressed state of the Jordanian economy in the late sixties and early seventies: the drain of skilled labour to developing countries, particularly the Gulf States, led to a shortage of locally trained technicians: this led to the reluctance of foreign companies to invest in the country because of high labour costs, and Jordan suffered from rising unemployment and hundreds of thousands of workers migrating.

Traditionally, Trans-Jordan was an agricultural economy until 1948, exporting cereals, fruits and vegetables to Palestine and abroad, via Haifa.

As the country is largely desert, agriculture was concentrated in the Jordan Valley, particularly in what is now 'occupied territory'. The Jordan Valley Authority aims at upgrading agriculture and living standards on the East Bank. The government has decided to intensify the search for commercially exploitable reserves of oil. The country's current oil production is small but guarded optimism about its potential has prompted two U.S. oil majors to sign prospecting agreements with Jordan.

Wildlife

Under legislation sponsored by King Hussein, national parks, wildlife reserves and biological stations have been established at Azraq, Shaumari, Petra, Wadi Rum and Aqaba.

There are more than 250 species of birds to be seen in Jordan. Azraq, a permanent source of water, is one of the most important bird sanctuaries in the world. The oasis is a stop-over for many varieties of migratory birds on their flight from Europe to India and Africa.

Mammals are sparsely distributed in the desert and rock areas of central, western and southern Jordan. These are normally desert gazelle, fox, and the sand rat, hares and jerboa.

The Gulf of Aqaba is rich in marine life, being especially noted for coral.

General Information

Government

Constitutional Monarchy.

Languages

The official language is Arabic but English is widely spoken; also some French.

Religion

The majority of the population is Moslem, but there is a sizeable Christian minority.

How to get there

By air: Royal Jordanian (formerly Alia) is the national carrier.
By road: From Europe through Turkey and Syria, there are good road conditions all the way to Amman. Taxis and buses run daily between Damascus and Amman. There is also an overland road linking Amman to Baghdad.
By sea: Jordan's only port is Aqaba on the Red Sea. Cargo vessels arrive from Europe and Asia; some carry passengers, but there are no scheduled passenger lines which call at Aqaba. The nearest sea port is Beirut.

Entry regulations

A valid passport with an entry visa is normally required for a visit to Jordan. Visas are not required by nationals of Algeria, Egypt, Iraq, Kuwait, Morocco, Syria and North Yemen. Visas are available at Jordanian embassies. Tourist visas are also obtainable at points of entry.

Cholera and smallpox vaccinations are required if arriving from infected areas.

Customs regulations

Import allowed on local currency is unlimited, provided it is not converted into foreign currency upon leaving Jordan and not deposited to the account of a non-resident. Foreign currency is also unrestricted provided it is declared on arrival. Export allowed on local currency, up to JD300; foreign currency up to the amount imported and declared.

Each visitor is allowed to take in 200 cigarettes, one bottle of spirit, one box of cigars. Articles for personal use such as portable typewriters, cameras etc, are admitted free of duty.

Climate

The summer, May to September, is hot and dry, but pleasantly cool in the evenings. The Jordan Valley (400m below sea level) is warm during the winter months and extremely hot in the summer. Rainfall during the months November to March.
What to wear: Clothes should be lightweight for summer and sun hats and sun glasses are also advisable. In winter warm woollens, coat and raincoat are necessary, particularly in Amman.

Currency

Jordanian Dinar (JD) divided into 1,000 fils.

Business hours

Most Moslem businesses close on Fridays, while Christian-owned businesses close on Sundays.
Government Offices: Saturday-Thursday 0830-1430.

105

Offices: May-October 0800-1300 and 1530-1930. November-April 0830-1330 and 1500-1830.

Banks: Saturday-Thursday 0900-1330. Cashiers close at 1230.

Shops: Saturday-Thursday 0800-1300 and 1500-1800.

Public holidays

Tree Day, 15 January
Arab League Day, 22 March
Labour Day, 1 May
Independence Day, 25 May
First day of Ramadan*, 7 April 1989
Eid al-Fitr*, 7-9 May 1989
King Hussein Accession to the throne, 11 August
Eid al-Adha*, 14-17 July 1989
Hijra*, 4 August
Al-Ashoura*, 3 August 1989
Prophet's birthday*, 13 October 1989
King Hussein's birthday, 14 November
The dates of the Moslem holidays, marked with an asterisk, are only approximate as they depend on sightings of the moon.

Transport

Jordan has an excellent network of roads and cars drive on the right. The service taxi (sharing) is a popular mode of transport providing regular daily runs along set routes within towns and throughout the country. Bus transport is available both within Amman and to most outlying districts. JETT, Jordan's official bus transport company, runs tours to Petra and Jerash in a new fleet of air-conditioned mini-buses.

Royal Jordanian operates scheduled flights from Amman to Aqaba (50 minutes).

Accommodation and food

Hotels offer a wide range of accommodation, both deluxe hotels and small inn type pensions or hostels.

There are tourist resthouses owned by the Ministry of Tourism and built near touristic sites and highways.

Meals at the majority of hotels and restaurants are mostly European but Jordanian dishes are offered on the menus. Oriental dishes are also available. Typical Jordanian dishes are *musakhan*, chicken in olive oil and onion sauce roasted on Arab bread, and *mensaf*, whole stewed lamb with yoghurt served on a bed of rice.

Consulates/Embassies in Amman

Algeria: 3rd Circle, Jabal Amman. Tel: 641271.

Australia: POB 35201, 4th Circle, Jabal Amman. Tel: 673246. Telex: 21743.

Austria: POB 815368, Amman. Tel: 644635. Telex: 22484.

Bahrain: Amman. Tel: 664148.

Belgium: Amman. Tel: 675683. Telex: 22340.

Brazil: POB 5497, Amman. Tel: 642183. Telex: 23827.

Bulgaria: POB 950578, Um Uzaina al-Janoubi, Amman. Tel: 818151. Telex: 22247.

Canada: POB 815403, Pearl of Shmeisani Bldg, Shmeisani, Amman. Tel: 666124. Telex: 23080.

Chile: Shmeisani, Amman. Tel: 661336. Telex: 21696.

China, People's Republic: Shmeisani, Amman. Tel: 666139. Telex: 21770.

Czechoslovakia: POB 2213, Amman. Tel: 665105.

Egypt: POB 35178, Zahran St, 3rd Circle, Jabal Amman. Tel: 641375.

France: POB 374, Jabal Amman. Tel: 641273. Telex: 21219.

Germany, Federal Republic: Al-Afghani St, POB 183, Jabal Amman. Tel: 641351. Telex: 1235.

Greece: POB 35069, Jabal Amman. Tel: 672331. Telex: 21566.

Hungary: POB 3441, Amman. Tel: 674916. Telex: 21815.

India: POB 2168, 1st Circle, Jabal

Amman. Tel: 637262. Telex: 21068.
Iran: POB 173, Jabal Amman. Tel: 641281. Telex: 21218.
Iraq: POB 2025, 1st Circle, Jabal Amman. Tel: 639331. Telex: 21277.
Italy: POB 9800, Jabal Luweibdeh, Amman. Tel: 638185. Telex: 21113.
Japan: Jabal Amman. Tel: 672486. Telex: 21518.
Korea, Democratic People's Republic: Amman. Tel: 666349.
Korea, Republic: 3rd Circle, Jabal Amman, Abu Tamman St, POB 3060, Amman. Tel: 642268. Telex: 29457.
Kuwait: POB 2107, Jabal Amman. Tel: 641235. Telex: 21377.
Lebanon: 2nd Circle, Jabal Amman. Tel: 641381.
Morocco: Jabal Amman. Tel: 641451. Telex: 21661.
Oman: Amman. Tel: 661131. Telex: 21550.
Pakistan: Amman. Tel: 622787.
Philippines: POB 925207, Shmeisani, Amman. Tel: 645161. Telex: 23321.
Poland: 1st Circle, Jabal Amman. Tel: 637153. Telex: 21119.
Qatar: Amman. Tel: 644331. Telex: 21248.

Romania: Amman. Tel: 663161.
Saudi Arabia: POB 2133, 5th Circle, Jabal Amman. Tel: 644154.
Spain: Jabal Amman. Tel: 622140. Telex: 21224.
Sudan: Jabal Amman. Tel: 624145. Telex: 21778.
Sweden: Shmeisani, Amman. Tel: 669177.
Switzerland: Jabal Amman. Tel: 644416. Telex: 21237.
Syria: POB 1377, 4th Circle, Jabal Amman. Tel: 641935.
Tunisia: Jabal Amman. Tel: 674307. Telex: 21849.
Turkey: POB 2062, Queen Zain ash-Sharaf St, 2nd Circle, Jabal Amman. Tel: 641251.
USSR: Amman. Tel: 641158.
United Arab Emirates: Jabal Amman. Tel: 644369. Telex: 21832.
United Kingdom: POB 87, Abdoun, Amman. Tel: 641261. Telex: 22209.
USA: POB 354, Jabal Amman. Tel: 644371. Telex: 21510.
Yemen Arab Republic: Amman. Tel: 642381. Telex: 23526.
Yugoslavia: POB 5227, Amman. Tel: 665107. Telex: 21505.

A desert police patrol

Hotels

NAME	ADDRESS	TELEPHONE	TELEX
AMMAN			
Alia Gateway	P.O. Box 39158	08/51000	23361
Amra	P.O. Box 950555	815071	22012
Jerusalem International	P.O. Box 926265	665121	22330
Holiday Inn	P.O. Box 6399	663100	21859
Inter-Continental	P.O. Box 35014	641361	21207
Marriott	P.O. Box 926333	660100	21145
Middle East	P.O. Box 19224	667160	21159
Plaza	P.O. Box 950629	665912	23266
Regency Palace	P.O. Box 927000	660000	22244
AQABA			
Aqaba Tourist House	P.O. Box 1060	315165	62308
Aquamarina Hotel Club	P.O. Box 96	316250	62249
Coral Beach	P.O. Box 71	313521	62227
Holiday Inn	P.O. Box 215	312426	62263
Miramar	P.O. Box 60	314339	62275
PETRA			
Petra Forum	P.O. Box 30	634200	64001

Amman

Amman, Jordan's capital city, has a population of over a million people. Biblically known as Rabbath-Ammon, and Philadelphia in Roman times, the city lies on seven hills that are dotted with Ammonite, Moabite, Greek, Byzantine, Roman and Islamic remains. The most impressive sight is the second century AD Roman amphitheatre in the middle of the city. Although it has been restored, the greater portion of the amphitheatre is original. Part of it is still used today to accommodate the Mosaics. Housed beneath the amphitheatre's tiers is the Costume and Folklore Museum.

The Citadel (Jebel el Qalat) towers over the city, and is the home of the Jordan Archaeological Museum whose exhibits include the relics dug up in the process of building modern Amman and from other sites within the Kingdom.

Amman is a new town which grew up at a rapid pace in the past 30 years. The layout of the city is modern and spacious. The *souq* area is in the heart of the city and includes scores of small shops and kiosks. For the young traveller some interesting though not strictly tourist sights are: the great youth centre, the King Hussein Medical Centre and the University and its hospital.

Agents run half-day tours from Amman to Mount Nebo, where Noah's Ark was reputedly hidden.

Near Amman, at Sabah, are important sites such as the once inhabited caves. East of Amman are a string of eighth century castles built by the Omayyads of Damascus as hunting lodges. The best preserved are Qasr Khareneh and Qasr Amr, with beautiful frescoes showing scenes of Omayyad times. Madaba is 30 kms south of Amman. Here you can see some of the finest Byzantine mosaics in the world. The most famous of these is the sixth century map of Palestine. Further south of Amman is the immense 15th century Crusader Castle in Kerak, on the tip of a hill; on one side the castle overlooks the Dead Sea.

Restaurants: There is no shortage of good restaurants in Amman.

Entertainments: The better nightclubs are located in the luxury hotels.

Sports: There are swimming pools and tennis courts at the Hussein Youth City, the Orthodox Club and the Royal Automobile Club. There are also courts at the YMCA and swimming pools at the Inter-Continental and Philadelphia hotels.

Tourist information: Tourist Authority Office, King Hussein St, Amman, tel: 42311.

Jerash

Just over 30 minutes by car from Amman to the north, over the scenic hills of Gilead in Jerash, lies a town of great historical interest. It is probably the most beautifully preserved Graeco-Roman city in the world and lay for hundreds of years beneath the sands before excavation and restoration began in the 1920s.

The most impressive sight is the Great Oval Forum, with a wide street of columns which lead towards the towering columns of the temple of Artemis. There are also the remains of several baths and pools, three theatres, and the triple arched gateway built in 129 AD to celebrate Hadrian's visit to the town.

Jerusalem and the West Bank

Since the war of June 1967, East Jerusalem and the West Bank have been under Israeli military occupation. Previously this area was Jordan's main tourist attraction.

Arab Jerusalem (al Kuds al Sharif) possesses the world's greatest religious shrines sacred to Christians, Moslems and Jews. Within the boundaries of al Haram al Sharif (the Nobel Sanctuary) stands the beautiful Dome of the Rock and the Al Aqsa Mosque dating from the Omayyad period. Close to al Haram al Sharif stands the Western (Wailing) wall, the last remnant of the Temple and the most sacred of Jewish shrines. Here also stands the Church of the Holy Sepulchre, built and often rebuilt on the site of Christ's crucifixion, and the Via Dolorosa, the narrow pathway along which Christ is said to have carried his cross to Calvary. Outside the walled city are the Garden of Gethsemane and the Mount of Olives.

In **Bethlehem** south of Jerusalem lies the birthplace of Christ marked by the

Church of the Nativity.

Hebron (al Khali), south of Bethlehem, is an ancient town with the famous al Ibrahimi mosque and the tombs of Abraham, Isaac and Jacob and their wives.

Nablus (Samaria) lies north of Jerusalem and is the home of about 350 surviving Samaritans. Jacob's Well stands at the entrance to the City; there are also numerous biblical sites such as Herod's Temple of Augustus and a Roman tribunal, stadium and theatre.

Jericho (Ariha) is half-an-hour's drive from Jerusalem and lies 400m below sea level in a landscape of salt encrusted desolation. Nearby on the River Jordan is the spot where John the Baptist is said to have baptised Jesus Christ. A few kilometres away lies the Dead Sea, the lowest body of water in the world.

Visiting the West Bank: Visitors to Jordan are allowed to travel in group tours across the River Jordan into the Israeli-occupied West Bank and then return to Jordan. Group tours are organised by local Jordanian travel agents in Amman. Holders of non-Arab passports travelling as individuals are permitted to make a one-way trip across the River Jordan and then have to continue their trip via Israel.

A land rich in archaeological treasures

The old and the new frequently live in harmony together

Aqaba and the Wadi Rum

Aqaba lies at Jordan's southernmost tip on the shores of the Red Sea, and is the country's only seaport. It is set against a rugged background of mountains, but the golden beach and blue waters are inviting to eyes that have seen nothing but desert on the journey there.

As a fun resort, Aqaba has much to offer; there is swimming in the Red Sea all the year round (in winter the temperature rarely falls below 20°C), also snorkelling, skin and scuba diving, boating, fishing and water skiing, The underwater scenery, which can be viewed through glass-bottomed boats, has coral formations and tropical fish.

The local airport is connected by regular weekly flights to Amman 325 km away (55 minutes flying time). There is also a regular taxi and bus service to Amman and vice versa.

Petra, 262 km south of Amman, was inhabited by the Nabateans from about 3000 BC,

Temples, palaces and tombs are everywhere hewn out of the mountainside. The most magnificent scene is that of the Treasury.

Although within easy reach of Amman, a day trip to Petra can be tiring. The only transport into Petra itself is by horseback, and it is a three-hour journey from the highway to the site. The visitor enters Petra through a *siq*, or a narrow passage, between walls of rock towering 70m overhead. The sights provide excellent photography. Within an hour's walk of Petra are the multi-tiered remains of **Beidha,** one of the world's oldest settlements.

Two hours' drive from Petra behind the mountains which surround Aqaba is **Wadi Rum,** the desert with the valley of the moon landscape. It is a large valley with eerie black and red crags and pink sands. In this century it became renowed as the Jordanian refuge and headquarters of T.E. Lawrence – Lawrence of Arabia.

KUWAIT

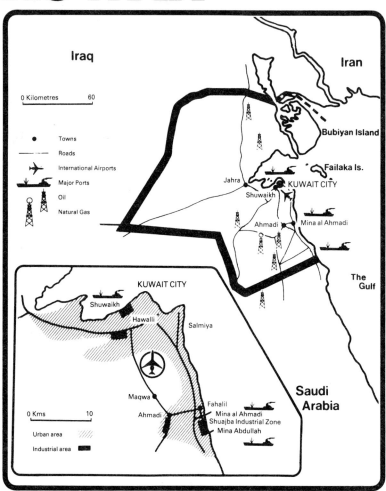

Area: 17,818 sq km
Population: 1.8 million (1988 estimate)
Capital: Kuwait City

Kuwaitis have a tendency to think of themselves as the sophisticates of the Gulf and perhaps, with some justification. The country which not long ago relied on its pearl fishing industry for survival is today a hectic business and banking centre with a stock market which features in the top ten *bourses* of the world by value. The country boasts the third largest proven oil reserves in the non-communist world but, despite the huge amounts of oil revenue earned by Kuwait, the government has long pursued an investment policy based on economic diversification.

A regional pacesetter

Seen from the air, the land is sand coloured, with a paler brown lacy edge of shore, and green-blue shallow sea, which becomes more blue as it leaves the shoreline and gains in depth. As the aircraft circles to descend, the high rise buildings of Kuwait City become more evident, and the water is seen to be patterned with oil tankers, cargo ships, a few dhows and a multitude of tiny pleasure craft. Kuwait was the first Gulf country to reap oil riches, and today is one of the most technologically advanced.

Oil, first thought to be present in 1914, was subsequently drilled and shipped out by the Kuwait Oil Company, a partnership between the Anglo Persian Oil Company (UK) and Gulf Oil (USA) from 1938. Kuwait's proven reserves are estimated to be about 73 billion barrels, second only in size to Saudi Arabia in the Middle East and sufficient to last over 200 years at current rates of extraction. The vast quantity of oil exported has resulted in a high per capita income for the citizens of the country, and a huge influx of consumer goods, foreign executives and workers. Of Kuwait's 1.8m population only about 40% are Kuwait citizens. Education is free and compulsory. Health care is also free and, as a result, the infant mortality and life expectancy rates in Kuwait are respectively among the lowest and highest in the Arab world. Kuwait City is a bustling American-style metropolis, with cinemas, restaurants, supermarkets and fast food outlets in abundance. Yet most Kuwaitis do not dress in the western style, preferring to retain the national dress – long white *dishdashas* and white headcloths, with *agals* to secure them.

The people of Kuwait are an ancient seafaring and merchant people; for thousands of years the *dhows*, *boums* and *baggalas* plied up and down the Gulf, travelling as far afield as Indonesia and Zanzibar with the trade winds. Pearling and fishing also played a major part in the country's economic survival, and around these seagoing occupations a thriving boat building industry grew up. Kuwait remained a shipbuilding centre until about 1950; since then the flood of oil wealth and modern technology has changed the pattern of life in the country. The skilled craftsmen who were trained to construct wooden dhows these days prefer to work as mechanics, run shops or work in the oilfields. Some traditional boats can still be seen in Gulf waters but they are mainly built by Asian craftsmen and operated more as pleasure

craft or relics of the past, than as commercial working vessels.

Unfortunately for the traditionalists, the ancient mud brick buildings of Kuwait City have almost all been knocked down and replaced with highrise concrete and glass towers in the rush to modernise. Little now remains of the old Kuwait. The old town wall, which once surrounded the city, is now reduced to five gateways and a few hundred yards of crumbling clay. It was largely demolished in the 1950s to make way for the expansion of modern Kuwait. Sheikh Kazal's Palace, built a century ago by Sheik Kazal al Khan, ruler of Muhammera, is now a broken down lodging house. All that remains of the old part of the city can be seen in the *souqs* and around the waterfront area, where some historic streets and houses miraculously escaped the bulldozers.

Serious implications

The Iran-Iraq war has had serious implications in Kuwait. Since the war began in 1979 Kuwait, along with its fellow Gulf Cooperation Council members, favoured an Iraqi victory. Kuwait enjoys full diplomatic relations with the Soviet Union (the only Gulf state to do so) and, in the past, enjoyed something of a reputation for its free press and support of leftist causes. However, a spate of Shia fundamentalist inspired terrorist incidents in the country have resulted in considerable anxiety in Kuwait's corridors of power. The hijack of a Kuwait Airways airliner, forced down in Iran before reaching Kuwait, on its way from Bangkok in April 1988, was aimed at securing the release of 17 Shia Moslems convicted for terrorist offences from Kuwaiti goals. After three weeks and the assassination of two Kuwaiti hostages, the remaining captives were released but the event brought sharply into focus the considerable problems Kuwaitis are having to deal with. The Gulf war forced a sharp contraction in Kuwait's business and banking markets. However, the new optimism for a permanent end to fighting between Iran and Iraq, is expected to lift private and public sector investment out of the doldrums given time.

General Information

Government

The head of state is the Amir, Sheikh Jaber al Ahmed al Sabah. Executive power is vested in the Amir, who exercises it through a Council of Ministers.

Language

Arabic is the official language. English is widely spoken.

Religion

Islam is the State religion. There are also Christian, Bahai, Hindu and Parsee minorities, which have their own places of worship.

How to get there

By air: Kuwait Airways is the national carrier.
By road: Kuwait has land borders with Saudi Arabia, Iraq and Iran.

Entry regulations

Transit passengers are allowed to stay for 72 hours without a visa provided they have a confirmed reservation at their next destination. Citizens of Kuwait, Bahrain, Oman, Qatar, the United Arab Emirates and Saudi Arabia do not require visas. All other nationalities must obtain visas or entry permits.

Custom regulations

Any amount of currency may be freely imported and exported.

500 cigarettes, personal effects and trade samples are admitted without duty, but the import and consumption of alcohol is strictly forbidden. For capital and consumer goods imported a customs duty of 4% *ad valorem* is levied.

Climate

Kuwait is located in the desert zone and has a very variable climate. Throughout the year, this climate produces wide differences in temperature, sparse rainfall and occasional dust storms.

The winter months (December-February) are fairly cold with winds coming from the north-west. The spring (March-May) is very pleasant with warm days and cool nights. During the summer months (June-September) it can be very hot, particularly in July and August when the temperature may reach 50°C. The autumn (October-November) can produce a wide variation in temperature from hot to quite cool. The nights are cool. There are occasional light rains towards the end of the season.

What to wear: Men will need short-sleeved shirts and lightweight trousers, plus a tropical suit for more formal occasions. For women, trousers and hip-length shirts with sleeves or dresses with long sleeves and below-the-knee hemlines are suitable; it is advisable to cover the body as much as possible. A sweater and a raincoat will be needed during the winter months.

Currency

Kuwait Dinar (KD) divided into 1,000 fils.

Business hours

Banks: Saturday-Wednesday 0800-1200. Thursday 0800-1100.
Offices: *Winter*, Saturday-Wednesday 0730-1230 and 1430-1800; Thursday

115

0730-1230. *Summer*, Saturday-Wednesday 0730-1200 and 1500-1800; Thursday 0730-1230.

Shops: Saturday-Thursday 0800-1230 and 1530-2030; Friday 0800-1200.

Press

Kuwait has a large selection of newspapers and magazines. The two leading English language dailies are The Arab Times, 2270, Safat, Kuwait City and The Kuwait Times, POB 1301, Safat, Kuwait City.

Public holidays

New Years Day, 1 January
National Day, 25 February
First day of Ramadan*, 7 April 1989
Eid al-Fitr*, 7-9 May 1989
Eid al-Adha*, 14-17 July 1989
Hijra*, 4 August 1989
Al-Ashoura*, 13 August 1989
Prophet's birthday*, 13 October 1989
The dates of the Moslem holidays, marked with an asterisk, are only approximate as they depend on sightings of the moon.

Transport

Road transport: Private car, taxi, service taxi (shared) and bus (plus a round town service by most hotels).

Consulates/Embassies in Kuwait City

Afghanistan: POB 33186, 73452 Rawdah, Mishref St No. 15, Block 5, House 7, Kuwait City. Tel. 5384522.

Algeria: POB 578, 13006 Safat, Istiqlal St, Kuwait City. Tel. 2519987. Telex 44750.

Austria: POB 33259, 73453 Rawdah, Kuwait City. Tel. 2552532.

Bahrain: POB 196, 13002 Safat, Riyadh St, Abdullah Salem District, Plot 4, Bldg 9, Kuwait City. Tel. 5318530. Telex 22649.

Bangladesh: POB 22344, 13084 Safat, Mansuria Block, 1 St 10, House 18, Kuwait City. Tel. 5330546. Telex 22484.

Belgium: POB 3280, 13033 Safat, Damascus St, Villa 12, Kuwait City. Tel. 2547161. Telex 22535.

Bhutan: POB 1510, 13016 Safat, Kuwait City. Tel. 5388451. Telex 30185.

Brazil: POB 21370, 13074 Safat, Istiqlal St, Kuwait City. Tel. 2549600. Telex 22398.

Bulgaria: POB 12090, 71651 Shamia, Kuwait City. Tel. 5643877. Telex 22122.

Canada: POB 24281, 13113 Safat, Block 1, 28 Quraish St, Nuzha, Kuwait City. Tel. 2511451. Telex 23549.

China, People's Republic: POB 2346, 13024 Safat, Dasman Nos 4 and 5, Kuwait City. Telex 22688.

Cuba: POB 26385, 13124 Safat, Bayan Block 5, Str. 5, House 16, Kuwait City. Tel. 5382024. Telex 44703.

Cyprus: POB 22034, 13081 Safat, Kuwait City. Tel 2433075. Telex 23781.

Czechoslovakia: POB 1151, 13012 Safat, an-Nuzha, Block 3, Kassima .No. 56, St 34, House 13, Kuwait City. Tel. 2548206. Telex 22243.

Denmark: POB 5452, Block No. 1, Dhahyat, Abdulla as-Salem District, Nisf al-Yousuf St, House No. 68, 13055 Kuwait City. Tel 2544988. Telex 22670.

Ecuador: POB 26745, Safat, Dahia, Block 1, ar-Rommi St, Villa No. 41, Kuwait City. Tel. 2562076. Telex 46117.

Finland: POB 26699, 13127 Safat, Kuwait City. Tel. 2463291. Telex 44948.

France: POB 1037, 13011 Safat, Jabriah, Block 12, Parcel 156-158, Kuwait City. Tel. 5319850. Telex 22195.

Gabon: POB 1230, 32013 Hawalli, Kuwait City. Tel. 5330952. Telex 30707.

German Democratic Republic: POB 5930, 13060 Safat, Gamal Abd an-Nasser St, Kuwait City. Tel. 4817055. Telex 22233.

Germany Federal Republic: POB 805, 13009 Safat, al-Mamoun St, Shamiya, Kuwait City. Tel. 814182. Telex 22097.

Greece: POB 23812, 13099 Safat, Block

2, St 2, House No. 21, Surrah. Tel. 5335861. Telex 22669.
Hungary: POB 23955, 13100 Safat, Shamia, Block 8, St 84, Villa No. 6, Kuwait City. Tel. 814080. Telex 22662.
India: POB 1450, 13015 Safat, 34 Istiqlal St, Kuwait City. Tel. 2530600. Telex 22273.
Indonesia: POB 21560, 13076 Safat, Nuzha District, Block 3, Nuzha Main St, Villa No. 32, Kuwait City. Tel. 2514588. Telex 22752.
Iran: POB 4686, 13047 Safat, 24 Istiqlal St, Kuwait City. Tel. 2533220. Telex 22223.
Iraq: POB 5088, 13051 Safat, Plot No. 26, Istiqlal St, al-Musa Bldg, Kuwait City. Tel. 2521066. Telex 22219.
Italy: POB 4453, 13045 Safat, F. Omar Bin al-Khattab St, al-Mulla Bldgs, Villa No. 6, Sharq, Kuwait City. Tel. 2445120. Telex 22356.
Japan: POB 2304, 13024 Safat, Plot No. 1, Damascus St, 13, Rawdah Area, House No. 5, Kuwait City. Tel. 2518155. Telex 22196.
Jordan: Daiyah, Istiqlal St, Embassies Area, Kuwait City. Tel. 2533500. Telex 30412.
Korea, Republic: POB 4272, 13043 Safat, an-Nuzha, Damascus St, Block 2, Div. 42, Villa No. 12, Kuwait City. Tel. 2531816. Telex 22353.
Lebanon: POB 253, 13003 Safat, 31 Istiqlal St, Kuwait City. Tel. 2619765. Telex 22330.
Libya: POB 21460, 13075 Safat, She'b Haroon ar-Rashid St, Kuwait City. Tel. 2520814. Telex 22256.
Malaysia: POB 4105, 13042 Safat, Villa 1, St 70, Block 7, Faiha, Kuwait City. Tel. 2546022. Telex 22540.
Mauritania: POB 23784, 13098 Safat, Mishrif Area, Parcel No. 6, Villa 37, Kuwait City. Tel. 5384849. Telex 22643.
Morocco: POB 784, 13008 Safat, Shuwaikh 'B', St 46, Kuwait City. Tel. 813912. Telex 22074.
Netherlands: POB 21822, 13079 Safat, Jabriah, Block No. 9, Plot No. 40A,

Kuwait City. Tel. 5312650. Telex 22459.
Niger: POB 44451, 32059 Hawalli, Surra, Block 2, Villa No. 270, Kuwait City. Tel. 2562232.
Nigeria: POB 6432, 32039 Hawalli, Rawdah, Parcel 4, St 44, Villa 14, Kuwait City. Tel. 2523658. Telex 22864.
Norway: POB 26967, 13130 Safat, Rawdah, Plot 5, St 50, Villa 12, Kuwait City. Tel. 2551566. Telex 23287.
Oman: POB 21975, 13080 Safat, Istiqlal St, Kuwait City. Tel. 2660029. Telex 22057.
Pakistan: POB 988, 13010 Safat, Hamza St, Villa No. 29, Dahia, Kuwait City. Tel. 2532101. Telex 44117.
Paraguay: POB 886, 13001 Safat, Kuwait City. Tel. 814462. Telex 22071.
Philippines: POB 26288, 13123 Safat, Rawdah, St 33, Area 3, Villa 10, Kuwait City. Tel. 2524398. Telex 22434.
Poland: POB 5066, 13051 Safat, Rawdah, Block 4, 3rd Ring Rd, Parcel No. 111, Kuwait City. Tel 2510355. Telex 23211.
Qatar: POB 1825, 13019 Safat, Istiqlal St, Dahia, Kuwait City. Tel. 2513599. Telex 22038.
Romania: POB 11149, Dasmah, 35152 Kifan, Zone 4, Mouna St. House 34, Kuwait City. Tel. 843419. Telex 22148.
Saudi Arabia: POB 20498, 13065 Safat, Arabian Gulf St, Kuwait City. Tel. 2531155. Telex 23458.
Senegal: POB 23892, 13099 Safat, Rawdah, Parcel 3, St. 35, House 9, Kuwait City. Tel. 2542044. Telex 22580.
Somalia: POB 22766, 13088 Safat, Abd an-Nasir St, Shuwaikh 'B', Kuwait City. Tel 2555567. Telex 23280.
Spain: POB 22207, 13083 Safat, Abdullah Salem District, St 12, Bldg 2, Kuwait City. Tel. 2512722. Telex 22341.
Sri Lanka: POB 16296, Qadisiah, House 31, Plot 6, Andalus St, Keifan, Kuwait City.
Sudan: POB 1076, 13011 Safat, Rawdah, Block 3, Abu Hayan St No. 26, Kuwait City. Tel. 2519299. Telex 22528.
Sweden: POB 21448, 13075 Safat, Faiha, Parcel 7, Shahba St, House 3, Kuwait

117

City. Tel. 2523588. Telex 22508.

Switzerland: POB 23954, 13100 Safat, Udailah St No. 32, Area 3, House No. 12, Kuwait City. Tel. 2551872. Telex 22672.

Syria: POB 25600, 13115 Safat, Rawdah, St No. 43, Plot 4, Villa 5, Kuwait City. Tel. 2531164. Telex 22270.

Thailand: POB 66647, 43757 Bayan, Jabriya Block 10, Area 12, Kuwait City. Tel. 5314870. Telex 44339.

Tunisia: POB 5976, 13060 Safat, Faiha, Plot 9, St 91, Villa 10F, Kuwait City. Tel. 2542144. Telex 22518.

Turkey: POB 20627, 13067 Safat, Bneid al-Gar, Hilton Hotel, Kuwait City. Tel. 2531785. Telex 44806.

USSR: POB 1765, 13018 Safat, Baghdad St, Midan-Hawalli, House No. 6, Kuwait City. Tel. 5642711.

United Arab Emirates: POB 1828, 13019 Safat, Istiqlal St. Plot 70, Kuwait City.

Tel. 2518381. Telex 22529.

United Kingdom: POB 2, 13001 Safat, Arabian Gulf St, Kuwait City. Tel. 2432047. Telex 44614.

USA: POB 77, 13001 Safat, Kuwait City. Tel. 2424151.

Venezuela: POB 24440, 13105 Safat, Dahia, Parcel No. 1, Nsif al-Yousuf St No. 72, Kuwait City. Tel. 5334578. Telex 22782.

Yemen Arab Republic: POB 4626, 13047 Safat, Rawdah, Block 3, Yousef as-Sabih St, Villa 15, Kuwait City. Tel. 2518827. Telex 44636.

Yemen, People's Democratic Republic: POB 5174, 13052, Safat, Parcel No. 1, Second Ring Rd, House 21, Kuwait City. Tel 2517898.

Yugoslavia: POB 20511, 13066 Safat, Shuwaikh 'B', al-Mansour St, Villa 15, Kuwait City. Tel. 4813140. Telex 23345.

Kuwaitis tend to think of themselves as the sophisticates of the Gulf . . . and with reason

Fun for all the family at Entertainment City

Hotels

NAME	ADDRESS	TELEPHONE	TELEX
KUWAIT			
Carlton Towers	P.O. Box 26950	2452740	46277
Golden Beach	Gulf Street	439521	2231
Kuwait Hilton	P.O. Box 5996	2533000	22039
Kuwait Regency	P.O. Box 1139	5628000	46082
Kuwait Sheraton	P.O. Box 5902	2422055	22016
Holiday Inn	P.O. Box 18544	4742000	46460
Meridien	P.O. Box 26302	2455550	44458
Messilah Beach Hotel	P.O. Box 3522	5624111	22215
Pullman	P.O. Box 21192	5634790	44310
Ramada Al-Salam	P.O. Box 24285	4835344	23596
SAS Hotel	P.O. Box 26199	5657000	44306

Accommodation and food

There are some excellent hotels in Kuwait and competition between them for the lucrative business traveller trade is keen. All major hotels offer the usual business support services, including telex, secretarial and translation services, and most now have their own restaurants serving Arabic, international and specialist cuisine, including Italian, Chinese and Japanese food or, for those who prefer it, 24 hour room service. It should be noted, however, that alcohol is totally banned in Kuwait.

What to see in Kuwait

Kuwait City's most prominent landmarks are the Kuwait towers which opened in 1977; in addition to much of the city's potable water supply, the shimmering blue towers also house a revolving restaurant which offers magnificent views of the city. Entertainment City, 25 kilometres outside Kuwait City, is a Disneyland-type theme park which offers fun for all the family. Entertainment City is a big favourite with Kuwaitis and foreigners alike, most of whom spend between half a day and a day experiencing the many rides and excursions on offer. Cinema and theatre are also popular diversions and at least one foreign language film is usually playing in the city. One of the oldest buildings in the city is the Seif Palace, the Amir's administrative headquarters, which stands on the sea front on Arabian Gulf Street. The palace, built in 1896, has undergone extensive restoration work. The spacious interior has a lot of mosaic tilework of traditional Islamic design with calligraphic inscriptions. Dasma Palace, constructed between 1915 and 1930, stands opposite the Kuwait towers and is now the private residence of the Amir Sheikh Jaber.

The Kuwait National Museum is well worth a visit. The museum houses an impressive collection of Islamic art from all over the world. There are also models of boats, pottery, seals and coins, in addition to several examples of magnificent wood carving. For sheer craftsmanship look out for the exquisitely carved wood window shutters and a magnificent door, carved several hundred years ago in Morocco. The museum also has an impressive planetarium where the hour long shows are given in different languages on different evenings. Most of the local treasures on display at the museum were found at Falaika Island. From discoveries made it is clear that Falaika was populated during the Bronze Age. The island can still be visited, ferries leave the mainland at Ras Al Ard every hour. At Al Jahra on the Basra Road there is a boat building centre, where *boums* and *sambuks* are still constructed in the traditional way, while an evening visit to the waterfront fishmarket gives the visitor some idea of the enormous variety of seafood available to Kuwaitis. South of Kuwait City the road leads to Fahalil, now a residential town, then on to Ahmadi, which was built as a settlement town for the expatriate employees of the Kuwait Oil Company (KOC).

Shopping: Kuwait City is extremely cosmopolitan. All basic and most luxury goods are available, in large shops or small general stores, often run by Indians or Pakistanis. For western style goods try the Souq al Watya, off Fahd Al Salem Street, or the Salhiya Commercial Complex on Hilali Street. The gold *souq* is well worth a visit and prices compare favourably with those in the west. The spice *souq* boasts a fascinating array of herbs, perfumes and spices while the *Souq* al Gharaballi is a more traditionalist market where the locals go to purchase their *dishdashes* and *bishts*, or cloaks, made up to their own specifications by one of the area's many tailors. This is also the place to purchase material from stalls displaying bolts of exotic silk, satin and sequined cloth, prices are competitive.

LEBANON

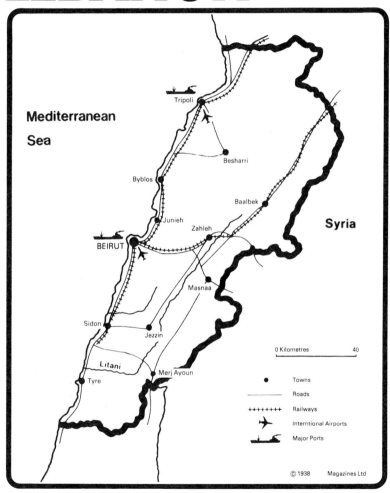

Mediterranean
Sea

Tripoli

Besharri

Byblos

Baalbek

Junieh

Zahleh

Syria

BEIRUT

Masnaa

Sidon

Jezzin

Litani

Merj Ayoun

Tyre

0 Kilometres   40

●   Towns

——————   Roads

++++++++   Railways

✈   Interntional Airports

⛴   Major Ports

© 1938   Magazines Ltd

Area: 10,400 sq km
Population: 3.5 million (approx)
Capital: Beirut

121

The tragedy of Lebanon is mourned throughout the Arab world. After thirteen years of civil strife, killing and destruction, Lebanon, and especially the capital city of Beirut is more divided today than it has ever been. Identity cards are required to pass from one side of Beirut to the other. Soldiers are on duty at the Green Line, which divides Moslem West Beirut from the Christian east of the city, the point where so many men, women and even children have met their fate with the aid of a sniper's bullet. In the once fashionable, now dilapidated Hamra area of West Beirut, people refer to the residents of Ashrafiya in East Beirut as being from "the other side" and vice versa. Though people commute daily from East to West to work in shops and offices, rarely would they venture to cross the no-man's land, a desolate stretch of road lined with scarred and shattered buildings, after sunset.

The bigger trading establishments – shops and offices – now have 'branches' on both sides. New cinemas and restaurants flourish on either side and life appears to continue in a haphazard, if dangerous fashion.

Most of the fashionable beaches and many of the high rent apartment blocks in the beach area have been occupied by refugees displaced from various parts of the city and especially south Lebanon.

It is a strange, somewhat surreal situation. On good days one can drive to the popular mountain resorts and partake of Lebanese food and drink. On the bad, practically nobody ventures out after lunch. And always at night the streets are almost deserted save the odd car travelling at speed down the main streets, occasionally eliciting a warning burst of gunfire.

The particular problems of the past 13 years are hard for the outsider to understand or disentangle, but a brief examination of the people and their history may help the reader to make some sense of the apparently senseless destruction.

Land of variety

For the traveller approaching by air or by sea the first sight of Lebanon is stunning if confusing. The impressive mountain ranges rise steeply above the horizon. Gradually the lower slopes and then the narrow coastal plain are discernible, after which the attention becomes fixed on the mass of buildings, many now in ruins, comprising Beirut and its suburbs.

Into this tiny country is packed such a variety of scenery that, before the war, there were few places to equal it in beauty and choice.

On the warm and humid coastal plain citrus fruit and bananas are cultivated. In places this plain is five or six kilometres wide; in others less than a kilometre, into which are packed a main road, a railway, and an almost continuous trail of small houses, plus the crops. Vegetables, radishes, and beans are grown in tiny patches, two metres square, irrigated daily and having high yields. The lower slopes of the mountains bear grapes, apricots, plums, peaches, figs, olives, and patches of barley, often on terraces painstakingly cut out and cultivated. The area is quite well-watered, the

Lebanon: Has the peace been shattered for ever?

mountains are of porous limestone, and the heavy winter rainfall on the seaward slopes of the Lebanon range soaks into them, then emerges as springs halfway down. Over the centuries these have been trapped, tamed, and led on to the terraces or into the villages also situated at the halfway mountain mark.

Four of the five *mohafazat*, or provinces, of the country, Akkar in the north, Kesrouan and Chouf in the centre, and south Lebanon have the configuration of coastal plain, well watered slopes, and mountain summits where little grows except apples. The famous cedars grow high in the mountains, but most are recent replants. Only at the village of the cedars high above Tripoli in the great semicircle of the Kornet es Saouda, where snow lingers all the year round, is to be found a forest of the ancient cedars of the Lord. About 25 are over 1,000 years old.

The Bekka, the fifth *mohafazat*, is the richest agricultural region of the whole Levant, and has been so since Roman times when it was one of the chief granaries of the Empire. To reach it one could take the road from Beirut to Damascus travelling up a steep highway to the highest pass on the Lebanon range, Dahr el Beidar. From the top there is an incredible view of the mountain sloping down to the flat, patchwork Bekka valley, and the barren, rainless slopes of the Anti-Lebanon mountains, beyond which lies the frontier with Syria.

The Litani river flows through the Bekka, and at the southern end a large dam and artificial lake have been constructed to provide electric power and a modern irrigation system for the plain. The fruits and vegetables once cultivated were more than the country could consume, and until the war were exported daily to the Gulf countries and Saudi Arabia, by air or by refrigerated truck.

The natural resources of the country are few, and the enterprise of the citizens is one of its greatest assets. Lebanese have traditionally sought their fortunes overseas, usually as merchants, in North and South America, West Africa, and more recently in the Gulf.

A population of minorities

Lebanon is the only country in the world whose population is composed exclusively of minorities: various sects of Christians, Sunni and Shi'ite Moslems, and the Druze. Rivalry between the various sects, each with different foreign affiliations, has led to conflict in the past, and was one, though not the only, cause of the civil war.

The Christians are Catholic, Orthodox, and Protestant, the Catholics are sub-divided into Latin (or Roman) Catholics, Chaldeans, Greek Catholics and the Maronites. The Latin Catholics are few and most are of foreign descent, with European connections and closely linked to the Franciscan order – who were made custodians of the Holy Places (Terra Sancta) after the Crusades.

The Chaldeans are a small offshoot of the Nestorians who reunited themselves to Rome in 1553 by acknowledging the supremacy of the Pope whilst keeping their own liturgy and customs. The Greek Catholics are a larger body, who broke away from the Greek Orthodox Church in 1760, and rejoined Rome under the same conditions. They permit clerical marriage before ordination as do the Maronites. But marriage is a bar to preferment in the Church because the archimandrites and Bishops are almost always chosen from members of the celibate monastic orders.

The Greek Orthodox have been long established in Lebanon, and Syria. Russian, Greek, and Arabic are languages in liturgical use in the Orthodox Church.

The Maronites are a turbulent sect, whose Patriarch has his residence at Bkerké – just north of Beirut. Their founder was a monk of northern Syria, St. Jean Maron, who founded a religous order in the sixth century AD which attracted many followers. Gradually they spread to Lebanon, built monasteries, and after the Moslem invasions of the seventh century withdrew to their mountain retreats refusing conversion, or indeed any contact with the Moslem enemies. They have a traditional alliance with France, dating from the 12th century; in 1182 they acknowledged Papal supremacy in return for independence in liturgy and canon law. In 1585 a Maronite College was set up in Rome. Many Maronites emigrated to North and South America in the late 19th and early 20th centuries. The communities in the Diaspora are both prosperous and patriotic, at a distance, towards their ancestral home. They have always sent money home, and some, after 20 or 30 years away (especially in West Africa) returned to their mountain villages, built comfortable houses, and sought to end their days prosperously and peacefully. Maronite political intransigence has lasted until today, and is to some extent responsible for the recent troubles.

There are fewer Protestants than other Christians in Lebanon, but they have considerable importance because the American University of Beirut was founded by American Protestant missionaries in 1872, and always attracted Protestant teachers. The best schools in Lebanon are still either French and Catholic, or English/American and Protestant. There are also fringe Protestant sects, and an Anglican church in Beirut, under the jurisdiction of the Anglican Bishop in Jerusalem.

The Armenians, although all the same race of Indo-Europeans from Turkey, can be Protestant, Gregorian (Orthodox) or Catholic. They took refuge in Lebanon in 1918/20 after many were massacred in Turkey and Northern Syria by Ottoman Turks. They are an industrious and cultured people, excellent craftsmen and musicians, and also talented bankers and financiers who have contributed largely to the prosperity of Lebanon and its pre-eminence until 1974 as a world banking centre. When the civil war started some emigrated.

Islam is divided into two sects, the Sunni and the Shia. Generally speaking, the western part of North Africa, Egypt, Syria and of course the Arabian peninsula is Sunni: representing the orthodox and legalistic aspects of the Faith; the eastern countries of Iraq and Iran are mostly Shia, and this is directed more towards the mystical face of Islam. It believes in holy men and women as minor prophets and even miracle workers, and the Sufi way of life is stronger. Sunni and Shia are both strongly represented in Lebanon. The old Moslem families of Beirut and Tripoli are Sunni, dating from the time of Ottoman hegemony before 1860, and the Shia are found in the poorer areas, southern Lebanon and the northern Bekka. They are now probably the largest community, and are becoming more prosperous, although still ruled by feudal landlords. Many from south Lebanon emigrated to West Africa and some to the Americas, and made considerable fortunes there: they exercise a considerable amount of political influence at home.

The Druze are found in the mountains of Lebanon, in the Djebel Druze in Syria, and in northern Palestine. They call themselves Muwahiddin (Unitarians) or Bani Ma'aruf (the Sons of Knowledge): the word Druze now generally used comes from one of the founders of their faith, a Persian called Darizi. Since they practise *takiyah*, or concealment of their faith, little is known about it by outsiders, although copies of their sacred books were abstracted in the early 19th century and may be found in the Vatican and Bodleian libraries. Not all the Druze are versed in the religion: there is a class of initiates, known as the Akl or Jawayhid, who meet on Thursdays to discuss both religious and community affairs. About 10% of the Druze are initiates, and admission is subject to strict tests. The first Druze were converts from Islam; their Deity is the indivisible source of Light, both spiritual and physical. They believe in reincarnation and far sight. The moral code is strict, and Druze women who marry outside the community are still ostracised. The Druze mountain villagers are very hospitable, and the villages well organised. They are good farmers and when they emigrate, usually do very well.

Beirut was once a sophisticated entrêpot.

History

The people of Lebanon make up its history and that history is long and turbulent. The cities of the sea coast, Byblos, Tyre and Sidon, are familiar from Egyptian history and from the Old Testament.

Lebanon was in ancient times Phoenicia, when the harbours were great trading centres, and Phoenician ships carried goods all over the Mediterranean. The cities of Carthage in what is now Tunisia, and Massilia (Marseilles) in present-day France were founded by Phoenician traders, and after the rise of the Roman Empire Phoenicians remained the sharpest merchants.

Beirut, then called Berytus, was a considerable Christian town with a university famed for its law faculty. Roman and then Byzantine rule endured until the Moslem conquests, when the mountain people remained Christian, and most of the coastal inhabitants became Moslem. The Arab empire endured until the Crusades when Norman military power established itself for almost two hundred years in the Levant, between 1099 and 1271. Then the Turks took over, and ruled in gradually increasing somnolence, until Napoleon's invasion of Egypt in 1799, when the Moslem world began to rediscover the West. Mohammed Ali Pasha came to power in Egypt in 1820, and brought Palestine, Lebanon and Syria under his hegemony. The victorious campaigns were fought by his son Ibrahim Pasha, a talented general, and it was only when the British, Austrians and Russians defended Beirut in 1840 by sending a fleet that the Egyptians were stopped.

In 1841, 1845 and 1860 three separate bouts of civil strife, mostly between Druze and Maronites, took place; in the 1860 troubles the Turks who were nominally in control openly aided the Druze, and conflict spread to Damascus where about 11,000 Christians were slaughtered. Finally, the European powers decided to intervene, along with Turkey. A joint French-Turkish force was sent to Beirut to restore order, and on 9 June 1861 an organic statute for Lebanon (*le grand Liban*) was signed in Istanbul between the European powers and the Ottoman government. It remained in force until the Turkish empire crumbled in 1917, and made Lebanon an autonomous Mutasarrifiyah of the Ottoman Empire. The Mutasarrif was a Christian and the inhabitants were officially permitted the free exercise of their religion, allowed to ring church bells, and have public religious processions. French educational influence became ever stronger, and when the Ottoman Empire was carved up, at the end of the First World War, the French received the mandates for Syria and Lebanon.

The Syrians bitterly resented French hegomony, but Lebanon became for a time almost a province of France. Some, even Lebanese, disclaimed Arab antecedents, loyalties, and the language; instead they referred to themselves as Phoenicians and sent their children to French schools where the elementary history books began '*Nos Ancêtres les Gaulois . . .*' The French did their best to impose their culture and civilisation in Lebanon, as they had done in Algeria, and were in some ways more successful, because of the so-called 'religious' link. But this ephemeral success was due to the Levantine desire for assimilation to European rather than Moslem Arab culture, reinforced by the Maronite community's fear of being swamped by a Moslem majority.

The country officially became an independent republic in 1946. The National Pact is an unwritten agreement between the various communities providing that the President of the Republic shall be a Maronite Christian, the Prime Minister a Sunni Moslem, the Speaker of the Chamber of Deputies a Shia Moslem, and the Foreign Minister a Greek Orthodox Christian, and so on. The Parliament, or Chamber of Deputies, has 99 members, each community being represented according to its strength in the country. However, no official census has been taken since 1946, because it would almost certainly show that the Shia Muslims were the largest in numbers and the Maronites fewer than they claim. So the deputies became less and less representative. Presidents of the Republic, are each supposed to hold office for six years, without the right of re-election. In 1958 Camille Chamoun tried to change the constitution and seek re-election. Civil strife broke out and lasted for about eight months, until Fouad Chehab, a former Commander-in-Chief of the army, was elected.

The Palestinians, during the early 1970s, exacerbated Lebanese community rivalry by bringing in a new political element. The PLO (Palestine Liberation Organisation) had its headquarters in Beirut. Many militant Palestinians also lived either in the UNWRA camps which once ringed the city, or, having prospered to a certain extent, in Beirut apartments. Some went to work in the Gulf, others found jobs in Lebanon, although there were always problems over work permits since most did not possess Lebanese nationality. Between 1948, the year of the exodus from Palestine, and 1955 when the Lebanese rules became much stricter, a good many Christian, and fewer Moslem Palestinians obtained the much coveted Lebanese identity card. This was deliberate government policy to increase the number of Christians.

The majority of Palestinians are involved in the cause, which has nothing to do with religious rivalry and everything to do with national feeling. Children were brought up to sing patriotic songs about Palestine; the Palestinian map and flag were prominently displayed in all classrooms and gradually guerilla forces, the Fedayeen, were trained in the camps of Lebanon, Syria, Jordan and the Gaza strip to attack and infiltrate enemy territory, Israel. The reader of any newspaper will be familiar with accounts of 'incidents' and 'reprisals'. The Lebanese government gave official lip service and support to the Palestinian cause. But as the Palestinians became more vociferous friction grew. The real cause, however, was that the Palestinians became something of a catalyst, bringing to a head many underlying problems and especially the socio-economic conflict between the 'haves' and 'have-nots'. The Palestinian armed presence presented a growing

Old soldiers and new martyrs.

threat to the privileges of those 'haves', mainly the Maronite Christians. And in turn it represented a means by which the 'have-nots' could perhaps gain some of those privileges, by force if necessary.

The Maronites were the most ferociously opposed to the Palestinians: the civil disturbances began in April 1975 when a bus carrying some Palestinians returning from a comrade's funeral passed near a Maronite church where a Maronite politician was addressing a meeting. The bus was attacked and its passengers massacred.

During 1975 and 1976 half of Beirut was destroyed, the country was torn apart, and at least 45,000 people killed. For about six months no public services functioned and the airport was closed. Order was restored by the Arab peace-keeping forces – mostly Syrian – who entered the country in June 1976 and occupied Beirut in November.

For a while it appeared that Lebanon was on the route to recovery; however, the invasion of Lebanon by Israel in 1982 brought to the fore the fragility of the situation. The Israelis managed to accomplish what they came for, and that was the expulsion of the PLO. But this did not provide a cure for Lebanon's warring religious factions, which still continues to this day and shows little sign of abating.

Even if a political solution is found, it will take many years to solve the severe social and economic problems.

The agriculture and scenery of Lebanon form the country's permanent attractions, and time and economic necessity may eventually help heal the wounds which now gape open. The Lebanese are traditionally the middlemen of the Mediterranean and of the rich Arab countries. Much of this business has been transferred abroad to Athens, to Bahrain, to Egypt and to London, but if the facilities can be restored, much of it could return to Lebanon.

General Information

Government

Lebanon is a Republic.

Languages

The official language is Arabic although French and English are frequently used.

Religion

All varieties of Islam and Christianity. There is total freedom of worship.

How to get there

Middle East Airlines is the country's national carrier.

MEA Buildings, P.O. Box 266, Beirut.

Entry regulations

Visas are required by all visitors except citizens of Lebanon and Syria. There are several categories. Transit visas, valid for 15 days from date of issue, allowing one entry and exit. Tourist or visitors' visas, valid for six months and allowing two entries. Business visas, granted on presentation of a letter from the firm which an individual represents, valid for six months and allowing multiple entries. Sometimes a 48-hour visa is issued by the immigration authorities at the airport to travellers arriving from places where there is no Lebanese representation; it can be converted to an ordinary visa at the police headquarters but it is advisable to check beforehand. The visitors' visa may become a Visa de Sejour for up to a year upon application.

Innoculation against yellow fever is required for travellers coming from areas where these diseases are endemic.

Climate

There are four distinct seasons in Lebanon, spring, from March to May, summer, from June to September, autumn, October and November, and winter which begins in December and usually lasts halfway through March. In winter there is a good deal of rain which turns to snow on the mountains; it is damp and draughty everywhere. Spring and autumn are both mild and pleasant. Summer is hot and humid on the coast, and cooler in the mountains.

What to wear: Warm clothes and a raincoat are necessary in the winter. During the rest of the year ligthweight, loose, cotton clothes are advisable.

Public holidays

New Year's Day, 1 January
St Maron Day, 9 February
Founding of Arab League, 22 March
First day of Ramadan*, 7 April 1989
Easter, 24-27 April 1989
Labour Day, 1 May
Martyr's Day, 6 May
Eid al-Fitr*, 7-9 May 1989
Eid al-Adha*, 14-17 July 1989
Hijra*, 4 August 1989
Al-Ashoura*, 13 August 1989
Assumption, 13 August 1989
Prophet's birthday, 13 October 1989
All Saints, 1 November
Independence Day, 22 November
Christmas, 25 December
Foreign Troops Evacuation Day, 31 December.

The dates of the Moslem holidays, marked with an asterisk, are only approximate as they depend on sightings of the moon.

Beirut

Until the civil war Beirut was one of the busiest and most prosperous cities of the Mediterranean. Reconstruction of the destroyed port and city centre always seems on the point of beginning but each time the situation takes a turn for the worse hope fades a little more. The modern town was never beautiful, but has a spectacular setting on the sea, with Mount Sannin, snow-capped for five months of the year, rising directly behind.

Beirut is far from being the sophisticated entrepôt it once was. The once elegant areas of the city – which boasted designer clothes shops selling the very latest in European fashions – are now tatty and down at heel. Little of the former ambience remains. However, the entrepreneurial Lebanese continue to trade wherever and whenever circumstances allow them to do so.

Other towns

Tripoli is the second city of Lebanon; it is divided into two parts, the port and the town outside. They are joined by 2km of road which runs amongst orange plantations; in spring the scent of the blossoms is almost unbearably fragrant. There is also an oil refinery, one of the two (the other being at Zahrani, south of Sidon). Tripoli has a provincial charm and cachet; excellent Arabic sweets and patisseries flavoured with orange flower water are made here, and a good many people work in the port or as fishermen.

Byblos is reputed to be the oldest town in the world; it was certainly a flourishing port in the time of the Phoenicians and the Egyptians, and has relics from these times, as well as Byzantine ruins and a Crusader castle and church. The harbour is still a resort of fishermen and pleasure craft – recently also of unofficial weapons importers. Here ancient tombs adjoin restaurants, and artefacts dredged from the sea floor decorate the port walls.

Beiteddine in the Chouf mountains between Beirut and Sidon, is the site of the palace built by the Amir Beshir, Prince of the Druze, in the early 19th century.

Baalbek is one of the best preserved temples of the Roman world still in existence. It is a complex of several temples, forming the City of the Sun, at the far end of the Bekka plain. A book written in 1926 describes it as 'the great Roman temple encircled by the mountains, towering above a grove of tall and gently waving poplars. I should doubt if there were another place on earth where natural and man-made beauty coincide as at Baalbek. Too often beautiful scenery is barren of beautiful architecture, while the great creations of man languish in negligible surroundings. But in this one spot nature and man have simultaneously achieved perfection. Baalbek was the Greek Heliopolis, or City of the Sun, and though the Roman temples are dedicated to Jupiter and Bacchus, it still belongs, in spirit, to the sun. The six soaring columns of the temple of Jupiter beyond are sand-coloured, washed by the sun, and look like pillars of sunlight solidified.' Until the outbreak of the war an annual international arts festival was held against this startling backdrop.

Arts and crafts

Lebanon is best known for its pottery, glass-blowing in various jewel colours, and metal work. At Jezzine in the mountains beyond Sidon animal bones are carefully carved into cutlery inlaid with metal and enamel, and shaped like birds. There are also weavers who make rugs, materials, and traditional Arab garments like abayas and kaftans. Much beautiful embroidery is done in the Druze and Christian mountain villages. However, the demand for many traditional goods dwindled with the death of the tourist trade.

OMAN

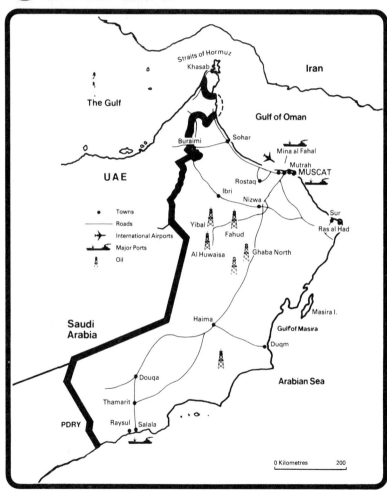

Area: 300,000 sq km
Population: 2 million (official estimate).
Capital: Muscat

It is a pity that though, both geographically and historically, Oman is one of the most interesting countries on the Arabian peninsula, entry for foreigners is not always easy. Visas are only granted, with few exceptions, to employees of firms working for the Sultanate, advisers, journalists, archaelogists and businessmen. Though a country with a long, proud history, Oman has been in a long period of isolation. When he succeeded his father in a bloodless coup in 1970, Sultan Qaboos was faced with the task of bringing his country into the mainstream of the 20th century, while fighting a war in Dhofar, his southern province, against leftwing guerilas of the Popular Front for the Liberation of Oman (PFLO). The war is now over, and Oman has already made great strides in development. An infrastructure of hotels and services is being built up.

A fertile coastal plain

Oman, on the south-east corner of the Arabian peninsula, has an area of 300,000 sq km and a coastline of over 2,700km, stretching from the South Yemen border in Dhofar, in the south, up to the United Arab Emirates in the north, which also divides it from the Musandam peninsula, a rocky, isolated promontory pointing up into the Strait of Hormuz.

The Hajir mountains divide Oman, forming a backbone reaching from the Musandam peninsula across to the south-eastern part of the peninsula, and these mountains are divided into two parts by the Sumail Gap. To the east of the high Hajir mountains lies the Batinah coast, a fertile, narrow plain, about 250 km long, peopled by those who have had contact with the outside world for centuries, descendants of Asian merchants, Baluchi traders, Arabs from other countries, a mixed population of different ethnic origins, more outward looking than the tribesmen of the interior, cut off by geography from the world. The Batinah, with its long beaches and many date palms, is intensely cultivated. Shepherds and goatherds gather under the shade of the palms. Fishermen bring in huge catches, going to sea in traditional *berasti* boats or *dhows*. Behind loom the mountains dominated by the Jebel Akhdar, the Green Mountains, 3,300 m high, and inhabited by fierce tribesmen who were loyal in the past to the Imam. Sohar, long ago the capital, was an important trading port in Oman's history.

Beyond the other end of the Batinah is Muscat, the capital, surrounded by mountains, and the natural harbour on whose steep cliffs sailors through the centuries, including Nelson when he was a midshipman, have cut or painted the names of their ships in huge letters. A new port at Mutrah, twin city to Muscat and the commercial centre, has been built, Mina Qaboos, and with Ruwi, recently grown from a small village with a military airport and ancient fort into a busy urban centre, comprises what is known as Greater Muscat.

Dhofar, the southernmost province, emerging even more recently from isolation because of war, is divided from the north by another huge desert, a vast area of stone and sand, with the Empty Quarter stretching to the west.

Dhofar is even more beautiful than the Batinah and the mountains of the interior of the north. Here too there is a coastal plain, with dramatic mountains behind, and Salalah, the main town and capital of the province beside the Indian Ocean. The monsoon brings rain, mist and drizzle, and the resulting green. The climate is sub-tropical, frankincense was grown and exported from here for centuries. The Kuria Muria islands lie out to sea, and the whole area is one of great beauty. In Salalah are found many black skinned Omanis, who are mainly descended from slaves brought to the Sultanate and then freed to settle in this lush country. Like the Shihu in the Musandam, they speak a different dialect. In the interior of Oman can be found nomadic Bedus.

Dress varies in Oman, due to this ethnic variety. Most men wear a long *dishdash*, a white shirt, covered sometimes with a cloak. The distinctive Omani curved dagger, the *Khanjar*, is treasured by all, and worn at the waist, tucked into a specially made ornate silver belt. Omanis usually wear turbans, often of brilliantly coloured Kashmir wool, sometimes of white cotton. Women wear the black cloak, called an *abaya*, outdoors, but the Baluchis sport brilliantly coloured cotton dresses. Many go unmasked, but there are others, particularly in the more puritan interior, who stick to the stiff, black masks.

A distinctive feature of Oman, as of the other Arabian countries, is the extensive irrigation brought by the Persians centuries ago, the *falaj*.

Fort Mirani, Muscat

History

Archaeologists working in Oman have discovered evidence that suggest part of the country's civilisation was probably pre-Arab. By the second century BC, due to its extremely important position at the place where the Indian Ocean and the Gulf meet, it had become an important Arab area, with trade to many areas, even as far as China. It was one of the first areas to embrace Islam during the lifetime of the Prophet. The Ibadhi sect was entrenched, and Imams were elected until the 17th century.

In the 16th century the Portuguese attacked this important coastal area to secure Muscat and other strategic coastal locations in order to protect their trade routes to India and the Far East. Muscat and Sohar were both conquered, and evidence of this is still to be seen in the two great Portuguese forts, Jalali and Merani, which guard the entrance to the harbour of Muscat and dominate the city to this day. There was civil war in the 18th century, which only ended when Ahmcd bin Said, elected Imam by both sides in this tribal controversy, and the ancestor of the present Sultan, came to power. From then, until Sultan Qaboos became Sultan, the country was known as Muscat and Oman, but then the name was changed to Oman, to make clear that the coastal community, Dhofar and the tribal interior were all one kingdom.

Varied wildlife

Probably one of the most interesting animals in Oman is the Arabian *tahr*, which lives in north Oman. It is so shy it is seldom seen; it belongs to the goat family, and looks like a gazelle, with a thick coat in winter.

Over-hunting has made the gazelle very rare, and the Sultan has taken steps to protect this and other threatened species. Foxes, wild cats, panthers, wolves, hyenas, porcupines are all found in Oman, and there is a rare black hedgehog, as well as many different sorts of bats, huge lizards, a distinctive spiny mouse, and many rare butterflies. The Bedu catch locusts, and eat them – you can often see mounds of them for sale in the *souqs*.

The camels of the Batinah coast are famous, and horses are bred in Oman too, with much interest being taken in them by the Sultan. There are many rare birds, including flamingos, ducks, geese and herons. There is plenty of marine life, and the seas abound in fish. Beautiful shells can be found on the miles of sands.

Economy

Economic development came relatively late to Oman. Although oil was discovered, and began to be exported during the lifetime of the previous Sultan, it was not until Qaboos came to power that oil revenues were put to great use in developing the country. Sultan Qaboos was obliged to start

Oman's development process from scratch. His father, the previous ruler, had placed little store by the benefits of modernisation. By 1970, when Sultan Qaboos came to power after the forced abdication of his father, work had already started on a hospital, schools, government offices, a few roads and a port. However, it was Qaboos who brought large scale development to the sultanate. The fruits of economic development are most apparent in the capital region, which by the turn of the century is expected to be home to between one-third and one-quarter of the entire population. Muscat's attractions of a hospital, schools and a university have already attracted a quarter of a million people to it, compared with a population of just 25,000 in 1970. Dhofar has also been transformed and although the benefits of economic change are not so striking in the country's interior they are none the less important. In 1970 few towns could boast electricity, running water or even adequate roads. Today, however, all major settlements enjoy these benefits. The current Five Year Development Plan (1986-90) concentrates on further rural development and also aims at reducing Oman's economic dependence on oil revenues by reviving fishing and agriculture.

Social services, health care and above all education are top priorities in the Sultan's plans and considerable resources are also being channelled into the operation of experimental farms and studies to determine how fertile areas can be made more profitable. Laudable results have already been achieved. In the first 15 years of Sultan Qaboos' rule (1970-1985) the number of schools increased from just three nationwide to 550; the number of students rose from less than 1,000 to 200,000; hospitals trebled in number to reach 15 and the total length of paved roads, which in 1970 amounted to just six miles, had reached 2,054 miles. However, since oil is the lynchpin of the Omani economy, the boom years of economic development coincided with the boom years of oil exportation. Unlike many of its Gulf Cooperation Council neighbours Oman does not have large reserves to fall back on and the recession of the 1980s has caused a certain amount of belt tightening which will slow further economic development markedly. Some new projects will go ahead and these are most likely to be in the light industry sector.

The Omanis are traditionally a seafaring people

General Information

Government

Power is in the hands of Sultan Qaboos bin Said who is the Head of State and the Prime Minister. He is Minister of Foreign Affairs and of Defence and presides over the Consultative Assembly.

Languages

Arabic is the official language but English is often spoken in government and business circles.

Religion

The majority are Ibadhi Moslems and about a quarter are Sunni Moslems.

How to get there

The national carrier of Oman is Gulf Air, jointly owned by Bahrain, Oman, the United Arab Emirates, and Qatar.

Entry regulations

Anyone travelling to Oman must obtain a visa from the Omani Embassy in the country where they are.

Applicants who already have connections in the Sultanate must attach to their application forms a letter from the firm or Government Department they wish to visit in Oman, giving the name or names of persons to be visited in Oman, the dates of their arrival in Oman and the duration of their stay there. Only in certain special cases will telexes be accepted in lieu of letters.

No application without the letters mentioned will be accepted. The application form is in triplicate with three passport size photographs and usual letter of recommendation from the company or firm.

A No Objection Certificate is required for persons going to the Sultanate of Oman on a visit to relatives or friends, to be obtained through friends or relatives in Oman. Visas for NOC holders are granted within 48 hours, and for others within three days, however, it is advisable to leave longer.

Vaccination against yellow fever is required for those coming from an infected area. TAB injections are advisable, as are anti-malaria tablets.

Customs regulations

There are no restrictions on the amount of foreign currency which may be taken into or out of Oman. Personal effects are allowed in duty free but it is forbidden to import alcohol.

Climate

Very hot and humid in summer, with June-July midday temperatures sometimes as high as 40°C, particularly on the coast where humidity is sometimes 85%. Muscat has 70 cm average rainfall; in Nizwa it is higher, while in Salalah the light monsoon rain falls from June to September. The best time to visit the area is from November to March.

What to wear: In winter light wool, with a jacket or shawl for the evenings, is suitable clothing. For the rest of the year, loose cool clothes are absolutely necessary, preferably cotton. To avoid offending local customs, men should not wear shorts and women's dresses should cover the knees, preferably with long sleeves. If wearing slacks a shirt or top should be worn that covers the hips.

137

Currency

Rial Omani (RO) divided into 1,000 baizas.

Business hours

The weekly holiday is Friday.
Banks: Saturday-Wednesday 0800-1200 and Thursday 0800-1100.
Government Offices: Saturday-Wednesday 0730-1400 and Thursday 0730-1300.
Offices: Saturday-Thursday, variable between 0830-1330 and 1600-1800.
Shops: 0800-1300 and 1600-1930.

Press

Oman Daily Observer, POB 580, Ruwi, is published daily in English while the English language Times of Oman, POB 3770, Ruwi, is published weekly.

Public holidays

New Year's Day, 1 January
First Day of Ramadan*, 7 April 1989
Eid al-Fitr*, 7-9 May 1989
Eid al-Adha*, 14-17 July 1989
Hijra*, 4 August 1989
Al-Ashoura*, 13 August 1989
Prophet's birthday*, 13 October 1989
National Day, 18 November
Sultan Qaboos' official birthday, 19 November
The dates of the Moslem holidays, marked with an asterisk, are only approximate, as they depend on sightings of the moon.

Consulates/Embassies in Oman

Algeria: POB 6942, Ruwi. Tel. 707337. Telex 3749.
Bangladesh: POB 6959, Ruwi. Tel. 708495. Telex 3800.
China, People's Republic: POB 3315, Muscat. Tel. 702451. Telex 3125.
Egypt: POB 5252, Ruwi. Tel. 600411. Telex 3438.
France: POB 591, Muscat. Tel. 737421. Telex 5223.
Germany, Federal Republic: POB 3128, Ruwi. Tel. 702482. Telex 3440.
India: POB 4727, Ruwi. Tel. 702957. Telex 3429.
Iran: POB 6155, Ruwi. Tel. 696944. Telex 5066.
Iraq: POB 4848, Muscat. Tel. 701349. Telex 3471.
Italy: POB 6727, Muscat. Tel. 703202. Telex 3727.
Japan: POB 6511, Ruwi. Tel. 603464. Telex 5087.
Jordan: POB 5281, Ruwi. Tel. 602561. Telex 5518.
Korea, Republic: POB 5220, Ruwi. Tel. 702322. Telex 3132.
Kuwait: POB 4798, Muscat. Tel. 706444. Telex 3455.
Malaysia: POB 6939, Ruwi. Tel. 706116. Telex 3747.
Morocco: POB 6125, Ruwi. Tel. 701977. Telex 3033.
Netherlands: POB 6302, Ruwi. Tel. 705410. Telex 3050.
Pakistan: POB 5451, Ruwi. Tel. 603439. Telex 5451.
Qatar: POB 8ʋ2, Muscat. Tel. 701802. Telex 3460.
Saudi Arabia: POB 4411, Muscat. Tel. 701111. Telex 3401.
Somalia: POB 4767, Ruwi. Tel. 701355. Telex 3253.
Sudan: POB 6971, Ruwi. Tel. 708790.
Tunisia: POB 5755, Ruwi. Tel. 704574. Telex 3641.
Turkey: POB 8511, Mutrah. Tel. 697050. Telex 5571.
United Arab Emirates: POB 1551, Muscat. Tel. 600302. Telex 3299.
United Kingdom: POB 300, Muscat. Tel. 738501. Telex 5216.
USA: POB 966, Muscat. Tel. 738006. Telex 3785.
Yemen Arab Republic: POB 3701, Muscat. Tel. 696966. Telex 3411.

Transport

Visitors are not permitted to travel into the interior or farther up the coast than Sib, about 50 km from Muscat, without prior permission from the Ministry of the Interior. Gulf Air flies daily to Salalah in Dhofar, but passengers must obtain permission in writing from the Office of the Governor and book a seat well in advance.

Taxis, probably the most expensive in the Gulf, operate between the airport and Mutrah/Muscat and inside the main towns. Prices should be negotiated first. Collective taxis operate on set routes but are rarely used by westerners. Hotels have hire cars.

There is a bus service which is frequent and very cheap.

Accommodation and food

It is advisable to book hotel accommodation well in advance and reconfirm before arrival. Prices, as in other Gulf areas, are high. A 10% service charge, plus 5% municipal tax, is usual. Tipping is not necessary.

Although alcoholic drinks may not be imported, they are available in hotels and restaurants.

Hotels

NAME	ADDRESS	TELEPHONE	TELEX
MUSCAT			
Al Bustan Palace	PO Box 8448	799666	5477
Muscat Inter-Continental	PO Box 7398	600500	5491
Gulf	PO Box 4455	560100	5416
Sheraton	PO Box 6260	799899	3353
RUWI			
Al Falaj	PO Box 5031	702311	3229
Ruwi	PO Box 5195	704244	3456
MUTRAH			
Mutrah	PO Box 4525	134401	5276
SEEB			
Seeb Novotel	PO Box 1069	510300	5199
SALALAH			
Holiday Inn	PO Box 18870	461777	7638

What to see in Oman

Muscat became the country's capital at the end of the 18th century, under the rule of Sayyia Ahmad bin Said. This old walled town is dominated by two well preserved 16th century Portuguese fortresses, Merani and Jalali. Merani is the headquarters of the Muscat Garrison and Jalali is the main jail of Oman. The town itself consists of impressive old houses, narrow streets and three beautifully carved original gates. Among the most important sights are the Ali Mousa Mosque, the New Mosque and the Sultan's Palace.

The Oman Museum is housed in a small building in the Ministry of Information and Culture area at Qurum, a few kilometres along the north-west coast of Muscat. It houses attractive modern displays covering Oman's archaeology, history and traditional culture. It aims to encapsulate, in a limited space, the culture and history of a complex society, and it does this in a series of five thematic exhibitions dealing with archaeology, the land and its people, Islamic architecture and arts and crafts.

Mutrah, 5 km from Muscat, is the centre of Oman's commercial life and Ruwi, 2 km away, is the administrative centre of the country.

Longer visits, with permission, can be made to visit ancient forts such as the ones at Nizwa, Bahla and Sohar, and to the beautiful mountains and desert country for bathing and picnics.

Restaurants: All the hotels have good restaurants, with Arab and international cuisine.

Entertainments: There are three aircon-ditioned cinemas in Ruwi and an open-air cinema at the Al Falaj Hotel, showing Arab, Indian, American and British films. There are a few nightclubs and bars, mostly in the hotels.

Sports: Spectator sports including hockey, football, volleyball and basket-ball at the new police sports stadium, Wattayah. Camel and horse races are held at the old airstrip at Seeb on Fridays and public holidays. There are many beautiful beaches where you can go swimming, sailing and skin-diving. There are also three private sports clubs offering a wide range of activities including fishing, water-skiing, tennis, squash and golf. The Omanis are keen sportsmen, and the local press carries details of what is on and where. Most international hotels have their own "in house" facilities although public facilities are also available.

Shopping: The main *souq* is in Mutrah where you can see many of Oman's traditional handicrafts on display. Silver and gold jewellery, Khanjars (Omani daggers), hand woven textiles, carpets and baskets. Most of the modern shops are in Ruwai, where large, Western-style department stores and supermarkets dominate the High Street.

Omani craftsman at work

QATAR

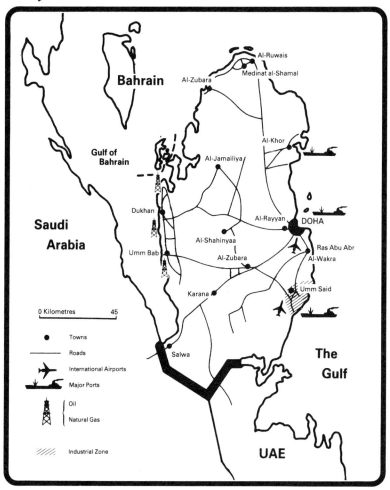

Area: 11,437 sq km
Population: 250,000
Capital: Doha

Qatar is the thumb shaped area of land which protrudes into the lower Gulf just below Bahrain. For generations the sparse population of the small sheikhdom relied chiefly on the sea for a living by fishing and pearling. The discovery of oil and its commercial exploitation, from 1948 onwards, revolutionised the old nomadic and seafaring lifestyle of the indigenous population. Today, Qatar is a thoroughly modern state. The capital, Doha, once an unimpressive little town of single story buildings, is an affluent city with a wide, palm tree lined corniche which follows the deep sweep of the bay. High rise office blocks, government ministries, banks and hotels overlook the shallow bay where wooden dhows are still much in evidence, a reminder of Qatar's proud seagoing history. Qatar's population is still small at around 250,000 but only about 25 per cent of this number are actually Qatari citizens, the rest are immigrant workers. Some 80 per cent live in Doha, which is a quieter, tidier and generally less hectic capital than others in the Gulf. Alcohol is forbidden and social life tends to centre around the family which can make it lonely for the visiting business executive. The local population, however, go out of their way to be friendly and crime is virtually unheard of.

Qatar does not grant tourist visas but bona fide business people are welcome in the country. Doha has an excellent National Museum – probably the best in the region – which traces the country's development through the generations. The Museum is centred around the Old Palace, where the current Emir lived as a child with his family. Its rooms are packed with personal collections and relics including all the ruler's medals and awards from foreign governments. A new three storey building houses permanent exhibitions of Qatar's life and culture, geology, the history of oil, a marine museum and aquarium. Qatar has miles of unspoilt sandy beaches for bathing and fishing, scuba diving and wind surfing. The number of restaurants in Doha has increased considerably over recent years although almost all are to be found in the city's leading hotels. Car rental desks can be found at Doha International Airport and in all major hotels but most visitors opt for hiring a driver with taxi or limousine on an hourly or a daily basis for the duration of their stay. There is no public transport system in the city.

A state in transition

The people of Qatar are of Arabian stock, a result of mainland migrations, largely in search of water. The first migration crossed from Kuwait in the 1870s and a second took place at the end of the 19th century when Al Ihsa tribesmen moved to Qatar during the period of Wahabi expansion in Saudi Arabia.

Qataris belong to three main Arab tribes: the Awamir, the Manasir and the Bani Hajir. The capital of Doha is situated on the mid-east coast and is small enough to be crossed on foot in less than one hour. Outside Doha there is little to attract the business visitor. Archaeological exploration is going on, mostly undertaken by Danish and British researchers and several interesting sites and cave paintings have been discovered. Examples of this work can be seen at Qatar's second town, Al Khor, which lies about 24 miles (40 km) north of Doha. The museum there has a permanent exhibition of artefacts discovered on site, some dating back to pre-historic and early Islamic civilisations. The small village of Umm Salal Mohammed, about 10 miles (16 km) north of Doha and dominated by an impressive 19th century fortress, has several examples of traditional Qatari architecture. The old village of Ruwais on the northern tip of the peninsula is one of Qatar's most important fishing centres while Wakrah, only a few miles outside Doha, is famous for its traditional architecture and magnificent new mosque.

Although Qatar is not without culture, many of its oldest traditions have been radically altered since the commercial exploitation of oil. Few nomads travel through the country with their herds these days, pearling has completely gone and, although fishing continues, boat building is no longer the preserve of Qatari craftsmen. For some years, particularly during the oil boom era of the Seventies, Qatar was caught up in a type of pseudo-Western culture in which the cinema and video predominated. However, great efforts are being made to preserve traditional culture in the form of poems, songs and dances and a strong theatre movement aims at producing indigenous plays.

Doha.

Qataris keep tradition alive in the national dance.

History

Qatar is known to have been inhabited by primitive man by the discovery there of relics dating back to 5000 BC. The country has a desert climate which is unsuitable for farming, although in recent years there have been giant steps forward in the local production of fruit and vegetable products. Successful cultivation of crops, however, remains labour intensive and without constant supervision and attention cultivated land would swiftly return to the desert. The country is surrounded on three sides by the sea and it is likely that the Qataris have always been involved in the fishing and pearling trades. Although the former continues today, pearling in Qatar suffered with Japan's exploitation of the cheap synthetic or cultured pearl. During the period of colonial expansion, Qatar was an important maritime entrêpot on the east-west spice, silk and slave routes.

Oil was discovered in 1940 and international exports of this precious new resource began in 1948. From 1961 to 1971 Qatar was a British protectorate but on 3 September 1972 treaty arrangements with the United Kingdom were annulled and Qatar became a fully independent sovereign state.

Economy

Although the government is diversifying industry, oil remains the lynchpin of the Qatari economy, accounting for 91% of export earnings and over 80% of government revenues. Decreased world demand for oil and the subsequent price decline of recent years have led to a marked deterioration in domestic economic activity. However, development of Qatar's offshore North Field, potentially the largest non-associated gas field in the world, will decrease domestic economic reliance on oil and Qatari economists are predicting a new economic boom when North Field export revenues begin to flow. The steady development of industries using hydrocarbons as fuel since independence in 1971 has given Qatar one of the most advanced heavy industrial sectors in the Gulf. In addition to oil refining and gas fractionating are fertilisers, petrochemicals and steel, all based at Umm Said, which has become the country's industrial centre. The Industrial Technical Centre (IDTC) was set up in 1973 to oversee the development of non-oil related industries. Incentives such as tax relief and low rents are offered in specified industrial zones to encourage new business ventures. Foreign participation is welcomed in industrial projects, with the general provision that the local partner holds at least 51% of the company's capital.

Boat building continues in Qatar but today it is mainly the preserve of Asian craftsmen.

General Information

Government

Qatar is an independent sovereign state ruled by Shaikh Khalifa bin Hamid al Thani, who came to power in February 1972. Shaikh Khalifa heads a 17 member Council of Ministers and a 30 member Advisory Council.

Languages

Arabic is the official language of the country but English is widely spoken and understood.

Religion

Islam is the official religion of the people and most Qataris are Sunni Moslems of the Wahabi sect.

How to get there

By air: The national carrier of Qatar is Gulf Air, jointly owned by Bahrain, Oman, Abu Dhabi and Qatar.
By road: It is possible to drive to Qatar from Saudi Arabia and the United Arab Emirates.

Entry Regulations

British nationals do not require visas for a stay of up to 30 days. But 72 hour visas for other nationals can be obtained at Doha airport providing a Qatari sponsor gives an undertaking and onward reservations are held. Visas are not required for nationals of Bahrain, Kuwait, Oman, Saudi Arabia and the United Arab Emirates. Other nationals require visas for entry to Qatar.

Yellow fever vaccination certificates are required for visitors coming from an infected area.

Customs Regulations

No alcohol may be imported. No limit on the amount of currency taken in or out.

Climate

Qatar has a very hot and humid summer with an average daily temperature of 41C. The best months in Qatar are October, November, April and May. January and February are the coldest months, when temperatures can fall as low as 7C. Rainfall, usually in the form of heavy showers, occurs generally between November and March.

Currency

Qatari Riyal (QR) divided into 100 dirhams. Most major credit cards are accepted by the top hotels but cash is still the preferred method of payment elsewhere.

Business Hours

Banks: Saturday-Wednesday 0730-1130 and Thursday 0730-1100.
Government Offices: Saturday-Thursday 0700-1300.
Offices: Saturday-Thursday 0730-1200 and 1500-1800.
Shops: Saturday-Thursday 0730-1200 and 1500-1800 or later.

Press

The English language Gulf Times is published in daily and weekly editions.

Public holidays

The Qataris are often regarded as being the traditionalists of the Gulf. They are

certainly very devout people and religious holidays are strictly observed. Accession of the Amir, 22 February
First day of Ramadan*, 7 April 1989
Eid al Fitr*, 7-9 May 1989
Eid al Adha*, 14-17 July 1989
Hijra*, 4 August 1989
Al Ashoura*, 13 August 1989
National Day, 3 September
Prophet's Birthday*, 13 October 1989
The dates of the Moslem holidays marked with an asterisk are only approximate as they depend on sightings of the moon.

Consulates/Embassies in Doha

United Kingdom: POB 3, Doha. Tel. 321991. Telex 4205
USA: POB 2399, Doha. Tel. 870701
France: POB 2669, Doha. Tel. 425216. Telex 4280
Germany, Federal Republic: POB 3064, Doha. Tel. 671101. Telex 4528
India: POB 2788, Doha. Tel. 672025. Telex 4646
Algeria: POB 2494, Doha. Tel. 446911. Telex 4604
Bangladesh: POB 2080, Doha. Tel. 671927. Telex 5102
Iran: POB 1633, Doha. Tel. 321930. Telex 4251
Iraq: POB 1526, Doha. Tel. 446877. Telex 4296
Japan: POB 2208, Doha. Tel. 831224. Telex 4339
Jordan: POB 2366, Doha. Tel. 425146
Korea: POB 3727, Doha. Tel. 320158
Kuwait: POB 1177, Doha. Tel. 832111. Telex 4113
Lebanon: POB 2411, Doha. Tel. 325193
Mauritania: POB 3132, Doha. Tel. 328831. Telex 4379
Morocco: POB 3242, Doha. Tel. 329182. Telex 4473
Oman: POB 3766, Doha. Tel. 329113. Telex 4341
Pakistan: POB 334, Doha. Tel. 425117
Saudi Arabia: POB 1255, Doha. Tel.

427144. Telex 4483
Somalia: POB 1948, Doha. Tel. 325758. Telex 4275
Sudan: POB 2999, Doha. Tel. 422627
Syria: POB 1257, Doha. Tel. 421873. Telex 4447
Tunisia: POB 2707, Doha. Tel. 421694. Telex 4422
Turkey: POB 1977, Doha. Tel. 865885. Telex 4406
Yemen Arab Republic: POB 3318. Tel. 671050. Telex 5130

Accommodation and Entertainment

Doha has only a few hotels but the competition between them is stiff and, as a result, all are excellent. However, it is advisable to make a reservation well in advance of a visit.

There is a wide range of recreational and sporting activities available in Qatar although mainly through private clubs. Your hotel receptionist is a good source of information about water sports and recreations, which are popular with Qataris and expatriates alike. The Gulf Cinema, on the C ringroad near Almana roundabout, shows English language films. The Doha Club, PO Box 366 offers swimming, tennis, squash, a games room and a restaurant.

The best food is usually to be found in the hotels, expect a first class selection of international cuisine, made with locally caught fish and home-grown fruit and vegetables.

The Qatar Museum is a must for any visitor and Wakrah, a now almost-deserted former fishing village has a tranquil beauty and magnificent new mosque that should be seen.

A spectacular new theatre in Doha offers a varied programme of music and drama. The Qatari people are exceptionally friendly and hospitable and will enjoy nothing more than giving you the benefit of their advice on where to go and what to see.

The Qataris are often regarded as the traditionalists of the Gulf.

Hotels

NAME	ADDRESS	TELEPHONE	TELEX
DOHA			
Gulf	PO Box 1911	432432	4250
Oasis	PO Box 717	424424	–
Ramada Renaissance	PO Box 1768	417417	4664DH
Sheraton	PO Box 6000	833833	5000
Sofitel Doha Palace	PO Box 7566	435222	5151

SAUDI ARABIA

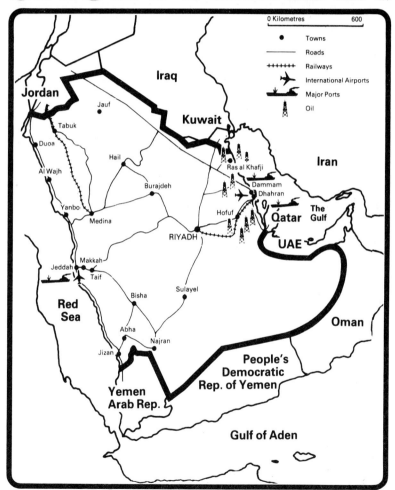

Towns
Roads
Railways
International Airports
Major Ports
Oil

Iraq

Jordan

Jauf

Tabuk

Duoa

Al Wajh

Hail

Yanbo

Burajdeh

Medina

Kuwait

Ras al Khafji

Dammam
Dhahran

Hofuf

RIYADH

Qatar

The Gulf

Iran

UAE

Makkah
Jeddah
Taif

Bisha

Sulayel

Red Sea

Abha

Najran

Jizan

Oman

People's Democratic Rep. of Yemen

Yemen Arab Rep.

Gulf of Aden

Area: 2,240,000 sq km
Population: 11,542,000 (official estimate)
Capital: Riyadh

The traveller in Saudi Arabia is of necessity a businessman, resident or pilgrim. Tourism as such does not exist for the western visitor.

For many people Saudi Arabia can be summed up in three words – desert, Islam and oil – but it is more than this. Certainly it has the largest sand desert in the world, the *Rub al-Khali* or Empty Quarter, but there are also the mountains of the Asir in the south-west, where green, fertile valleys have supported agricultural communities for centuries, and the coastal plains of the Gulf with its coral reefs and traditions of pearl diving.

The Holy City of Makkah dominates one of the few passes from the Nejd in the centre of the country through the stark mountains of the Hejaz bordering the Red Sea coast. Millions of pilgrims descend on Makkah every year from all over the world and Saudi Arabia is proud of its continuing role as the focal point of Islam. Yet from the point of view of the visitor this can have its drawbacks, for the 18th century conservative fundamentalism of the Wahabi sect still prevails, making it difficult, particularly for women, to move about the country freely. Non-Moslems are forbidden to enter the holy city.

Earnings from oil exports resulted in rapid modernisation particularly in the boom years of the 1970s, and communication between the main towns is quite good. Development in fact proceeded at such a pace in the commercial and diplomatic centres of Jeddah and Riyadh, that much of the old character of the cities has been lost. Efforts are being made to preserve the traditional architecture of the holy centres of Makkah and Medina. In essence, Saudi Arabia is a land of contrasts where the past exists, sometimes uncomfortably, beside the present.

Desert and Development

The Arabian peninsula is thought to have once been part of a much bigger continent which also included Africa, and certainly the wildlife and vegetation of the southern and western areas support this theory. It broke away after large rifts appeared which now form the Red Sea and the Gulf of Aden. The whole land mass then tilted and the western edge was lifted as the eastern side was lowered. The west was also the subject of further disturbances which produced the extensive lava fields which occur all along that side of the peninsula.

Thus, behind the very narrow coastal strip (Tihama) along the Red Sea, is a formidable mountain range with plateaux of up to 2,000m. The southern part of this range, the *Asir* region, has some peaks of over 3,000m. East of these mountains, in the north is the *Nejd* – a semi desert area with scattered oases. Further south this gradually changes to sand desert eventually becoming the Empty Quarter which is completely uninhabitable. Along the Gulf coast is a low-lying and relatively fertile plain, giving way further inland to limestone ridges.

Saudi Arabia is one of the driest countries in the world with an average annual rainfall of only 20 cm. Most of this falls in the south-western province of Asir – the only well watered region of the whole country – often the *Rub al-Khali* (Empty Quarter) gets no rain at all. There are no permanent rivers with outlets to the sea in the Kingdom.

Summer daytime temperatures are between 45°C and 50°C and even higher in the desert areas, but drop dramatically at night and in winter. Night time winter temperatures in the north can fall to −7°C.

In the semi-desert area the population is mainly nomadic, although there have long been small villages and towns in the central *Nejd* area. Most permanent settlement, however, has been in the coastal districts – in the *Hejaz* and *Asir* bordering the Red Sea and along the Gulf coast. The rapid expansion of the main towns bears witness to the development and modernisation which resulted from oil wealth. In the 1930s, for instance, the land could only support a population of about two million, yet now this has increased dramatically with the advent of irrigation and the exploitation of underground water resources.

Dispersed communities

The heart of Saudi Arabia is the *Nejd* (highlands), or central province. It has always been somewhat isolated from the rest of the peninsula because of the mountains to the west and the desert on the other three sides. This and its poverty never made it worthwhile, for the various civilisations which held sway in the region through the centuries, to conquer it. For this reason it is considered by many to be the only remaining example of true Arab society. The Najdis have traditionally lived by camel and sheep herding. Tribal traditions and allegiance, which are still strong throughout Saudi Arabia, are perhaps the best preserved in this area. The watchtowers which grace all the high points and the remnants of walls around the towns and villages are a reminder of a warfaring past.

To the west, the *Hejaz* (barrier), or western province, provides a contrast with its mountains and narrow coastal strip. It had long been a centre of trade and commerce and was conquered by successive civilisations from the Nabateans through the Babylonians, Jews and Christians to the Ottomans. Now, the Hejaz is most important because of the Islamic holy cities of Makkah and Medina which attract pilgrims from all over the world. The *Hajj* (pilgrimage) diversified the population even more, as generations ago, did the negro slaves brought in from Africa. The Hejaz is also an important commercial centre.

Perhaps the most picturesque area of Saudi Arabia is the *Asir* (difficult) region, or south-west province. It was called the difficult region because the very high mountains made access almost impossible in the past, but now a modern highway links it to the rest of the country. Asir is the main agricultural area of Saudi Arabia; it gets plenty of rain as a result of the monsoons. The hillsides are terraced to prevent soil erosion.

The population is mainly settled except in the Tihama lowlands to the west of the province where there are still some nomadic tribes. But tribal allegiance is also strong in the settled communities and there is a long history of feuds and fighting. The way of life, however, is altogether different from the other parts of Saudi Arabia, with brighter forms of dress and unique architecture.

The eastern province on the Gulf coast is different again.

History

Saudi Arabia's history before the birth of the Prophet Mohammad is essentially a tribal one, although the peninsula was also influenced by the various civilisations which held sway in the Middle East from the Sumerians through the Assyrians and Persians to the Romans. The only really settled urban centres, however, were on the west coast where the towns of Medina, Makkah and Taif became fairly important trading centres.

Within a century of the birth of Mohammad in 571 AD Islam had spread as far as Spain to the north and India to the east, yet its effect on the Arabian peninsula itself was in some ways temporary. The unification of tribes which it effected soon broke down, but the Islamic unity of the Middle East lasted longer, reducing the importance of Arabia as a trading centre.

In the 16th century the peninsula became nominally under the control of the Ottoman empire but its influence was never strong, especially in the central Nejd area. Even before the First World War Britain had established a foothold along the Gulf coast of Arabia and the (British) government of India had good relations with the Nejd.

When Turkey entered the war in 1914, the British enlisted Arab help against the Ottomans, eventually persuading Sherif Hussain of Makkah to lead an Arab revolt, which was successfully launched in 1916. The following year saw the increasing power of Ibn Saud, the ruler of the Nejd, and descendant of the puritanical and fundamentalist Wahabis of the 18th century. It was Ibn Saud who finally united the various provinces into the modern Kingdom of Saudi Arabia after displacing Sherif Hussain from the Hejaz in 1926.

Asir.

Heads are shaved in preparation for the pilgrimage.

Islamic traditions

The Saudis insist that their culture resides not in material things but in their Islamic religion and the perfection of the Arabic language. When Islam replaced the animism of the Arab tribes in the seventh century, it incorporated many features from the old society. The Prophet Mohammad, who was born of the Quraish tribe, sought to end tribal feuds by advocating unity in Islam, but the traditions were strong and tribal allegiance is still a powerful influence today.

The beauties of the Arabic language are best exhibited in its poetry. This was a powerful force in pre-Islamic days and played a fundamental role in inter-tribal relations. It extolled the virtues of heroic deeds arising out of tribal conflict and was also thought to have some mystical power which could be used either to benefit or destroy. This last aspect was frowned on by Islam, but in its form and to some extent in its content the poetry has survived, particularly in the nomadic communities.

Since Islam forbids the representation of the human form, decoration in Saudi Arabia, whether of houses, clothes or jewellery, is mainly performed with geometric patterns or illuminated Arabic writing.

The Islam of Saudi Arabia is conservative and fundamentalist, based on the revivalist movement of Nejd leader Shaikh Mohammad Ibn Abdel-Wahhab which swept the area in the 18th century. This still has a profound effect on Saudi society, particularly on the position of women, who do not venture outside the house without covering themselves from head to foot in the traditional black robes (*abaya*) which also cover all the face except the eyes.

Yet there are regional differences. In the Asir, the women wear gaily-coloured dresses and are not veiled at all. The architecture of the region is also notable for most of the houses are built with louvred walls as a means of weather-proofing. Inside and out, the walls are decorated with colourful paintings, usually done by the women.

The way of life in the Nejd, home of the Wahabis, could not offer a greater contrast. Here all the traditional Arab and Islamic values predominate still. Poetry, much of it unwritten, is deep rooted and tribal loyalty is important. Marriages are arranged, as they are in many other parts of Saudi Arabia. The old sports of falconry, horse racing and camel racing are still followed avidly.

For the foreign visitor, the Hejaz has possibly the most to offer. In addition to Makkah, the site of the holy Ka'ba which attracts Moslem pilgrims from all over the world each year, there is the other holy city of Medina and the beautiful mountain resort of Taif. Moreover, at Mada'in Saleh there are the well-preserved remains of a Nabatean city carved out of the mountainside like the famous rose city of Petra in Jordan.

Throughout the country some traditional handicrafts are still produced. There is fine bronze and brass ware, in particular incense burners and coffee mortars. Finely worked gold and silver jewellery is made and in the eastern provinces huge brass-bonded chests are to be found. Possibly the most typical metal work are the daggers and swords made in various sizes and designs – all richly decorated. In many other areas, however, the traditionalist crafts have been largely displaced by imports from Asia and the Far East, which enjoy healthy trade relations with the Kingdom.

Saudi Arabia's traditional way of life has dramatically altered with the rapid modernistion and development of the country. This is particularly true in the big towns where much of the old architecture has disappeared to make room for the new office blocks and apartment buildings, while many of the old *souq*-type street markets have given way to new department stores.

Traditional dress, on the other hand, is well established, for although Western clothing is often seen in the towns, it is usually being worn by visiting businessmen or expatriate workers. Saudi men generally prefer to wear the traditional white robes and head-dress (*ghotra*).

Wildlife

Saudi Arabia is not generally thought of as important with respect to wildlife, yet it is the home of at least two fairly rare species of animal – the sand cat, and the oryx, a large antelope with straight antlers. The ibex (mountain goat) is still be found in the northern Hejaz mountains and in the remote areas of the south the Dorcas gazelle and sand gazelle can sometimes be seen. The

Few Bedouin camel herders remain in Saudi Arabia.

cheetah and caracal lynx also used to roam the country but these are threatened with extinction because of hunting. The government hopes to reintroduce these endangered species, which are now protected, back into the wild.

Economy

Although Saudi Arabia has made determined efforts to diversify its economy, oil is still the most vital sector, not really surprising since Saudi Arabia has one quarter of the world's known oil resources. Petrochemical products, fertilisers, plastics and steel produced at the massive complexes of Yanbu on the Red Sea and Jubail on the Gulf coast are also an important source of export earnings. Since 1970 the country's economy has been organised in a series of Five Year Plans. In the boom years of the 1970s and early 1980s, when world oil prices reached their peak, Saudi Arabia was a hive of frenetic activity. It was during this period that huge numbers of expatriate workers flocked to the kingdom in pursuit of lucrative contracts in construction, transport and telecommunications.

Today, with most of its infrastructure complete, development projects have declined to more realistically sustainable levels. Many of the foreign workers have left and the emphasis of economic development, as directed by the current Five Year Plan, (1985-90), is the development of the private sector to provide new stimulation for economic growth.

Agriculture is a major growth area, with about one quarter of the country's workforce involved in this sector. Despite very real climatic constraints the Saudis have achieved remarkable results in agricultural productivity. With the help of hefty government subsidies the kingdom has achieved self sufficiency in wheat production and indeed, in recent years, has recorded a significant surplus which has been made available for export.

155

General Information

Government

Absolute Monarchy. The ruler is King Fahd Ibn Abdul Aziz.

Languages

Arabic is the official language; English is understood in business circles.

Religions

Centre of Islamic faith. The majority follow the Sunni faith, except in the Eastern Provinces where a large number of people follow Shia rites. Saudi Arabia includes Makkah (birthplace of Mohammad) and Medina (burial place of Mohammad).

How to get there

By air: Saudia is the national carrier of Saudi Arabia.
By road: Saudi Arabia shares land borders with Jordan, Iraq, Kuwait, Qatar, the UAE, Oman and the Yemens. In 1986 the completition of the causeway with Bahrain provided a direct road link between the Kingdom and its near neighbour.

Entry regulations

All visitors must be in possession of a valid passport and a current visa, obtainable from Saudi embassies abroad.

Nationals of Bahrain, Kuwait, Qatar and the United Arab Emirates do not require visas.

Obtaining a visa is often a long and arduous process, involving finding a sponsor and justifying the purpose of the trip to the satisfaction of the embassy officials.

Customs regulations

There is no restriction on the amount of currency that may be taken into or out of the country. Articles for personal use including 600 cigarettes, 100 cigars, or tobacco are allowed in duty free. The import of alcoholic beverages and pork products is strictly prohibited.

Climate

Saudi Arabia has a desert climate. In Jeddah it is warm and humid for most of the year. Riyadh, much more inland, is hotter than Jeddah in the summer and colder in winter, when occasional heavy rainstorms occur.
What to wear: Lightweight clothing is adequate in Jeddah for most of the year. In Riyadh and the Eastern provinces, tropical clothing is necessary from mid-April to mid-October. During December and January warmer clothing and raincoats are necessary.

Currency

Saudi riyal divided into 100 halalah or 20 qursh.

Business hours

Banks: Saturday-Wednesday, 0830-1200. Government Departments: Saturday-Wednesday, 0730-1430. Thursday and Friday are official holidays.
Offices and Shops: No standard hours. Roughly as follows: Jeddah 0900-1330 and 1630-2000 (Ramadan, 2000-0100). Riyadh 0830-1200 and 1630-1930 (Ramadan, 1930-2330). Eastern Province, 0730-1200 and 1430-1800 (Ramadan, 1900-2300).

Press

Saudi Arabia has a number of English language publications the most popular of which are The Arab News, POB 4556, Jeddah, and The Saudi Gazette, POB 5576, Jeddah. Both are published daily.

Public holidays

First day of Ramadan*, 7 April 1989
Eid al-Fitr*, 7-9 May 1989
Eid al-Adha*, 14-17 July 1989
National Day, 23 September (not official)
Hijra*, 4 August 1989
Al-Ashoura*, 13 August 1989
Prophet's birthday*, 13 October 1989
The dates of the Moslem holidays, marked with an asterisk, are only approximate as they depend on sightings of the moon.

Transport

By air: All internal services are run by Saudia which operates services between Jeddah, Riyadh and Dhahran. Air journeys from Jeddah to Riyadh and from Riyadh to Dhahran take on average 75 and 45 minutes respectively.

By road: Good roads link the main towns. Taxis are readily available in the main centres. Car hire facilities are limited. Taxi fares in the country are officially controlled and rates are displayed both at the airport and in the downtown centre. It is, however, necessary to bargain with the driver as the official rates are not usually observed.

By rail: Riyadh and Dammam are linked by a railway with a daily passenger service in each direction. The journey takes eight hours (compared with five hours by road).

Accommodation and food

All hotels are air-conditioned and all rooms have private baths. Hotel tariffs fluctuate. All the large hotels have excellent restaurants at which a variety of western and oriental dishes are served.

Consulates/Embassies in Jeddah

Afghanistan: Tariq al-Madina, Kilo No. 3, Jeddah. Tel: (2) 53142.
Algeria: POB 94388, Riyadh 11693. Tel: (1) 788-7171. Telex: 202828.
Argentina: POB 94369, Riyadh 11693. Tel: (1) 465-2600. Telex: 405988.
Australia: POB 94400, Riyadh 11693. Tel: (1) 488-7788. Telex: 405944.
Austria: POB 94373, Riyadh 11693. Tel: (1) 477-7445. Telex: 406555.
Bahrain: POB 94371, Riyadh 11693. Tel: (1) 488-0044. Telex: 407055.
Bangladesh: POB 94395, Riyadh 11693. Tel: (1) 465-5300. Telex: 406133.
Belgium: POB 94396, Riyadh 11693. Tel: (1) 488-2888. Telex: 406344.
Brazil: POB 94348, Riyadh 11693. Tel: (1) 488-0018. Telex: 406711.
Burkina Faso: POB 94300, Riyadh 11693. Tel: (1) 454-6168. Telex: 403844.
Burundi: POB 94355, Riyadh 11693. Tel: (1) 464-1155. Telex: 406477.
Cameroon: POB 94336, Riyadh 11693. Tel: (1) 488-0022. Telex: 406688.
Canada: POB 94321, Riyadh 11693. Tel: (1) 488-2288. Telex 404893.
Chad: POB 94374, Riyadh 11693. Tel: (1) 465-7702. Telex: 406366.
China (Taiwan): POB 94393, Riyadh 11693. Tel: (1) 488-1900.
Denmark: POB 94398, Riyadh 11693. Tel: (1) 464-9516. Telex 404672.
Djibouti: POB 94340, Riyadh 11693. Tel: (1) 454-3182. Telex: 406544.
Egypt: (Interests served by Sudan): POB 94333, Riyadh 11693. Tel: (1) 465-2800.
Ethiopia: POB 94341, Riyadh 11693. Tel: (1) 479-0904. Telex: 406633.
Finland: POB 94363, Riyadh 11693. Tel: (1) 488-1515. Telex: 406099.
France: POB 94367, Riyadh 11693. Tel: (1) 488-1755. Telex: 403830.
Gabon: POB 94325, Riyadh 11693. Tel: (1) 454-9500. Telex: 406766.
Gambia: POB 94322, Riyadh 11693. Tel:

(1) 454-9156. Telex: 406767.
Germany, Federal Republic: POB 8974, Riyadh 11492. Tel: (1) 465-4800. Telex: 402297.
Ghana: POB 94339, Riyadh 11693. Tel: (1) 464-1383. Telex: 406599.
Greece: POB 94375, Riyadh 11693. Tel: (1) 465-5026. Telex: 406322.
Guinea: POB 94326, Riyadh 11693. Tel: (1) 231-0631. Telex: 404944.
India: POB 94387, Riyadh 11693. Tel: (1) 477-7006. Telex: 406077.
Indonesia: POB 94343, Riyadh 11693. Tel: (1) 488-9127. Telex: 406577.
Iran: POB 94394, Riyadh 11693. Tel: (1) 482-6111. Telex: 406066.
Iraq: POB 94349, Riyadh 11693. Tel: (1) 491-2929. Telex: 406522.
Ireland: POB 94349, Riyadh 11693. Tel: (1) 488-1383. Telex: 406655.
Italy: POB 94389, Riyadh 11693. Tel: (1) 454-3429. Telex: 406188.
Japan: POB 4095, Riyadh 11491. Tel: (1) 488-1100. Telex: 405866.
Jordan: POB 7455, Riyadh 11693. Tel: (1) 454-3727.
Kenya: POB 94358, Riyadh 11693. Tel: (1) 488-2484. Telex: 406455.
Korea, Republic: POB 94399, Riyadh 11693. Tel: (1) 448-2211. Telex: 405858.
Kuwait: POB 2166, Riyadh 11451. Tel: (1) 488-3401. Telex: 401301.
Lebanon: POB 94350, Riyadh 11693. Tel: (1) 465-1000.
Libya: POB 94365, Riyadh 11693. Tel: (1) 454-4511. Telex: 401049.
Malaysia: POB 94335, Riyadh 11693. Tel: (1) 401-3050. Telex: 401033.
Mali: POB 94331, Riyadh 11693. Tel: (1) 465-8900. Telex: 406733.
Malta: POB 94361, Riyadh 11693. Tel: (1) 463-2345. Telex: 406422.
Mauritania: POB 94354, Riyadh 11693. Tel: (1) 465-6313. Telex: 406466.
Mexico: POB 94391, Riyadh 11693. Tel: (1) 476-1200. Telex: 406111.
Morocco: POB 94392, Riyadh 11693. Tel: (1) 465-4900. Telex: 406155.
Nepal: POB 94384, Riyadh 11693. Tel: (1) 402-4758. Telex: 406288.

Netherlands: POB 21683, Riyadh 11485. Tel: (1) 488-0011. Telex: 403820.
New Zealand: POB 94397, Riyadh 11693. Tel: (1) 476-6602. Telex: 405878.
Niger: POB 94334, Riyadh 11693. Tel: (1) 464-3116. Telex: 406722.
Nigeria: POB 94386, Riyadh 11693. Tel: (1) 465-4111. Telex: 406177.
Norway: POB 94380, Riyadh 11693. Tel: (1) 488-1904. Telex: 406311.
Oman: POB 94381, Riyadh 11693. Tel: (1) 465-0010. Telex: 406222.
Pakistan: POB 6891, Riyadh 11693. Tel: (1) 476-7266. Telex: 406500.
Philippines: POB 94366, Riyadh 11693. Tel: (1) 454-0777. Telex: 406377.
Portugal: POB 94328, Riyadh 11693. Tel: (1) 464-4688. Telex: 404477.
Qatar: POB 94353, Riyadh 11693. Tel: (1) 464-5400.
Rwanda: POB 94383, Riyadh 11693. Tel: (1) 454-0808. Telex: 406199.
Senegal: POB 94382, Riyadh 11693. Tel: (1) 454-2144. Telex: 406565.
Sierra Leone: POB 94378, 11693. Tel: (1) 463-3149. Telex: 406744.
Singapore: POB 94378, Riyadh 11693. Tel: (1) 465-7007. Telex: 406211.
Somalia: POB 94372, Riyadh 11693. Tel: (1) 454-0111.
Spain: POB 94347, Riyadh 11693. Tel: (1) 488-0606. Telex: 406788.
Sri Lanka: POB 94360, Riyadh 11693. Tel: (1) 463-4200. Telex: 405688.
Sudan: POB 94337, Riyadh 11693. Tel: (1) 482-9666.
Sweden: POB 94382, Riyadh 11693. Tel: (1) 448-3100. Telex: 406266.
Switzerland: POB 9265, Riyadh 11413. Tel: (1) 488-1291. Telex: 406055.
Syria: POB 94323, Riyadh 11693. Tel: (1) 465-3800. Telex: 406677.
Thailand: POB 94359, Riyadh 11693. Tel: (1) 463-4325. Telex: 406433.
Tunisia: POB 94368, Riyadh 11693. Tel: (1) 465-4585.
Turkey: POB 94390, Riyadh 11613. Tel: (1) 465-6452. Telex: 406622.
Uganda: POB 94344, Riyadh 11693. Tel: (1) 454-4910. Telex: 406588.

United Arab Emirates: POB 94385, Riyadh 11693. Tel: (1) 482-6803. Telex: 401458.

United Kingdom: POB 94351, Riyadh 11693. Tel: (1) 488-0077. Telex: 406488.

USA: POB 9041, Riyadh 11413. Tel: (1) 488-3800. Telex: 401363.

Uruguary: POB 94346, Riyadh 11693. Tel: (1) 491-2285. Telex: 406611.

Venezuela: POB 94364, Riyadh 11693. Tel: (1) 476-7867. Telex: 405599.

Yemen Arab Republic: POB 94356, Riyadh 11693. Tel: (1) 464-2077.

Yemen, People's Democratic Republic: POB 94319, Riyadh 11693.

Zaire: relations broken off, May 1982; interests served by Belgium.

Hotels

NAME	ADDRESS	TELEPHONE	TELEX
RIYADH			
Al Khozama	P.O. Box 4148	4654650	400100
Al Mutlaq Novotel	P.O. Box 3525	4762193	405266
Atallah Sheraton	P.O. Box 1975	4543300	401415
Hyatt Regency	P.O. Box 18006	4771111	402963
Inter-Continental	P.O. Box 3636	4655000	401076
Marriott	P.O. Box 16294	4779300	400983
Minhal Sofitel	P.O. Box 17058	4782500	403088
Riyadh Palace	P.O. Box 2691	4054444	200312
JEDDAH			
Albilad Movenpick	P.O. Box 6788	6828282	603010
Al Fau Holiday Inn	P.O. Box 10924	6611000	400755
Alhamra Sofitel	P.O. Box 7375	6602000	600749
Al Harithy Frantel	P.O. Box 7584	6670520	600687
Alsalam Ramada	P.O. Box 6582	6314000	6013275
Hyatt Regency	P.O. Box 8483	6519800	602688
Kaki	P.O. Box 2559	6312201	601738
Khojah Residence	P.O. Box 16955	631800	605127

[Hotels]

Marriott	P.O. Box 6448	6714000	405135
Red Sea Palace	P.O. Box 2552	6428555	404790
Sands	P.O. Box 7030	6692020	400789

AL KHOBAR-DHAHRAN

Algosaibi	P.O. Box 51	8942466	870008
Carlton Al Moaibed	P.O. Box 1235	8575455	870064
Gulf Meridien	P.O. Box 1266	8646000	–
International	P.O. Box 428	8918555	801272
Ramada Palace	P.O. Box 381	8915444	801227

TAIF

Al Hada Sheraton	P.O. Box 999	7541400	751092
Massarrah Inter-Continental	P.O. Box 827	7328333	750055

DAMMAM

Alhamra	P.O. Box 1411	8333444	–
Oberoi	P.O. Box 5397	8345555	802071

JUBAIL

Holiday Inn	P.O. Box 10167	3417000	832222
International	P.O. Box 215	3610645	831027

YANBU

Hyatt	P.O. Box 300	3223888	461053
Radwa Holiday Inn	P.O. Box 452	3223767	661086

MAKKAH

Ajyad Makkah	P.O. Box 6020	5368444	540471
Inter-Continental	P.O. Box 1496	5434455	54006

[Hotels]			
MEDINA			
Sheraton	P.O. Box 1735	8230240	470076
KHAMIS MUSHAYT-ABHA			
Khamis Al Frantel	P.O. Box 892	2233466	906122
Abha Inter-Continental	P.O. Box 1496	5434455	54006

Riyadh

Riyadh has been the capital of Saudi Arabia since the Kingdom was first set up in the 1920s. It has been the site of settlements in the Nejd for centuries but has really expanded in the past 60 years. It is an essentially modern city well served by roads, a railway and airport and with plenty of hotels. Apart from the Royal Palace and an interesting museum, it boasts what is debatably the biggest commercial airport in the world.

Jeddah

Jeddah, Saudi Arabia's commercial and diplomatic capital, has been a port for more than 1,200 years. Now it is the biggest port on the Red Sea with a population of about 500,000. Like Riyadh, it has expanded so fast that it has lost much of its character, although there is something of the old quarter left. Some 50 embassies are located in Jeddah. It is well served by roads and has good hotel accommodation.

All visitors should visit the *souq*. There are fruiterers with giant fresh dates, hookah smokers, coppersmiths, incense sellers, jewellers and the like.

At prayer time recordings blare out from the mosques and devout shop-keepers rush off, leaving their wares untended. (Theft, as a result of the law of the Koran is minimal.) Those who don't are occasionally rapped by the religious police who wander around with their canes. The *souq* is a melting pot of old and new, women balancing baskets on their heads walk beside 20th century luxury stores.

The only thing to do at the weekend – Thursday afternoon or Friday – is to follow the mob to the beach. Jeddah has its much frequented Creek. But a drive out of town on a flat sandy road will lead you to various spots on the Red Sea where foreigners repair. You can collect white coral, sport a bikini, or watch the Pakistanis and Arabs fishing as they immerse themselves fully clothed. You may prefer the swimming pool at your hotel, or the men-only health club.

Traffic in Jeddah is a hazard. It is as much as a driver's life is worth, you are told, to knock you down. Nevertheless it takes an insane kind of courage to walk into that seething mass of dodgem cars and gesture to them with your bare hand to stop. But this is the only way to reach the other side. Being in a car is not much more secure, but again you quickly learn to relax.

Having put your life into your driver's hands, a further problem arises in that street names, by and large, are non-existent. Destinations can only be reached if you have detailed directions via a major landmark. But without these, it is best to get your quarry to meet you at your hotel or to send his own driver.

Makkah

Makkah is built some 700m up in the mountains of the west where it dominates a pass through to the Nejd from the coast. Because of its strategic siting, it was settled long before Islam made it the focus of world attention. As Mohammad's birthplace it has the Sacred Mosque which houses the *Ka'ba* (House of God) which brings in over a million pilgrims each year. Although the city has expanded fast and is now easily accessible by road, an effort has been made to preserve the traditional architecture. Makkah also has a new and impressive Islamic conference hall.

Medina

The second holy city of Islam, Medina is also in the mountains but somewhat to the north of Makkah. It is the only settlement in that area and is able to support a permanent population because of its reserves of underground water. The city is also a centre of learning – where students of religion can attend one of the city's three colleges of theology. Medina is also the home of the green-domed Great Mosque.

Oil is still the lynchpin of the Saudi economy.

SYRIA

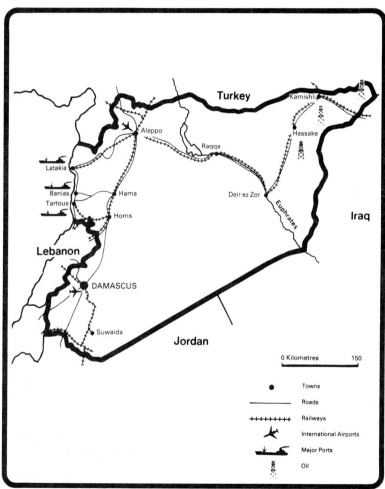

Area: 184,050 sq km
Population: 10.6 million (official estimate)
Capital: Damascus

Variety in a changing landscape

The country that is today known as Syria was carved by politicians from the much larger territory of 'greater' Syria at the end of the First World War. Before it came to be applied exclusively to the present republic, the term Syria referred to a geographical entity which included Lebanon, Palestine and Trans-Jordan. This area lay within the natural boundaries formed by the Taurus mountains to the North, the Syrian and Sinai deserts to the east and south, and the Mediterranean to the west – a factor which enabled free movement between coast and hinterland and largely accounted for geographical Syria's prosperity and long-standing trading tradition.

Modern Syria is less advantageously placed. With the loss of the seaports of Beirut and Tripoli to Lebanon in the post-war carve-up and later on the loss of Iskerderum to Turkey, the Syrian centres of Damascus, Homs and Aleppo were no longer within such easy reach of their natural maritime outlets and Syria itself has been left to develop alternative facilities at Lattakia, Tartous and Banias, along a truncated stretch of the coast.

If, historically, movement has always been possible across Syria from east to west through the various breaks in the country's coastal mountain ranges, the same cannot be said of passage from north to south. For although, topographically, Syria consists of five distinct zones all running roughly parallel with the shoreline along a north-south axis, no single strip is so homogeneous as to offer a continuous north-south route.

The fertile but narrow coastal plain, for example, varies from around 30 km in width in some places to no more than a few metres in others and the road that runs along the shore has to branch inland when it reaches the environs of Lattakia.

These idiosyncrasies also have their effect on climate and the distribution of Syria's population, which is made up of different religious groupings. Immediately next to the coastal strip in the North are the Nusairiya mountains, which, though relatively low, have very steep slopes – the 1,000 m drop down to the newly-developed agricultural area of the Ghab on the eastern flank is particularly sudden.

As a result these mountains have traditionally afforded a number of vantage points. The Crusaders chose one to build their *Krak des Chevaliers*, a castle which can be seen from 30 km away or more. And they have provided places of refuge, particularly for the long-established indigenous community of Nusairis or Alawis, a sect that combines elements of Shia Islam with other non-Islamic beliefs and observances. Altogether, Syria's Alawis number something over half a million.

To the south of the Nusairiya mountain range, but separated from it by the valleys of the Orontes (or Asi) river and the Nahr al-Kabir and lying much further inland behind the border with Lebanon, stand the mountains of the Anti-Lebanon, extending southwards to Mount Hermon and the Golan Heights.

Palmyra: relics of ancient civilisations

Further south is the Jabal (mountain) al-Duruz, named after another very secretive sect, the Druze, who have inhabited this area from the early 18th century. The Druze, of whom there are about 175,000 in Syria, consider themselves Moslems, but in terms of religious activity they keep themselves so much apart that outsiders know little about their customs. As a community, with other members living in Southern Lebanon and northern Israel, they are an offshoot of the Ismaili sect, itself a movement which broke away from the main body of Shia Muslims in the eighth century.

The Orontes river flows some of the way along the great Red Sea rift valley which traverses Syria alongside the Nusairiya mountains, crosses through the Bekaa valley in Lebanon and continues southwards all the way to East Africa. The Euphrates flows from Turkey, through Syria and on to Iraq and provides water for major hydro-electric and irrrigation projects in all three countries – a demand which has proved a source of friction, actual and potential, amongst the three riparian states.

The southern part of Syria, in contrast, is much less fortunate in its rainfall and rivers, which explains the huge diversity of Syria's weather and vegetation and the rapid degradation from fertility to desert as one moves east from the Damascus region. Mount Hermon for example (also called Jabal al-Shaikh) stands over 3,000m high and is snow-capped for most of the year. On its southern side lies the productive soil of the Hawran plateau, which provides wheat and pasture and was once the granary of 'greater' Syria. That was before dry farming developments in the Jezira over the past half century or so, proved that this latter spacious, relatively flat, triangular plain in Syria's north-eastern corner was better equipped to furnish the bulk of the country's cotton and grain.

The Hawran nevertheless remains, along with the Damascus oasis, one of the most densely populated areas of the country and presents a striking contrast with the vast wasteland of the Syrian desert to the east. Stretching at its widest point for some 1,200 km, this desert separates Syria from the populated river valleys of Iraq and is itself punctuated only by the sites of such ancient settlements as Palmyra, which then and now provides a resting place on the well-worn trade route between the Mediterranean and the Gulf. In the olden days it was the wells of the Kalamoun hills which branch out north-eastwards from Damascus to Palmyra that dictated the desert route, and modern roadways have followed the same path.

Syria's varied topography is reflected in the sharp distinctions between its urban, rural and nomadic populations. The country's principal cities, Damascus, Homs, Hama and Aleppo, are situated in valleys and plains where movement has been easier and there has been a greater intermingling of cultural and racial influences. These were the areas where Greek, Roman and Arab influences had their greatest cultural impact.

The inhabitants of these cities have traditionally formed something of an urban elite, which has coincidentally tended to follow the mainstream of religious thought, namely Sunni Islam, orthodox versions of Christianity or Judaism.

Outside the urban centres, however, the lifestyle changes radically and more minority sects are found. The hundreds of tiny, ragged children standing in the village doorways are a testimony, both to Syria's exceptionally high birth rate and the persisting poverty of many of its rural inhabitants.

It is not that farming in Syria is unprofitable but the agricultural sector has perhaps been the most vulnerable to the internal political upheavals that have taken place from independence. The tradition of large land-holdings worked by poorly-rewarded sharecroppers is clearly illustrated by the fact that 95% of land around Aleppo was farmed in this fashion up until the late 1950s. Re-organisation of land tenure on such a scale has not been without its ups and downs.

As for Syria's nomads, they, like nomads everywhere, have lost many of their customary tracks and haunts in the face of new roads, railways, and irrigation schemes. Nevertheless, their contribution to the economy, particularly in providing wool for export, is recognised and their existence further exemplifies the diversity of Syria's ethnic and religious groupings.

In terms of language, there is not only Arabic – although Arabic is spoken by about 90% of the population – but also Kurdish, Circassian, Armenian and Assyrian. The Kurds in Syria are few, an overflow from the territory of Kurdistan which, with its own language, culture and national dress but sharing the Moslem religion, straddles Iraq, Iran and Turkey and spreads into northern Syria as well. Like the Kurds the Circassians too are mountain folk who moved into Syria in large numbers from Turkey during the present century, when the Syrian -Turkish frontier was drawn. Many Armenians and

Assyrians have likewise come to Syria from Turkey and Iraq. Other immigrants to Syria have been the Palestinian refugees, many of whom live around Damascus.

Ummayad Mosque, Damascus. The head of St. John the Baptist is reputed to be enshrined in this 8th century tomb

Culture and history

Greater Syria was too rich and too important strategically to be left to its own devices for long by political and military forces outside. The site of human habitation for over 150,000 years – displaying signs of very early human advances in the domestication of animals, the cultivation of wheat and the use of copper – the area is also thought to have provided the world with its first consonantal alphabet.

Syria's trading tradition, promoted first and foremost by the Phoenicians of the coast, whose sturdy merchant ships were built from the renowned cedar trees of Lebanon, gave its people the opportunity to benefit from and disseminate the cultural and intellectual achievements of the ancient civilisations in nearby Egypt and Mesopotamia and beyond. But, as these exchanges grew, they soon attracted foreign powers and by 1600 BC an area stretching up as far as Damascus had come under the administrative grip of the Egyptian empire.

At about the same time the north was being overrun by Hittites, moving in from Anatolia. But, gradually, both Egyptian and Hittite domination receded, giving way to Assyrian and later Chaldean influence from what is now Iraq. Of all these incursions, however, with their inevitable cultural impact, the only group to leave any lasting ethnic imprint were the Arameans. For, despite the lack of any literary or other Aramean cultural heritage to speak of, the Arameans can be described as the forerunners of modern Syrians in much the same way as the Phoenicians are the acknowledged ancestors of the modern Lebanese. Originally they were nomads who had migrated from Arabia to the Euphrates, eventually settling around Damascus by around 1200 BC. They too were merchants whose travels enabled them to spread the innovatory Phoenician alphabet, which they adopted, together with their own language, Aramaic – the language of Christ which has survived in one small group of villages north of Damascus to the present day. Syriac, which evolved from Aramaic, is also still used as the liturgical language for Syrian Christians.

A new influence, that of the Greeks, had started to reach Syria before the arrival of Alexander the Great, but it was Alexander's conquest in 331 BC which launched a completely new phase in Syrian history – a phase marked by the spread of Greek learning and the deliberate mingling of Greek and oriental cultures. The Roman conquest of the area took place two and a half centuries later and the centre of the Syrian 'province' was moved to Antioch.

Nevertheless, it is Damascus, the capital of the Aramean kingdom, which has served as the most consistent pivot for developments in Syria for as long as 4,000 years. So far as is known it is probably the oldest continuously inhabited capital of the world. Indeed, nowhere is the succession of outside influences more clearly illustrated than in the capital, where the same ancient sites have been adapted and venerated by Greeks, Romans, early Christians and Moslem Arabs in turn.

The best example is perhaps the famous Ummayyad mosque, where once there stood a temple devoted to the god of thunder and lightning, Haddad, the chief deity of the Arameans. The original building was enlarged and converted by the Romans into a temple of Jupiter but was then destroyed by the Byzantines who erected the Cathedral of John the Baptist in its place. But, when in 636 AD the first conquering Arab army entered Damascus bringing with it the teachings of Islam, the Christians relinquished their rights to the Cathedral, allowing it to be transformed into a mosque, which bears the name of the Ummayyad dynasty, the first caliphs of the Moslem world to succeed the four specially-revered caliphs who followed immediately after the Prophet Mohammad. Damascus, as the seat of the Ummayyads, thus became imbued simultaneously with an Arab and Islamic identity.

Syria's special propensity for assimilating diverse cultures enabled it to play a unique role in transmitting elements of one body of learning into another. Just as it had acted as middleman between the Pharaonic and Mesopotamian civilisations, so it managed to translate and promote

Drink seller, Damascus

Graeco-Roman scholarship within the framework of Islam. And so, in the 10th and 11th centuries the Crusaders were able to leave their mark, penetrating easily among the many local principalities that had grown up. These invaders in their turn were overtaken by the Mamluks who, from their base in Egypt, defended Syrian territory against damaging Mongol attacks and ruled the area until the 16th century when their place was taken by the Ottoman Turks. This early Ottoman imprint is still to be seen today in the Tikiyeh mosque in Damascus – its great dome, two slender minarets and series of separate domed alcoves designed by the Turkish architect Sinan and built in the 1550s on the orders of Sultan Suleyman the Magnificent.

From the early 1880s, however, Syria's fortunes took yet another turn with similarly crucial cultural implications, when Ibrahim Pasha, the son of Mohammad Ali of Egypt, snatched Syria from the Ottoman Sultan and, imposing a strong centralised administration, allowed Western missionaries and educationists to establish themselves in the area.

This process, combined with other factors, led indirectly to an Arab cultural renaissance in the late 19th century, which in turn paved the way for the Arab nationalist movement that was to follow, fanned and inflamed by the three decades of French administration that came into force after the Sykes-Picot agreement of 1916. Syria has customarily seen itself as the pulsating heart of Arab nationalism.

Economy

Despite its relatively recent dismemberment (the memory of which goes a long way to explaining modern Syria's acute interest in events in neighbouring Lebanon and Jordan) Syria still has much to gain economically from its geographical position.

From the point of view of tourism and its own foreign trade, Syria is conveniently close to Europe and indeed the bulk of Syrian trade exchanges now take place with countries of the EC. In terms of exports alone, there is also a promising future for Syrian-manufactured foodstuffs, textiles and durable consumer goods in the Arab market next door. For the time being, however, and until the necessary industrialisation takes place, Syria's chief exports are raw materials.

Cotton was for many years the leading source of foreign exchange, taking over from cereals as the country's most valuable crop shortly after the Second World War when high cotton prices on world markets stimulated large-scale cotton production on largely virgin soil in the Jezira. Cotton was superseded by oil in 1974, when oil prices were quadrupled, and oil now accounts for some 50% of the country's export income.

15th century Mamluk Mosque in Old Damascus

General Information

Government

Socialist popular democracy. Power is in the hands of the Baath Party led by President Lt Gen Hafiz Assad.

Languages

Arabic is spoken over most of the country but Kurdish is widely used along the northern frontier and Armenian in the cities. French and English are also spoken.

Religion

More than 90% of the population is Moslem, mainly Sunni and Shiite, Ismaili, Druze, Alawite and Yazidi minorities. Less than 10% of the population is Christian, divided among Greek, Armenian and Syrian Orthodox and Catholic persuasions and the Maronites. A tiny fraction are Jewish.

How to get there

By air: Syrian Arab Airlines is the national carrier.
By road: An international highway reaches Syria via Ankara, Adana and Iskanderum in Turkey. The country is also linked by good roads to Amman in Jordan.
By sea: Syria's ports handle only commercial vessels and there are no passenger lines linking them with the European ports.

Entry regulations

A visa is necessary to enter Syria and this can be obtained from Syrian consular offices abroad. Arab nationals do not require visas.

Customs regulations

Only a limited amount of Syrian currency (£S200) is allowed to be carried by the visitor in or out of the country. There is however no restriction on the import or export of foreign currency.

Articles for personal use are admitted free of duty but it is advisable to fill out a customs declaration. Goods admitted free of duty are 200 cigarettes or 50 cigars or 250gms of tobacco and a quarter of a litre of spirits.

Climate

Syria's climate is characterised by hot dry summers and fairly cold winters. Nights are often cool throughout the year.
What to wear: Lightweight clothing is essential in the summer, and heavy winter clothing is advisable from November to March. Sunglasses and protective headgear are a necessity in the summer.

Currency

Syrian Pound (£S) divided into 100 piastres.

Business hours

Friday is the weekly holiday.
Government offices and Banks: Saturday-Thursday 0800-1430.
Offices: *Summer* Saturday-Thursday 0830-1300 and 1700-2000. *Winter* Saturday-Thursday 0900-1400 and 1600-1900

Press

The Syria Times, Corniche Meedan, BP5452, Damascus is published daily in English.

Public holidays

New year's Day, 1 January
Union Day, 22 February
Revolution Day, 8 March
Evacuation Day, 17 April
Labour Day, 1 May
Martyr's Day, 6 May
Egypt's Revolution Day, 23 July
Christmas Day, 25 December.

Consulates/Embassies in Damascus

Afghanistan: Imm. Muhammad Amin Abd ar-Rabou, 2nd Floor, rue al-Bizan, West Malki. Tel: 713103.

Algeria: Raouda, Imm. Noss, Damascus. Telex: 411344.

Argentina: Raouda, rue Ziad ben Abi Soufian, BP 116, Damascus. Telex: 411058.

Australia: 128A rue Farabi, East Villas, Imm. Dakkak, Mezzeh, Damascus. Tel: 662603. Telex: 419132.

Austria: Raouda, rue Chafik Mouayed, Imm. Sabri Malki, BP 5634, Damascus. Tel: 337528. Telex: 411389.

Belgium: rue Ata Ayoubi, Imm. Hachem, Damascus. Tel: 332821. Telex: 411090.

Brazil: 76 rue Ata Ayoubi, Damascus. Telex: 411204.

Bulgaria: 4 rue Chahbandar, Damascus.

Canada: Hotel Méridien, ave Kouatly, Damascus. Tel: 718. Telex: 412422.

Chile: 43 rue ar-Rachid, Damascus. Telex: 411392.

China, People's Republic: 83 rue Ata Ayoubi, Damascus.

Cuba: 40 rue Ar-Rachid, Imm. Oustwani and Charabati, Damascus. Telex: 419155.

Cyprus: Abd al-Malek al-Morouan, Jaded ar-Rais, Abou Roumaneh, BP 3853, Damascus. Tel: 332804. Telex: 411411.

Czechoslavakia: place Abou al-Ala'a al-Maari, Damascus.

Denmark: Imm. Patriarcat Grec-Catholique, rue Chekib Arslan. Abou Roumaneh, BP2244, Damascus. Tel: 331008. Telex: 419125.

Finland: Hawakir, Imm. Yacoubian, West Malki. POB 3893, Damascus. Tel: 338809. Telex: 411491.

France: BP 769, rue Ata Ayoubi, Damascus. Tel: 332627. Telex: 411013.

German Democratic Republic: 60 ave Adnan al-Malki, Damascus. Tel: 713860. Telex: 411261.

Germany, Federal Republic: 53 rue Ibrahim Hanano, Imm Kotob, Damascus. Tel: 713860. Telex: 411065.

Greece: 1 rue Farabi, Imm. Tello, Mezzeh, Damascus. Tel: 244031. Telex: 411045.

Holy Sea: 82 rue Masr, BP 2271, Damascus (Apostolic Nunciature). Tel: 332601.

Hungary: 13 rue Ibrahim Hanano (Imm. Roujoulé), Damascus. Tel: 337966. Telex: 419151.

India: 40/46 ave Adnan al-Malki, Imm. Noueilati, Damascus. Tel: 718203. Telex: 411377.

Indonesia: 19 rue al-Amir Ezz ed-Din, Damascus. Telex: 419188.

Iran: Mezzeh Outostrade, nr ar-Razi Hospital, Damascus. Telex: 411041.

Italy: 82 ave al-Mansour, Damascus.

Japan: 15 ave al-Jala'a, Damascus. Telex: 411042.

Jordan: rue Abou Roumaneh, Damascus. Telex: 419161.

Korea, Democratic People's Republic: rue Fares al-Khouri-Jisr Tora, Damascus.

Kuwait: rue Ibrahim Hanano, Damascus. Telex: 419172.

Libya: 36/37 Abou Roumaneh, Damascus.

Mauritani: ave al-Jala'a, rue Karameh, Damascus. Telex: 411264.

Morocco: (relations broken off by Syria, July 1986).

Netherlands: place Abou al-Ala'a al-Maari, Imm. Badr Diab, Damascus. Tel: 336871. Telex: 411032.

Pakistan: rue al-Farabi, East Villat, POB 9284, Damascus. Tel: 662391.

Panama: Malki, rue al-Bizm, Imm. as-Zein, Apt 7, Damascus. Tel: 714305. Telex: 411918.
Poland: rue Georges Haddad, Imm. Chahine, Damascus.
Qatar: POB 4188, Abou Roumaneh, place Madfa, Imm. Alllawi No. 20, Damascus. Tel: 336717. Telex: 411064.
Romania: rue Ibrahim Hanano No. 8, Damascus. Telex: 411305.
Saudi Arabia: ave al-Jala'a, Damascus. Telex: 411906.
Somalia: ave Ata Ayoubi, Damascus. Telex: 419194.
Spain: 81 ave al-Jala'a, Imm. Sawaf, Damascus. Telex: 411253.
Sudan: Damascus. Telex: 411266.
Sweden: rue Chekib Arslan, Abou Roumaneh, Damascus. Telex: 411339.
Switzerland: Malki, 31 rue M. Kurd Ali, Damascus. Tel: 715474. Telex: 411016.
Tunisia: Villa Ouest, Jaddat Chafei, No.6 Mezzeh BP 4114, Damascus. Tel: 660356. Telex: 431302.
Turkey: 56-58 ave Ziad bin Abou Soufian, Damascus. Tel: 331370
USSR: Boustan al-Kouzbari, rue d'Alep, Damascus. Telex: 411221.
United Arab Emirates: rue Raouda No.62, Imm. Housami, Damascus. Telex: 411213.
United Kingdom: (relations broken off by UK October 1986).
USA: rue al-Mansour 2, Damascus. Telex: 411919.
Venezuela: BP 2403, Abou Roumaneh, rue Nour Pacha, Imm. Tabbah, Damascus. Tel: 335356. Telex: 411929.
Viet-Nam: 9 ave Malki, Damascus. Tel: 333008.
Yemen Arab Republic: Abou Roumaneh, Charkassieh, Damascus.
Yemen, People's Democratic Republic: Damascus.
Yugoslavia: ave al-Jala'a, Damascus.

Changing lifestyles in Syria

Transport

By air: Syrian Airlines operates domestic services between Damascus, Aleppo, Palmya, Deir ez Zor and Latakkia.

By road: There are good asphalted roads linking all the major towns. regular bus services and shared taxis are available to all parts of the country. In Damascus, taxis are readily available but fares should be negotiated with the driver before the journey.

Accommodation and food

There are a great number of hotels in the country but not more than a handful are worth mentioning. It is however advisable to book in advance.

There are numerous good restaurants in Damascus and Aleppo serving a variety of oriental and European dishes.

Damascus

Damascus is also often referred to as Al-Sham, the same name as is given to the Syrian region as a whole. Sited to the east of the Anti-Lebanon mountains, which form the rugged, dun-coloured backdrop to the city scene, 4,000-year-old Damascus owes its existence originally to the Barada river and its many tributaries. This does not mean there is any visual comparison with the other river-bank capitals such as Prague, London or Baghdad, however, for where the Barada runs through the heart of Damascus it is very narrow and shrinks in summertime to a trickle. Nor can the city any longer be said to be 'nestling' against the Jabal Kasioun, since housing and other developments have started to creep further up the dusty hillside, where rows of what are now rather thirsty-looking saplings will eventually enhance the view.

The clamour and crush of the city centre – which gradually abates as one moves out into the tree- lined residential areas – is a constant reminder of the fact that the population of the capital and its immediate suburbs has swollen rapidly in recent years and currently stands at about 1.3 million.

The central feature of Damascus is the Ummayyad mosque (see History), which is also the site of St. John the Baptist's tomb. The mosque with its richer interior and spacious courtyard is approached through the covered al-Himidiyah bazaar. Another relic of the city's Christian past is to be found at the House of Hanania in old Damascus, the refuge of St. Paul the Apostle. Hanania's House, with its underground chapel, is located off the famous Via Recta, the Street called Strait. Also of histrorical interest are the Sulaimaniya mosque (see History) and the 18th century Al-Azm palace which now houses a museum of Syrian folklore. The remains of the country's ancient civilisations can be found at the National Museum, which also holds a splendid collection of Islamic art – including many historic copies of the Koran with elaborate calligraphy and illuminations.

Aleppo

Aleppo is possibly even older than Damascus, being referred to in an ancient manuscript dating back to the third millennium BC. Its population, at around a milllion, is below that of the capital but in terms of their historical remains and their _souqs_, the two cities are clearly rivals. Aleppo's citadel, a fine example of Arab military architecture with particularly remarkable carved ceilings, stands on the old site of a Hittite acropolis and represents one of the city's principal attractions. The city has had its present Arabic name 'Halab' in one form or another since at least the time of the Hittites and possibly before. Early on it was the centre of a prosperous kingdom but its evolution has been interrupted both by the pillaging of invading armies and the destruction wrought by the last earthquake in 1822. Aleppo has retained its importance today mainly because the cession of the Sanjak of Alexandretta to Turkey in 1939 consolidated its position as northern Syria's major town. The visitor to Aleppo will be quickly impressed by the number of mosques – only Cairo is thought to match it in this respect. The city is also known for its old-style houses and their characteristic courtyards and fountains.

The *souq*, ten miles of meandering, low corridors, lined with shops packed with goods of every description, is one of the oldest and best preserved, and possibly the most fascinating in the entire Middle East. Some parts appear to have remained unchanged by time, even the goods sold seem as if they have just been unloaded from one of the ancient camel trains traversing Syria. There are about 20 traditional *hammans* or public baths, some of the ancient *khans* or rest houses, still in a fine state of preservation, shops, schools, graveyards and courtyards. It is a fascinating city where the visitor can spend days wandering about without seeing the same thing twice. Also Aleppo's archaeological museum, a modern well lit building in which objects and artefacts of Syria's rich and varied cultural past are displayed with care and imagination, should not be missed.

Homs and Hama

Homs, situated on the main Damascus-Aleppo highway, is Syria's third largest city. Like other centres throughout the country it can boast a rich past. Homs is now best-known as the site of Syria's first oil refinery and houses a number of big industrial plants.

Hama, some 45 km from Homs on the Orontes, retains a rather more colourful image with its famous, rhythmically-groaning wooden water wheels and its orchards. Of neolithic origins, Hama became the northern capital of the Arameans and is also notable for its Al-Azm Palace and museum of ethnography, which is well worth a visit.

Lattakia

Lattakia was first built by the Phoenicians and although, in centuries gone by, it had come under Assyrian, Babylonian, Greek and Roman rule, it is chiefly characterised by its Roman remains, its Temple of Bacchus and Triumphal Arch. The population of Lattakia, itself Syria's principal port, is comparable in size with that of Hama. As regards climate, the Lattakia region, with its thick forests, is spared the rigours of a continental climate by its sea breezes which raise the

The Hejaz railway at Damascus

175

temperature in winter and moderate the summer heat to a bearable level.

Palmyra

Mention of Palmyra (or Tadmur) dates back to the 19th century BC. Located 155 km from Homs in the Syrian desert, it was the capital of the famous Queen Zenobia, whose ambitions provoked the Romans into achieving what other armies had for so long failed to do and crush the Palmyran kingdom. The ruins of its ancient buildings – best known of which is the Temple of Bel – are to be found over a wide radius from the town centre and are so stunning and well-preserved they are considered to be among the finest not only in Syria but in the whole of the Middle East.

Hotels

NAME	ADDRESS	TELEPHONE	TELEX
ALEPPO			
Baron Hotel	Baron St	10880	31020
Pullman Al Shahba	P.O Box 1350	239630	331444
Tourisme Hotel	Saad alah al-Djabri St	10156	–
DAMASCUS			
Airport	Opposite Airport	225400	11060
Chams Palace	P.O. Box 7570	232300	–
International	Bahba St	112400	11062
Kattan	Jamhourieh St	112513	–
Meridien	P.O. Box 5531	7187304	411379
New Semiramis	Jamourieh St	113813	11373
Sheraton	P.O. Box 4795	229300	411404
LATTAKIA			
Meridien	P.O. Box 473	29000	451124
PALMYRA			
Meridien	Homs Rd	37000	441041

TURKEY

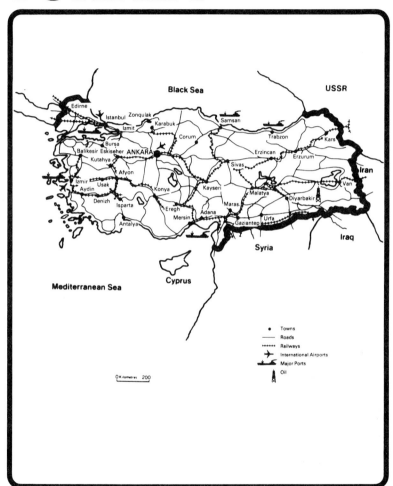

Area: 780,576 sq km
Population: 50,664,458 (official estimate).
Capital: Ankara

Turkey is a gateway between Europe and the East and the cradle of many civilisations of which Hittites, Greeks, Romans, Persians, Arabs, Crusaders and Turks have all left their mark. This land of historical contrasts envelops the restful Aegean countryside, the ochre stretches of the Antolian Plateau, the sombre forests of the Black Sea coast and the spectacular landscapes of Cappadocia.

A huge country

With an estimated 50.6 million people Turkey is the most populous country in the Middle East although even here the population density if far below the level of Western European countries. Like its largest city, Istanbul, Turkey straddles two continents.

Asia Minor, or Anatolia, accounts for 97% of the country. It forms a long peninsula (1,650 km from east to west, 800 km from north to south) bordered to the north by the Black Sea and the Marmara, to the west by the Aegean and to the south by the Mediterranean. Two east-west mountain ranges, the Pontic in the north, the Taurus in the south, enclose the central Anatolian plateau, but join up in a vast mountainous region in the far east of the country. Here the two great rivers of antiquity, the Tigris and the Euphrates, rise. The central plateau is surrounded by a fertile coastal region.

The undulating country of Thrace (European Turkey) is divided from Anatolia by the Sea of Marmara and the Bosphorus and Dardanelles straits. Turkey has land frontiers with Bulgaria, Greece, the Soviet Union, Iran, Iraq and Syria.

History and culture

The country's history is complex. At Catal Höyük, in central southern Turkey, remains of a neolithic settlement dating to 6000 BC have been found. The first settlement at Troy has been dated around 3000 BC. In the second millenium BC the Hittites established a great empire in Anatolia. They were followed by the Phrygians, the Lydians and the Persians. Alexander the Great conquered the entire Anatolian peninsula after defeating the Persians in 334 BC. Then came Roman hegemony, and in 324 AD, Constantine selected Byzantium to be the New Rome: for 16 centuries it was the capital of an empire.

The Selojuk Turks, migrating from their homelands in central Asia, arrived on the scene in the 11th century, eventually establishing a Sultanate in Konya with control of most of Asia Minor. Another Turkish group, the Ottomans, established their first principality in 1301, and went on to capture Byzantium in 1453. In the 16th century, Sultan Suleyman the Magnificent was Europe's most powerful monarch, his empire extending as far as Hungary and Saudi Arabia and including most of North Africa.

The Ottoman Empire survived until the first world war before its collapse.

Renouncing all claims to the Arab parts of the empire, Kemal Ataturk drove a Greek invasion out of Asia Minor in 1922, and the following year proclaimed the Turkish Republic. Two brief periods of military rule aside, Turkey has been a multi-party democracy since 1950.

The Turks' cultural traditions are almost entirely Asiatic and Islamic, super-imposed on the classical and Christian cultures they found in Anatolia. The modern Turkish Republic is committed to a policy of westernisation, initiated by Ataturk. Yet the mass of the people are small townsfolk or peasants, their way of life essentially Middle Eastern; they are pious Moslems (99% of the population are Moslems, even though the state is secular), and are fiercely nationalistic. The more sophisticated Turks of the cities consider themselves more European than Middle Eastern.

A huge social and economic gap yawns between the rural masses and the westernised city dwellers. More than half the population cannot read. The past 10 years has seen mass migration into the big cities – Istanbul, Ankara and Izmir – which are surrounded by extensive shanty towns.

The four million or so Kurds who live in the mountains of the east are the largest ethnic minority. Arabic-speaking Moslems and Christians are to be found in the province of Hatay (Alexandretta), which joined the Republic in 1039. Armenian, Greek and Jewish minorities live in Istanbul, where they are largely engaged in business.

The domestic political situation in Turkey is stable, with the Motherland Party, a coalition of conservative and liberal elements holding an overall majority. During the period 1950-1980, the army intervened on three occasions to resolve political crises and restore stability. The latest such move was in 1980. In an attempt to avoid extremist and destabilising policies, the present constitutional framework – introduced in 1982 – bans extremist activities and gives the military a continuing role in political affairs through the National Security Council. Presidential authorisation is still required for some governmental decisions relating to national security and foreign affairs.

Since the 1983 elections which restored civilian democratic government, following a three year period of military rule, Mr Turgut Ozal, head of the ruling Motherland party, has pursued an economic programme characterised by fiscal restraint, vigourous encouragement of exports and tourism, and the initiation of structural reform of the industrial sector, including a reduction of state control. In April 1987, Turkey, which is an associate member of the European Economic Community (EEC), applied formally for full membership. However, this has presented the Community with a number of difficult political and economic issues, and the application remains under consideration.

Economy

In recent years economic performance has strengthened significantly. Over the past two decades the contribution of agriculture has declined from 34%

of GDP to 19%, but the sector remains in many respects the mainstay of the economy and has considerable growth potential. About 60% of the country's workforce are employed in the agricultural sector. Turkey produces a large food surplus and agricultural output accounts for about 25% of exports. The main crops are wheat, sugar-beet and cotton. Fruit, tobacco and hazelnuts (of which Turkey is the world's largest producer) are also important exports.

Industry has shown strong growth in recent years. The sector is dominated by large state-owned industries although a privatisation programme is now underway. Recently the main emphasis has been on processing domestic agricultural produce and the important local textile industry, although cars, electrical engineering and chemicals have grown significantly in importance. The construction sector has been hit by declining orders from oil producing countries in the Middle East but some major infrastructural projects are proposed which, if implemented, could go far to revive the flagging construction sector's fortunes.

Turkey has substantial mineral resources including, zinc, lead and some rare materials such as borax. There are limited oil reserves which provide one-eighth of domestic requirements. New legislation has been introduced to encourage further oil exploration and there are plans to extend hydro-electric capacity. One of the government's main aims is to promote tourism. New regions have been opened up and hotel capacity expanded. Inflation remains a persistent problem in the country. Although continuing to decline slowly the rate is still high by international standards.

Nearly half of Turkey's trade is with the EEC although trade with the countries of the Middle East has been increasingly steadily over recent years.

Turkey is the most populous country in the region

General Information

Government

Republic

Languages

The official language is Turkish which is spoken by 90% of the population. There are also small Kurdish and Arabic speaking groups.

Religion

Most of the population is Moslem. There are small Christian (Greek Orthodox, Gregorian, Roman and Catholic) and also Jewish communities.

How to get there

Turk Hava Yollari (THY) is the national carrier of Turkey.

By road: Turkey is connected with Greece, Bulgaria, Iran and Iraq.

By rail: There are scheduled services to Istanbul from Paris and Munich.

By sea: Turkish Maritime Lines have a regular passenger service to Istanbul from Ancona and Venice. There is also a regular service all the year round to Istanbul and Izmir by the Italian Adriatica Line from French and Italian ports.

Entry regulations

A valid passport but visas are not required.

Customs regulations

There are no restrictions on the import of foreign currency or its export. Only a small amount of Turkish currency may be taken in or out of the country.

Articles for personal use are allowed in free of duty. This includes 200 cigarettes or 500 grammes of tobacco or 100 cigars; one litre of alcoholic liquor or two litres of wine. The export of antiquities without a licence is prohibited. The total retail value of souvenirs should not exceed $350 unless accompanied by proof that the foreign currency has been changed at banks or an authorised exchange bureau.

Climate

Winters tend to be very cold, whereas the summer months are usually hot. The southern coastal districts, sheltered by the Taurus mountains, have a milder winter but are hotter and more humid in the summer.

What to wear: In winter warm clothing is essential throughout the country. In the summer tropical clothing is recommended in the southern areas, and lightweight clothing in the northern areas.

Currency

Turkish Lira (TL) divided into 100 Kurash.

Business Hours

Business hours in Turkey tend to vary. In large cities such as Istanbul and Ankara the European Monday-Saturday working week is usually observed, while away from the cities, Middle East business hours are more frequently observed.

Public holidays

New Year's Day, 1 January
National Sovereignty Day, 23 April
Spring Day, 1 May
Youth and Sport Day, 19 May

Freedom and Constitution Day, 17 May
Ramadan begins*, 7 April 1989
Eid al-Fitr*, 7-9 May 1989
Victory Day, 30 August
Eid al-Adha*, 14-17 July 1989
Republic Day, 29-30 October.

Press

Turkey's leading English language daily
is the Turkish Daily News, Tanus Cad
49/7, Kavaklidere, Ankara.

Embassies in Turkey

Afghanistan: Cinnah Cad. 88, Çankaya,
Ankara. Tel: (41) 277698.
Albania: Nenehatun Cad. 89, Gazios-
manpaşa, Ankara. Tel: (41) 274954.
Algeria: Şehit Ersan Cad., Ankara. Tel:
(41) 278700. Telex: 42053.
Argentina: Iran Cad. 57/1, Çankaya,
Ankara. Tel: (41) 271322.
Australia: Nenehatun Cad. 83, Gazios-
manpaşa, Ankara. Tel: (41) 286715.
Austria: PK 230, Atatürk Bulvari 189,
06680 Kavaklidere, Ankara. Tel: (41)
342172. Telex: 42429.
Bangladesh: Karyağdi Sok. 18, 06690
Ankara. Tel: (41) 388396.
Belgium: Nenehatun Cad. 109, Ankara.
Tel: (41) 361653. Telex: 42258.
Brazil: Alaçam Sok. 10/2-4-5, Çankaya,
Ankara. Tel: (41) 262930. Telex: 42657.
Bulgaria: Atatürk Bulvari 124, Ankara.
Tel: (41) 267455.
Canada: Nenehatun Cad. 75, Gazios-
manpaşa, Ankara. Tel: (41) 361275.
Telex: 42369.
Chile: Cinnah Cad. 78/1, Çankaya,
Ankara. Tel: (41) 389444.
China, People's Republic: Yukari
Ayranci 8, Durak Hoşdere Cad. 147,
Ankara. Tel: (41) 264081.
Czechoslovakia: Atatürk Bulvari 245,
Ankara. Tel: (41) 265887.
Denmark: Kirlangiç Sok. 42, 06700
Gaziosmanpaşa, Ankara. Tel: (41)
275258. Telex: 42377.
Egypt: Atatürk Bulvari 126, Kavaklidere,
06680 Ankara. Tel: (41) 266478.

Finland: Galip Dede Sok. 1/20, Farabi,
Ankara. Tel: (41) 265921.
France: Paris Cad. 70, Kavaklidere,
Ankara. Tel: (41) 261480. Telex: 42385.
German Democratic Republic: Karli Sok.
3, Gaziosmanpaşa, Ankara. Tel: (41)
338444. Telex: 42735.
Germany, Federal Republic: Atatürk
Bulvari 114, Ankara. Tel: (41) 265465.
Telex: 42379.
Greece: Sölen Sok. 8, Çankaya, Ankara.
Tel: (41) 275207.
Holy See: POB 33, 06552 Çankaya,
Ankara. Tel: (41) 390041.
Hungary: Gazi Mustafa Kemal Bulvari,
10, Ankara. Tel: (41) 252122.
India: Kirlangiç Sok. No. 9, Gaziosman-
paşa, Ankara. Tel: (41) 278140. Telex:
42561.
Indonesia: Abdullah Cevdet Sok. 10,
Çankaya, Ankara. Tel: (41) 382190.
Telex: 43250.
Iran: Tahran Cad. 10, Ankara. Tel: (41)
274320.
Iraq: Turan Emeksiz Sok. 11, Gazios-
manpaşa, Ankara. Tel: (41) 266118.
Telex: 42577.
Israel: Farabi Sok. 43, Çankaya, Ankara.
Tel: (41) 263904. Telex: 42560.
Italy: Atatürk Bulvari 118, Ankara. Tel:
(41) 265460. Telex: 42624.
Japan: Nenehatun Cad. 66, Ankara. Tel:
(41) 274324. Telex: 42435.
Jordan: Dede Korkut Sok. 10, Çankaya,
Ankara. Tel: (41) 272362.
Korea, Republic: Cinnah Cad. Alaçam
Sok. 9, 06690 Çankaya, Ankara. Tel:
(41) 264633. Telex: 42680.
Kuwait: Kader Sok 6/3, Çankaya,
Ankara. Tel: (41) 274318. Telex: 43238.
Lebanon: Cinnah Cad. 11/3, Çankaya,
Ankara. Tel: (41) 263729. Telex: 46063.
Libya: Ebuziya Tevfik Sok. 5, Çankaya,
Ankara. Tel: (41) 274892. Telex: 43270.
Malaysia: Nenehatun Cad. 115, Gazios-
manpaşa, Çankaya, Ankara. Tel: (41)
274062. Telex: 43616.
Mexico: Iran Cad. 45/2, Çankaya,
Ankara. Tel: (41) 675056. Telex: 42278.
Morocco: Reşit Galip Cad., Incirli Sok.

II, Gaziosmanpaşa, Ankara. Tel: (41) 1376020. Telex: 42869.
Netherlands: Köroğlu Sok. 16, Gaziosmanpaşa, Ankara. Tel: (41) 274326. Telex: 42612.
Norway: Kelebek Sok. 18, Çankaya, PK 82, Kavaklidere, Ankara. Tel: (41) 379950. Telex: 42244.
Pakistan: Iran Cad. 37, Ankara. Tel: (41) 271410.
Poland: Atatürk Bulvari 241, Ankara. Tel: (41) 261694.
Portugal: Cinnah Cad. 28/3, 06690 Ankara. Tel: (41) 275055. Telex: 42771.
Romania: Bükreş Sok. 4, Çankaya, Ankara. Tel: (41) 271241. Telex: 42760.
Saudi Arabia: Abdullah Cevdet Sok. 18, Çankaya, Ankara. Tel: (41) 271587. Telex: 42456.
Somalia: Abdullah Cevdet Sok. 26/2, Çankaya, Ankara. Tel: (41) 269369. Telex: 43392.
Spain: Abdullah Cevdet Sok. 8, Çankaya, PK. 1030 Yenişehir, Ankara. Tel: (41) 380392. Telex: 42551.

Sweden: Katip Çelebi Sok. 7, 06692 Kavaklidere, Ankara. Tel: (41) 286735.
Switzerland: Atatürk Bulvari 247, Ankara. Tel: (41) 274316.
Syria: Abdullah Cevdet Sok. 7, Çankaya, Ankara. Tel: (41) 273342. Telex: 42888.
Thailand: Cinnah Cad. 61, 5–6 Kavaklidere, Ankara. Tel: (41) 391929. Telex: 46096.
Tunisia: Kuleli Sok. 12, Gaziosmanpaşa, Ankara. Tel: (41) 274536. Telex: 42215.
'Turkish Republic of Northern Cyprus': Incirli Sok. 20, Gaziosmanpaşa, Ankara. Tel: (41) 379538. Telex: 42575.
USSR: Karyağdi Sok. 5, 06692 Kavaklidere, Ankara. Tel: (41) 392122. Telex: 46151.
United Kingdom: Şehit Ersan Cad. 46/A, Çankaya, Ankara. Tel: (41) 274310. Telex: 42320.
USA: Atatürk Bulvari 110, Ankara. Tel: (41) 265470.
Venezuela: Cinnah Cad. 78/2, Çankaya, Ankara. Tel: (41) 389440. Telex: 42453.

Ephesus

Hotels

NAME	ADDRESS	TELEPHONE	TELEX
ADANA			
Buyuk Surmeli	Kurukopru, Ozler Cad. 142	21944	62282
ANKARA			
Buyuk Ankara	Ataturk Bulvari 183	171106	42398
Bulvar Palas	Ataturk Bu. 141	175020	42613
Dedeman	Bakanliklar	171100	42408
Kent	Buklum Sok. 1	184220	42424
Keykan	Mithatpasa Cad. 4	302195	–
Marmara	Fevzi Cakmak Sok. 12	231361	42275
Mola	Ataturk Orman Ciftligi	183140	42294
Stad	Izmir Cad. 27/1	116644	42248
Tunali	Baruthane Meydani	274082	42142
Yeni	Tunali Hilmi Cad. 119	106812	–
ANTAKYA			
Atahan	Hurriyet Cad. 28	1036	–
Guney Palas	5 Temmuz Cad. 13	3696	–
ANTALYA			
Antalya Oteli	Fener Cad. Hasim Iscan Mah.	5600	56111
BURSA			
Akdogan	1 Murat Cad. 5 Cekirge	24755	–
Celik Palas	Cekirge Cad. 79	19600	32121

[Hotels]

ICEL

Mersin	Gumruk Meydani	2200	67180

ISTANBUL

Anka	Molla Gurani Cad. 42	256002	–
Buyuk Tarabya	Tarabya	621000	26203
Cinar	Yesilkoy	732910	22208
Divan	Cumhuriyet Cad. Harbiye	464020	22402
Hilton	Cumhuriyet Cad.	467050	22379
Keban	Siraselviler Cad. 51 Taksim	433310	–
Macka	Eytam Cad. 35 Macka	401053	23114
Olkay	Millet Cad. 187 Topkapi	250332	23209
Park	Gumussuyu Cad. 6 Taksim	436010	22826
Per Palas	Mesrutiyet Cad. 98-100	452230	22029
Sheraton	Tepebasi	489000	22729
Sozmen	Taksim	234006	22014
Washington	Millet Cad. 258 Capa	262415	–

IZMIR

Anba	Cumhuriyet Bul. 124	144380	52449
Buyuk Efes	Cumhuriyet Mey.	144300	52341
Etap	Cumhuriyet Bul. 138	144290	52463
Izmir Palas	Ataturk Bul.	132100	52631
Karaca	Karaca 1379 Sok. 1/12-A	131498	–
Kilim	Ataturk Bulvari	145340	52631
Kismet	1377 Sokak 9	144385	–

Transport

By air: There is an extensive internal network and Turkish airlines operate regular services between the main airports.

By sea: There are regular steamship services between Istanbul and all the large coastal towns.

By rail: Istanbul is linked by rail with a number of coastal towns including Izmir, Mersin and Iskenderun. There is a daily express service between Istanbul and Ankara.

By road: Taxis are available in all the main cities; the most economic way is travel by shared taxis (dolmus) which operate between Istanbul and Ankara and other nearby towns. Self drive cars are readily available, The asphalt highways are well maintained.

Bus services link most of the major towns.

Accommodation and food

Hotels, motels and pensions are plentiful throughout Turkey. There are also many camping sites and holiday villages and mountain hotels established in special localities. All accommodation is classified and there is an official guide issued by the Ministry of Tourism and Information. Besides the official list there are many other places throughout Turkey.

Most hotels have their own restaurants. There are also a large number of other eating places. Turkish food is world famous. It is a happy combination of the culinary traditions of a pastoral people originating from Central Asia and the influences of the Mediterranean world. Turkish cuisine is noted for its pure quality stemming from the freshness of the fruit, vegetables, meat and fish in a country that produces all its own foodstuff. Lamb is a basic meat and figures on all menus. Pieces threaded on a skewer and grilled over charcoal are the famous *sis kebab*. The other, *doner kebab*, is pieces of lamb packed tightly round a revolving spit. Fish and shellfish are very fresh and *barbunya* (red mullet) and *kilic biligi* (swordfish) are delicious. Also be sure to sample *dolma* (vegetables and vine leaves stuffed with pine nuts and currants), *ayran* (a refreshing yoghourt drink) and *karniyarik* (aubergine stuffed with minced meat).

Ankara

On a hill overlooking Ankara is the monument to Ataturk, father of the Turks. Around Ankara are traces of civilisation stretching back to the Hittites who ruled in the second millenium BC and the Phrygians, a Thracian people who dominated the Anatolian plateau in the first millenium BC.

Mirroring all Anatolia's civilisations is the Archaeoligical Museum with its unique collection of proto-Hittite sun discs and stag cult figures. The museum is housed in an Ottoman bazaar and Han or caravanserai (inn).

Ruins of Roman baths and a Roman temple can also be seen in the capital city.

Istanbul

The largest city, and capital of the Byzantine and Ottoman Empires, Istanbul is at once superlatively beautiful and staggeringly squalid. The old city is divided from the modern business centre where the principal hotels are situated by a heavily populated inlet, the Golden Horn, crossed by the picturesque, archaic Galata Bridge. A third part of the city, largely residential, lies across the Bosphorus in Asia.

Justinian's sixth century cathedral of the Holy Wisdom Aya Sofya, became a mosque after the Turkish conquest, but is now a museum. The mosaics in the gallery should not be missed. The 14th century mosaics and frescoes in the Kariye Camii (near Edirnekapi) are a must. Mosaics from the same period are to be seen in the Fethiye Camii (near Edirnekapi).

Sultan Ahmed Mosque, Istanbul

The old city abounds in Ottoman mosques, the finest, the 16th century Suleymaniye designed by the famous Ottoman architect Sinan, includes a library and museum of Islamic art. The Sultan Ahmet or Blue Mosque dates from the following century, and has fine tile work. The tiles in the Rustempasa mosque are also excellent.

The former home of the Ottoman Sultans, the Topkapi Palace, lies at the tip of the headland on which the old city stands. The various kiosks stand in delightful gardens, with a view across the Bosphorus to the massive Selimiye Barracks, where Florence Nightingale nursed soldiers wounded in the Crimean War. In the beauty of this setting, it is hard to conjure up the dark plots hatched within the palace walls.

An unfailing source of fascination for western visitors is the extensive covered bazaar Kapali Carsi, where expensive jewellers, antique dealers, leather and carpet merchants bargain endlessly.

Visitors tired of the noise and bustle of the city can take a boat from the Galata Bridge either up the Bosphorus, with its Ottoman villas on either side, or to the peaceful Princes' Islands – where bathing is reasonable. Bathing at the Black Sea village of Kilyos is not recommended, due to the dangerous currents.

Izmir

Turkey's third city and main export port, Izmir, was founded by Alexander the Great. The citadel, on the top of Mount Pagus, affords a view of the beautiful Gulf of Izmir. The agora of Hellenistic and Roman Smyrna is worth a visit, so is the Archaeological Museum, which houses finds from old Smyrna and other cities of ancient Ionia. In late August and September, an international trade fair is held in the Kultur Park, and finding hotels can be near impossible then.

Bursa

Lying at the foot of Bithynian Olympus (Uludag), Bursa is one of the most attractive cities in Turkey: a cluster of Ottoman houses, mosques and mausolea, set among cypresses and cool springs. Throughout the period of Ottoman greatness, Bursa acquired a wealth of architectural monuments. Most notable are the Yesil Camii (Green Mosque) built by Sultan Mehmet I in 1424. Opposite is Mehmet's mausoleum, the Yesil Turbe. The Yildirim Beyazit mosque (circa 1400) and Ulu (great) mosque are also not to be missed.

Uludag is Istanbul's principal ski resort, and is equipped with a cable car, well worth a visit even in summer. Easily accessible from Bursa is the attractive lakeside town of Iznik – ancient Nicaea.

Erdine

The 16th century architect Sinan built here what is seen as his finest mosque, the Selimiye Camii. The old mosque (Eski Camii), dating from early 15th century, and the mosque of Beyazit II (late 15th century) should also be seen.

Antalya

The only ancient city of Pamphylia to retain importance today, Antalya is a delightfully shaded city with abundant water, and an attractive old harbour. The extensive old Ottoman town with its narrow streets and timber houses is one of the best preserved of its kind. Well kept public gardens on the cliff tops afford a superlative view across the Gulf to the rugged mountains of ancient Lycia. An ethnographic museum now occupies what was once a church, and subsequently a mosque, with a distinctively grooved minaret, Yivli Minare Camii. The new archaeological museum, to the west of the town, houses finds from the ancient cities of the region. Avoid Antalya in high summer.

Antakya

The capital of the Roman province of Syria, Antioch on the Orontes, where the disciples were first called Christians, has a mild climate, even in high summer, and the surrounding country, particularly to the south, near ancient Daphne (*Harbiye*), is of considerable beauty.

The museum boasts a collection of late antique mosaics unrivalled anywhere, and no visitor should leave Turkey without seeing them. Outside the city, there is an ancient rock church, known as St. Peter's cave. Also worth seeing are the attractive old section of the town, and the view from the citadel.

Erzurum

Most notable monuments in this high Eastern city are the 12th century Ulu Camii mosque, and the famous Selcuk double-minareted religious school, the Cifte Minare Medressi.

Kars

Visit the 10th century Church of the Holy Apostles (now a museum) at the foot of the citadel. Thirty miles away, on the Soviet frontier, lies the old Armenian capital of Ani, founded in the 10th century, and now deserted. Permission to visit must be first obtained from the military authorities in Kars.

A remarkable collection of frescoed Armenian churches is to be found in beautiful natural surroundings.

Kayseri

At the foot of an extinct volcano, Erciyes Dagi (Mt. Argaeus), Caesarea was the capital of Roman Cappadocia, and a prominent city in both Selcuk and Ottoman times. Notable Selcuk monuments are the mosques, Ulu Camii and Honat Hatun Camii, and the religious school Huand Medressi, now the archaeological museum. A Selcuk mausoleum, the Doner Kumbet, should also be seen.

Konya

Iconium fell to the Selcuk Turks in the late 11th century. It then served as capital of their Sultanate until the middle of the 13th century, when the Selcuks were defeated by the Mongol hordes. Konya finally was annexed to the Ottoman empire in 1466/7.

From the Selcuk period date the Alaeddin mosque, and three religious schools, the Buyuk, Karatay, Ince Minare and Sircall.

Konya's most famous monument is the monastery of the Mevlana, or whirling dervishes. Founded here by a 13th century mystic, this sect found its most direct route to God through ecstatic whirling, accompanied by music. This is annually re-enacted at a December festival, when Konya is flooded by tourists.

Diyarbakir

Near the banks of the Tigris, Diyarbakir is distinguished by its massive basalt mediaeval walls. The Ulu Camii mosque is either an Arab structure or earlier.

Mardin

Worth a visit for the striking view it affords over Iraq. See the Selcuk Sultan Isa Medresesi. In the region of the nearby town of Midyat, the palaeochristian monasteries of Tur Abdin should be visited.

Urfa

There is little to be seen of the ancient Edessa. At the foot of the ruined crusader citadel is a large pool of sacred carp. Abraham is said to have stopped here. He also halted for several years at Charan, now Harran, a small village south of Urfa with distinctive Syrian 'bee-hive' houses.

Van

Apart from the archaeological museum, there is little of great interest in the city, but the lake it is situated on is both enormous by European standards (nearly 3,750 sq km), and of considerable beauty. Along the shores lies the dead city of Eski Ahlat, and on the opposite side of the lake there is the small island of Ahtamar, where a beautiful 10th century Armenian basilica stands.

Central Anatolia

The Konya-Kayseri road is fairly free of traffic, and is marked by a succession of spectacular Selcuk caravanserais (inns), with remarkable carving in a very beautiful warm stone; most notable is Sultanhani.

Perhaps the most extraordinary phenomenon in all Anatolia, however, is the bizarre rock formation in Cappadocia, a result of erosion of volcanic rock thrown up by Erciyes Dagi. The resulting 'lunar' landscape became a refuge for ascetics from the fourth century, and churches have been carved out of the rock; in several cases they are frescoed. Most notable examples are in the Goreme and Peristreme (Ihlara) valleys. Equally bizarre are two entire underground cities six miles apart, connected by a tunnel, Kaymakli and Derinkuya. There is no clue from above that these even exist. As one observer put it, they are a colossal monument to fear. While in this area, visit the Dervish monastery at Hacibektas.

Central Anatolia also boasts numerous Hittite cities. The most notable are Hattusas (Bogazkoy) and Alacahoyuk, near Ankara. Further south, the most ancient city ever unearthed can be seen at Catalhoyuk.

Trabzon

A pleasant Black Sea port and small town beautifully sited, Trebizond was the romantic last outpost of the Byzantine world. Do not miss the late 13th century frescoes in the church of Aya Sofya. East of Trabzon, the road to Rize and Hopa, near the Soviet frontier, is spectacular. Visit the beautifully sited tea research institute Cay Arastirma Enstitusu in the otherwise fairly ordinary town of Rize. Inland from Trabzon, do not miss the deserted Byzantine monastery of Sumela, at the head of a spectacular gorge. This region of Turkey is unique, and should be given priority by the visitor, even though it frequently rains.

Aegean

Crossing over the Dardenelles from the Gallipoli peninsula, the graves and memorials to those who died during the Gallipoli campaign in the First World War can be seen. Gallipoli itself, now Gelibolu, is an attractive fishing village and a good place to stay.

South of the straits lie the remains of the ancient city of Troy, now Truva. Nine levels have been discovered. The city described in Homer's Iliad is the sixth.

Pergamum, now Bergams, is less old, and its period of glory was the second and third centuries BC, when it was the capital of a Western Anatolian Empire. Its library rivalled Alexandria's, and a cut-off of papyrus supplies led to the use of pergamini (parchment) instead. Principal sights are the *Asclepion* (temple of the god of medicine), a second century AD basilica temple, the Kizil Avlu, and the Acropolis.

The most important city of the Roman province of Asia, however, was Ephesus – founded originally in the 13th century BC. The temple of Artemis was famous throughout the ancient world. To be seen today on either side of the ancient street are a theatre, odeon, baths and gymnasium. Notable finds from the site are in the museum in the nearby township of Selcuk.

Smaller sites of Ionian cities on the west coast are Foca, Priene, Assos, Miletus and Didyma.

Pleasant resorts are Ayvalik, Cesme, Kusadasi, Bodrum and Marmaris. The last three are usually very crowded in high summer.

Inland, spectacular and unique water-falls at Pamukkale should not be missed.

Mediterranean

In the inaccessible mountains of Lycia, west of Antalya, the rock churches at ancient Myra are well worth the trouble. Twenty miles from Antalya is the spectacular site of Termerssos.

In the Pamphylian plain, the remains of three ancient cities should be seen, Perge, Aspendos and Side. These sites are all in remarkable condition. The theatre of Aspendos is almost undamaged, and is regularly used today. The theatre of Side is recommended on a moonlit evening. Side is a rapidly expanding resort centre, and has numerous guest houses and motels.

Driving along the beautiful coast road (non-stop beaches), one passes the resort town of Alamya. At the bottom of the 'bump', at Anamur, there is a remarkable crusader fortress.

Inland from the Silifke are the remains of Olba Diocaesarea (Uzuncaborc), with a notable temple of Zeus. But the most spectacular site is undoubtedly that of ancient Korykos. Twin castles dwarf the theatre, palace and necropolis. North of Kiz Kalesi, yawn the two pits known locally as heaven and hell, Cennet ve Cehennem, Obrugu: a ruined Armenian chapel lies by a grotto, and a narrow hole nearby, where condemned sinners were consigned.

One of the Turkish government's main aims is to promote tourism.

UAE

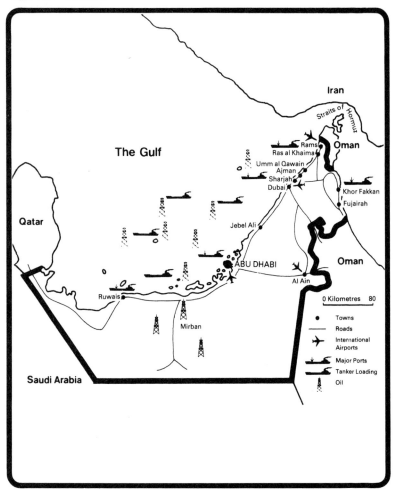

Area: 77,700 sq km
Population: 1.6m (official estimate)
Principal Towns: Abu Dhabi, Dubai, Sharjah and Ras al-Khaimah

192

Covering an area of 85,000 square kilometres, the UAE has coastlines on the Arabian Gulf and, on the other side of the peninsula, on the Gulf of Oman. The early history of the land which makes up the UAE has not yet been completely catalogued. However, archaeological finds have shown that communities have been thriving in the area since the earliest times. Some of the country's archeological sites have been tentatively dated as far back as 5000 BC.

Trading Links

Islam came to the area soon after the death of the Prophet Muhammad in 632 AD and Arab historians in the Eighth Century refer to Ras al Khaimah (then known as Julfar) as a port used by the Muslim armies. By the beginning of the 16th Century the Gulf had become an important region for European traders, providing a vital link between the sea routes to India and the Far East and the overland route to Europe via Basra. The Portuguese were the first Europeans to invade the Gulf. They conquered Ras al Khaimah and rebuilt the fort there in 1631. But Portugal was not the only European nation anxious to establish a foothold in the region. The Dutch, the French and the British were all fighting for dominance of the area and, by the middle of the 18th century, the latter had attained a clear supremecy over the European contenders. However, if the British felt they had managed to settle the issue, their self-congratulations were swiftly proved premature. Members of the region's indigenous seafaring and trading population – most notably tribesmen of the Qawasim – bitterly resented the incursions into their sealanes and many ferocious clashes between British and local vessels ensued. A treaty, which agreed to freedom for all shipping in the Gulf, was signed between Britain and the area's tribal chiefs in 1820 and an uneasy peace was established. Some 15 years later the British intervened to orchestrate a maritime truce between rival regional tribesmen. This truce was signed by the sheikhs of Dubai, Abu Dhabi, Sharjah, Ajman and Umm al Qaiwan and, because of it, the region became known as the Trucial coast.

Trucial States

In 1892 Britain signed separate but identical treaties with each of the Trucial State sheikhs. Under the terms of these agreements the rulers bound themselves and their heirs to recognise Britain's position in the region to the exclusion of all others. They agreed not to cede, mortgage or dispose of any of their territories to anyone except the British Government, without British consent. In return Britain agreed to provide the sheikhs and their people with protection. It was over 70 years after the signing of those treaties that Britain would begin to loose her grip on the Trucial States and the rest of the Gulf region.

In 1968 the British announced their intention to withdraw from the region within three years. In the meantime they had set up a Trucial States Council through which the sheikhs could work out a common administrative policy with the aim of setting up a federation. Abu Dhabi and Dubai took the first tentative steps towards the setting up of such a body with their agreement to form a joint union to deal with matters including foreign affairs, defence and social services. The other Trucial States were invited to join the union, as were the neighbouring states of Bahrain and Qatar. The nine formed a Supreme Council of Rulers later in the year but the organisation's success was short lived. By 1970 it was clear that Bahrain and Qatar would best serve their own interests as independent states, which is of course what they later, successfully, became. Finally, in July 1971, after considerable international pressure had been put on the remaining seven states to become aligned, six of them – Abu Dhabi, Dubai, Sharjah, Ajman, Fujairah and Umm al Khaimah – announced the formation of the United Arab Emirates and the new country became fully independent in December. The seventh emirate, Ras al Khaimah, joined up with its neighbours in 1972.

Economy

Since those historic events the UAE has gone from strength to strength. The Supreme Council, which comprises the rulers of the seven emirates, is the highest federal authority. The Council is presided over by Sheikh Zayed bin Sultan al Nahayan, the Ruler of the Abu Dhabi, while a Council of Ministers, appointed by the President, has executive powers. The Federal National Council – a consultative assembly made up of 40 members appointed by the Emirates – acts as a forum for debating government policies. Under the Government's direction a wide range of new industries has blossomed, among them petrochemicals, aluminium, fertilisers and oil refining but the UAE's economy, like those of its Gulf neighbours, is oil based. Efficient exploitation of its natural energy reserves – together with a sound investment programme – has enabled UAE citizens to enjoy one of the highest per capita incomes in the world. Oil liftings have declined steadily in line with world demand although proven reserves of some 32 billion barrels are sufficient to provide around 75 years of production at current output levels.

As oil liftings decline gas has been playing an increasingly important economic role and since proven gas reserves are estimated to be in excess of 30 trillion cubic feet, the UAE's status as a major energy producer is assured well into the next century.

In 1981, the UAE joined Bahrain, Saudi Arabia, Kuwait, Oman and Qatar in forming the Gulf Cooperation Council (GCC). One of the Council's principal aims has been to promote economic integration within the GCC area and an economic agreement allows for the free-movement of locally produced goods within the six member states. A number of joint projects have already been successfully established in the region and others, expected to provide considerable new commercial opportunities, are planned.

Banking centre

The rapid economic growth of the late 1970s encouraged a hectic expansion of local and foreign banks. At the start of the big oil boom in 1973 there were 20 commercial banks in the country; by 1975 there were 46 and two years later in 1977 there were 53, of which 24 were locally and 29 foreign owned. At this rate of growth the UAE became one of the world's most overbanked countries with the Currency Board (itself dating from only 1973) lacking the authority to control the situation effectively. Nevertheless, following the collapse of two institutions in 1977, the Board banned the creation of any new banks.

In 1980 the Currency Board was converted into the UAE Central Bank, with greater powers of supervision and regulation of the country's banking system, although it lacks the resources to function as a lender of last resort. This inadequacy has been mitigated in practice by the readiness of the governments of Abu Dhabi and Dubai to provide finance for this purpose. The Central Bank's efforts to deal with the consequences of overbanking have concentrated on reducing the number of branch offices, particularly those of foreign banks, and on encouraging mergers, especially among the smaller local banks. The financial authorities have been concerned about the scale of outflows of private capital, affecting the liquidity of the domestic banking system and the balance of payments. The Central Bank has therefore suspended certain dollar/dirham swap facilities, and has been issuing Certificates of Deposit, yielding high competitive returns, in an attempt to provide a domestic investment opportunity.

Bank profits in general have suffered from the slowing down of economic activity, and non-performing loans have become a frequent and serious problem. The Central Bank's efforts to help deal with this situation have been hampered by the lack of appropriate legislation as well as legal uncertainty over the rights of banks to charge interest, particularly compound interest.

As far as public finance is concerned, there has been a marked improvement in the coordination of national fiscal policy since 1980 when the Central Bank was established. Virtually the sole basis of the federal budget has been a commitment by Abu Dhabi and Dubai to contribute 50% of their oil revenues. The main function of the Federal Budget is to channel funds from Abu Dhabi and Dubai to the smaller emirates.

A series of cost cutting measures have begun to bite although the discomfort is not yet acute. In line with declining oil earnings a number of federal projects have been delayed, scaled down or cancelled in an effort to reduce expenditure, with these cutbacks having the greatest effect on the smaller Emirates. Indeed, since 1984 the concept of a budget setting out revenue and expenditure estimates at the beginning of the fiscal year has been in practice abandoned, with Federal Departments working to instructions to keep monthly expenditures within those of the previous year.

A traditional Arab greeting between friends

However, despite a fairly comprehensive programme of cutbacks, the UAE continues to retain its position as a regional leader in the field of transportation. Sea, air and general international freight traffic through the ports of Dubai, Sharjah and Fujairah continues to prosper.

Abu Dhabi

Abu Dhabi is flat and sandy, with huge buildings springing up rapidly as the oil wealth increases. The ruler Sheikh Zayed has a philosophic attitude to the riches he controls. He is reputed to have said to a foreign diplomat 'King or beggar, everything is brief, and changing'. He travels the world – preferring Pakistan next to his own country as good hunting territory.

Abu Dhabi is the largest of the Emirates; within its boundaries is the desert town of Al Ain, part of the Buraimi oasis, where there are underground water, date plantations and an experimental farm where vegetables and fruit, especially cucumbers, tomatoes, melons and beans are grown in artificially cooled greenhouses. Al Ain has a museum of ancient archaeological discoveries in an old fort converted for the purpose. Other museums exist in Dubai and Fujairah. Al Ain is 160 km from Abu Dhabi town, linked to it by a four lane highway, bordered with oleander bushes.

Dubai

Dubai is first of all remarkable for its deep-water creek, 16 km long, which causes it to be called the Venice of the Gulf. The creek now has two bridges and a tunnel to cope with the ever-increasing traffic. On either side are tall concrete buildings and crowds of people who seem to be eternally crossing the creek in small flat-bottomed ferry boats.

It is no secret that the fortunes of Dubai were founded on the gold trade with India, perfectly legal until the fast boats carrying bars of bullion came within Indian territorial waters.

Sharjah

Sharjah is the former headquarters of the Trucial Oman Scouts, who before independence were responsible for maintaining order in the region. Now there is a federal force, and the airport, which before 1939 used to be a staging-post for Imperial Airways on the route to India, has been replaced by vast runways for jumbo jets. Sheikh Sultan has begun vigorous development of his emirate since 1974, when oil was produced from Abu Musa island, just off the coast. A deep-water port is at Khor Fakkan, which has the advantage of being on the Batinah coast, facing the Indian Ocean. Ships do not, therefore, have to pass through the already overcrowded and hazardous Straits of Hormuz into the Gulf.

Ras al-Khaimah

Ras-al-Khaimah is the fourth emirate, in size, population and prosperity. Its ruler is rapidly developing its hotels, commerce, and housing. The largest agricultural research station in the UAE is at Digdagga, where students come from all over the Gulf. Improvement of crops and livestock, as well as their adaptation to the difficult climatic conditions, is carried out, and although the Emirates will never be totally green, they may well become self-sufficient in fruit and vegetables.

The smaller emirates

Fujairah, Ajman and Umm al Qaiwain are the smallest of the sheikdoms comprising the UAE. Fujairah is situated on the Batinah coast and has local tourist and agricultural potential. The other two Emirates were small fishing villages that are now beginning to be brought into the prosperity of the region.

Modern roads now link the Emirates, and one across the Hajar mountains links Fujairah and Khor Fakkan to the rest of the UAE.

General Information

Federation

President: Sheikh Zayed bin Sultan (Abu Dhabi). Vice-President: Sheikh Rashid bin Said Al-Maktoum (Dubai).

Language

Arabic is the language of the country. English is widely spoken and understood.

Religion

Islam is the State religion. Christian, Hindu and Parsee minorities exist and have their own places of worship.

How to get there

Gulf Air – jointly owned by Bahrain, Oman, Qatar and Abu Dhabi – is the national carrier. Emirates is the official carrier of Dubai.

Entry regulations

Citizens of the UK, Bahrain, Kuwait, Oman, Qatar and Saudi Arabia require only valid passports, not visas. Citizens of all other countries require visas, to be obtained from the nearest UAE embassy. Sponsors within the country are required. Business visitors without visas may be admitted for up to a week if they are met at the airport by a sponsor bearing proof of identity which should be a passport if the sponsor is not a UAE citizen. The visitor must surrender his own passport, and leave from the place of entry. Regulations are liable to change at short notice, and intending travellers should therefore keep up to date with them.

Customs regulations

There are no restrictions on the import or export of currency. Visitors are allowed to bring in 200 cigarettes and personal effects are allowed in duty free.

Climate

Hot and humid in the summer and mild in the winter. From December to the end of March the climate is pleasant while from May to October it is very hot and damp. The annual average rainfall is negligible.
What to wear: For most of the year lightweight or light clothing is adequate. From the end of November to the end of March medium weight clothing is suitable during the day and warm clothing is advisable in the evening.

Currency

UAE Dirham (Dh) divided into 100 fils.

Business hours

Friday is the weekly holiday.
Government offices: Winter 0800-1400 Saturday-Wednesday and 0800-1200 Thursday; Summer 0700-1300 Saturday-Wednedsay and 0700-1100 Thursday.
Oil companies: *Abu Dhabi:* 0700-1400 Saturday-Wednesday and 0700-1300 Thursday; *Northern Emirates:* Summer: 0830-1300 Saturday-Thursday; Winter: 0830-1300 and 1600-1800 Saturday-Thursday.
Banks: *Abu Dhabi:* 0800-1200 Saturday-Wednesday and 0800-1100 Thursday; *Northern Emirates:* 0800-1200 Saturday-Thursday.
Private firms and shops: *Abu Dhabi:* Summer 0800-1300 and 1600-1930 Saturday-Thursday; Winter 0800-1300 and 1530-1900 Saturday-Thursday; *Northern Emirates:* Summer 0900-1300 and 1630-2000 Saturday-Thursday; Winter 0900-1300 and 1600-2000 Saturday-Thursday.

Press

Emirates News, P.O. Box 791, Abu Dhabi, The Gulf News, P.O. Box 6519, Dubai, and The Khaleej Times, P.O. Box 11243, Dubai, are all published daily in English.

Public holidays

New Year's Day, 1 January
First day of Ramadan*, 7 April 1989
Eid-al Fitr*, 7-9 May 1989
Eid-al Adha*, 14-17 July 1989
Hijra*, 4 August 1989
Al-Ashoura*, 13 August 1989
National Day, 2 December
Prophet's birthday*, 13 October 1989
Christmas Day, 25 December
Boxing Day, 26 December
The anniversary of the accession of Shaikh Zayed, on 6 August, is celebrated in Abu Dhabi only.
The dates of the Moslem holidays, marked with an asterisk, are only approximate as they depend on the sightings of the moon.

Consulates/Embassies in Abu Dhabi

Algeria: POB 3070, Abu Dhabi. Tel: (2) 326700. Telex: 22720.
Argentina: POB 3325, Abu Dhabi. Tel: (2) 364131. Telex: 23998.
Australia: POB 559, Abu Dhabi. Tel: (2) 821800. Telex: 23309.
Austria: POB 3095, Abu Dhabi. Tel: (2) 324103. Telex: 22675.
Bangladesh: POB 2504, Abu Dhabi. Tel: (2) 368375. Telex: 22201.
Belgium: POB 3686, Abu Dhabi. Tel: (2) 824090. Telex: 22860.
Brazil: POB 3027, Abu Dhabi. Tel: (2) 365352. Telex: 23815.
Canada: POB 6166, Abu Dhabi. Tel: (2) 723800. Telex: 22446.
China, People's Republic: POB 2741, Abu Dhabi. Tel: (2) 211174. Telex: 23928.

Denmark: POB 6666, Abu Dhabi. Tel: (2) 325900. Telex: 23677.
Egypt: POB 4026, Abu Dhabi. Tel: (2) 822950. Telex: 22258.
France: POB 4014, Abu Dhabi. Tel: (2) 331100. Telex: 22325.
Gabon: POB 2653, Abu Dhabi. Tel: (2) 822889. Telex: 22438.
Germany, Federal Republic: POB 2591, Abu Dhabi. Tel: (2) 331630. Telex: 22202.
India: POB 4090, Abu Dhabi. Tel: (2) 337700. Telex: 22620.
Indonesia: POB 7256, Abu Dhabi. Tel: (2) 369233. Telex: 22253.
Iran: POB 4080, Abu Dhabi. Tel: (2) 343257. Telex: 22344.
Iraq: POB 4030, Abu Dhabi. Tel: (2) 369900. Telex: 22367.
Italy: POB 6752, Abu Dhabi. Tel: (2) 328640. Telex: 23861.
Japan: POB 2430, Abu Dhabi. Tel: (2) 344696. Telex: 22270.
Jordan: POB 4024, Abu Dhabi. Tel: (2) 338632. Telex: 24411.
Kenya: POB 3854, Abu Dhabi. Tel: (2) 366300. Telex: 24244.
Korea, Republic: POB 3270, Abu Dhabi. Tel: (2) 338337. Telex: 24237.
Kuwait: POB 926, Abu Dhabi. Tel: (2) 376888. Telex: 22804.
Lebanon: POB 4023, Abu Dhabi. Tel: (2) 323863. Telex: 22206.
Malaysia: POB 3887, Abu Dhabi. Tel: (2) 338112. Telex: 22630.
Mali: POB 3792, Abu Dhabi. Tel: (2) 462252. Telex: 23161.
Mauritania: POB 2714, Abu Dhabi. Tel: (2) 462724. Telex: 22512.
Morocco: POB 4066, Abu Dhabi. Tel: (2) 345863. Telex: 22549.
Netherlands: POB 6560, Abu Dhabi. Tel: (2) 321920. Telex: 23610.
Pakistan: POB 846, Abu Dhabi. Tel: (2) 342631. Telex: 23003.
Philippines: POB 3215, Abu Dhabi. Tel: (2) 345664. Telex: 23995.
Qatar: POB 3503, Abu Dhabi. Tel: (2) 338900. Telex: 22664.
Saudi Arabia: POB 4057, Abu Dhabi.

Tel: (2) 365700. Telex: 22670.
Somalia: POB 4155, Abu Dhabi. Tel: (2) 464813. Telex: 22624.
Spain: POB 6474, Abu Dhabi. Tel: (2) 829250. Telex: 23340.
Sri Lanka: POB 6534, Abu Dhabi. Tel: (2) 366688. Telex: 23333.
Sudan: POB 4027, Abu Dhabi. Tel: (2) 822750. Telex: 22706.
Sweden: POB 2609, Abu Dhabi. Tel: (2) 337772. Telex: 23277.
Switzerland: POB 6116, Abu Dhabi. Tel: (2) 343636. Telex: 22824.
Syria: POB 4011, Abu Dhabi. Tel: (2) 378768. Telex: 22729.
Tunisia: POB 4166, Abu Dhabi. Tel: (2) 343852. Telex: 22370.
Turkey: POB 3204, Abu Dhabi. Tel: (2) 463372. Telex: 23037.
USSR: POB 8211, Abu Dhabi. Tel: (2) 721797.
United Kingdom: POB 248, Abu Dhabi. Tel: (2) 326600. Telex: 22234.
USA: POB 4009, Abu Dhabi. Tel: (2) 336691. Telex: 22229.
Yemen Arab Republic: POB 2095, Abu Dhabi. Tel: (2) 822800. Telex: 23600.
Yemen, People's Democratic Republic: POB 840, Abu Dhabi. Tel: (2) 368162. Telex: 23600.

Transport

Regular Gulf Air services link Abu Dhabi, Dubai, Sharjah, and Ras al-Khaimah. Small aircraft and helicopters may be chartered. Emirates has regular domestic flights.

The roads are good; taxis or private and rented cars may be used. There are now taximeters in Abu Dhabi which simplify the old bargaining system.

Businessmen wishing to drive hired cars must obtain a temporary driving licence from the Traffic Police. Passport, two passport photographs and UK licence must be produced.

Accommodation and food

Hotel charges are amongst the highest in the world, though the scarcity which prompted these has eased off considerably and some hotels are offering cheaper rates so as to attract more customers.

Local fruit and vegetables are available; there is excellent local fish at an ever-increasing price, although dates remain a staple of the diet. Hotels serve both Arab and European food, and there are Chinese and Indian restaurants. The various supermarkets supply frozen foods from all over the world.

Tipping: Practically all hotels, restaurants and clubs add fairly high service charges to the bill, therefore tips are not generally required.

What to see in the Emirates

The Emirates are a spectacular combination of sea, desert and oases. This is not generally regarded as a tourist country – although the number of tourists travelling to the Emirates is increasing annually – but one in which people live and do business. In summer the fierce heat prevents easy movement out-of-doors, at least during the day, but at other seasons the creek of Dubai, the sea corniches both in Dubai and Abu Dhabi, the beaches and fishing harbours along both coasts, and the Hajar mountains, are all worth exploring. Fishing boats are still built in the traditional fashion, the ancient forts survive as relics of a more turbulent past, and traditional sports have taken on a new lease of life. These include boat races for about thirty rowers in each craft, much resembling an elongated whaler, horse and camel racing and falconry. Traditional dances are performed on public holidays; football has become very popular, as has water skiing and speed boating. There is an abundance of game fish in the Gulf, and people are beginning to show interest in fishing for sport rather than as a livelihood.

Inland, the Al Ain oasis is well worth visiting; the road there is a well

Camels, once a source of transportation and food, are still popular in the UAE, as racing animals

engineered highway, and Sheikh Zayed has a fine stud of Arab horses.

The ports, at Khor Fakkan, Sharjah and Dubai, are most impressive, and certainly worth visiting, whatever the traveller's business may be.

Falconry is the chief diversion of the Sheikhs and a good many other citizens.

There are cinemas, discotheques in some of the hotels, but no casinos.

Almost every kind of manufactured goods from all over the world can be bought in the shops and supermarkets of the UAE, and enterprising merchants will certainly seek out new products if the customers demand them. Since customs duties are so low all electrical goods are cheaper here than in most countries, though transportation costs make food and clothes more expensive.

201

Hotels

NAME	ADDRESS	TELEPHONE	TELEX
ABU DHABI			
Centre	P.O. Box 7136	333555	–
Corniche Residence	P.O. Box 279	211200	23750
Gulf	P.O. Box 3766	377260	22904
Hilton	P.O. Box 877	361900	22212
Holiday Inn	P.O. Box 3541	335335	23030
InterContinental	P.O. Box 4171	363777	23160
Meridien	P.O. Box 6066	826666	4391244
Nihal	P.O. Box 3789	829900	–
Sheraton	P.O. Box 640	823333	23453
AJMAN			
Beach Hotel	P.O. Box 874	423333	69519
AL AIN			
Hilton	P.O. Box 1333	614410	33505
InterContinental	P.O. Box 16031	654654	34034
DUBAI			
Carlton Tower	P.O. Box 1955	227111	–
Chicago Beach	P.O. Box 11416	480000	47490
Hilton	P.O. Box 927	370000	46670
Hyatt Regency	P.O. Box 5588	23800	47555
InterContinental	P.O. Box 476	227171	45779
International	P.O. Box 10001	245111	47333

[Hotels]

Metropolitan	P.O. Box 4988	440000	46999
Ramada	–	421010	48333
Sheraton	P.O. Box 4250	281111	46710

DUBAI-HATTA

Hatta Fort	P.O. Box 9277	23211	47999

DUBAI-JEBEL ALI

Jebel Ali	P.O. Box 9255	35252	48000

FUJAIRAH

Hilton	P.O. Box 231	22411	89018

JABAL DHANNAH/RUWEIS

Ramada	P.O. Box 11828	71600	52201

KHOR FAKKAN

Oceanic	P.O. Box 10444	85111	89089

RAS AL KHAIMAH

Ras Al Khaimah	P.O. Box 56	52999	–

SHARJAH

Carlton	P.O. Box 1198	523711	68012
Continental	P.O. Box 3527	371111	–
Coral Beach	P.O. Box ????	351011	–
Grand	P.O. Box 6059	356557	68204
Holiday International	P.O. Box 5802	357357	68305
Marbella Club	P.O. Box 5017	357123	68281

YEMEN AR

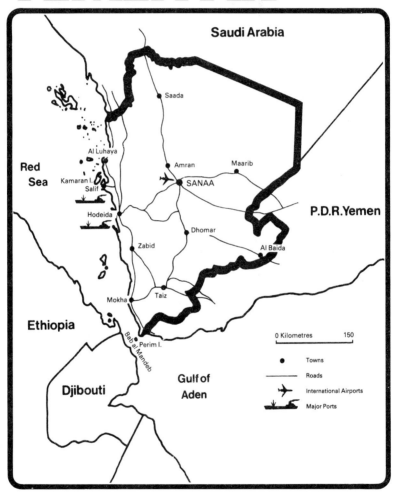

Area: 200,000 sq km
Population: 9,274,173 (1986 official estimate)
Capital: Sanaa

A traveller shown scenes from the North Yemeni countryside out of context would be hard put to guess that this is the Arabian peninsula. Shown scenes not too far inland from the Red Sea he or she might be more likely to opt for 'somewhere in East Africa' – 'outside Nairobi' or 'northern Tanzania'. Indeed, Yemen – a country in which chilly mountain heights slope down to a hot humid coast – forms the clearest living reminder of the fact that Arabia and Africa were once part of the same continent.

Helped by its rugged topography and peculiarly protective architecture to fend off outside influences until well into the present century, Yemen is also today the last refuge of those who would like to see the old Arabia before it is bulldozed into oblivion. Fortunately they still have time. For the risk that Yemen too will be razed to make way for the ubiquitous concrete and glass of modern building has been averted. The present authorities are well aware that the foreigner comes to Yemen in search not of beaches or night life but of beautiful scenery, extraordinary architecture and a strong sense of the past. Anxious to promote tourism on this basis they are attempting to make the country more accessible and more comfortable, while retaining the characteristics that make a visit to the Yemen, or Arabia Felix as it was once known, so worthwhile.

Terraced agriculture

The Arabia Felix of ancient times was probably more fertile than it is now, because of the presence of the great Maarib dam which, built in the seventh century BC, continued to function for well over a millennium until it was swept away, leaving irreparable damage, in the sixth century AD. The dam which was partially restored to its former glory by a $90m restoration programme, completed in 1986, was originally considered one of the wonders of the world and is referred to in the Koran, together with the 'marvellous gardens' that grew 'to the right and to the left'. The luxuriant vegetation of the surrounding area was almost legendary – early travellers invariably remarked on the abundance and variety of fruit. This internally-generated prosperity combined with the quantity of spices and precious gold entering the country from across the Indian Ocean, help to explain how this part of Arabia earned the classical epithet 'felix'. Even now, however, the description is not entirely inappropriate. Admittedly the complete breakdown of the ancient irrigation system, the erosion of many mountainside farming areas and the departure of a large proportion of Yemen's farming population in search of more lucrative work in Saudi Arabia and elsewhere has meant an inevitable decline. Yemen, though potentially a source of food for the rest of the peninsula, now has to import cereals and other foodstuffs to feed itself. But the aerial view of the terraces, their contours rippling out across the basalt of the central plateau and their shades of green, brown and gold reflecting great fertility, comes as a tremendous relief after the interminable deserts of Saudi Arabia and pinpoints what is still Yemen's best but possibly most underrated asset – its good soil and farming skills.

Central Yemen, the home of this agricultural tradition and the site of most of the major towns, ranges in height from around 200 m to the 4,000 m peak of Jabal Nabi Shoueb, the highest mountain in the whole of the Middle East. This high part of the central plateau vies only with the coastal ranges of Lebanon as the wettest part of the whole Arabian massif. The diurnal temperature variations at these heights are extreme and in Sanaa, the capital, situated at over 2,000 m above sea level, temperatures can fall below freezing at night.

To the west, in striking contrast, lies the Tihama, the flat coastal strip where rainfall is negligible and where the rain torrents and rivers flowing down from the mountains lose themselves in the sand. Some fertile patches are interspersed along the strip, flourishing in the alluvium left by the seasonal floods. In general, however, this narrow plain – which is barely 80 km across at its widest point – is intensely hot and humid and is sparsely populated, except for the ports of Mokha and Hodaida. The same is also true of the east, where the mountains suddenly drop away to the Rub al-Khali (Empty Quarter) and where, although the climate is more temperate, water is very scarce.

Perhaps because of its topography, the mountainous south-western corner of Arabia that today forms Yemen has generally been controlled as a unit in its own right, separate from the rest of the peninsula, throughout history. For the same reason, since the coming of Islam, the people of the region have represented an isolated outpost of Shia Islam on the edge of the Sunni stronghold of Saudi Arabia. Yet the Yemeni Shia, the Zaidis, are in many ways closer to their Sunni brethren than Shia in other parts of the Moslem world. They are not given to mysticism or saint worship or to the extravagant self-punishment with which other Shia sects usually mark the month of Muharram. Nor are they rigidly opposed to intermarriage with their compatriots, the Sunni Moslems, who themselves being of the Shafei school are not as strictly puritan as their Saudi neighbours farther north. Other than the small group of Ismailis far inland and the Yemeni Jews, almost all of whom have left for Israel, the Zaidis and Shafeis are the Yemen's only sects. And, in terms of numbers, they are believed to be fairly evenly balanced, although, until the demise of the Imams, the Zaidis gained status from the fact that the secular ruler of the country was also their spiritual leader.

More important than any division of the population on sectarian lines, however, are the distinctions between the urban and rural ways of life and the highland and lowland peoples. The Shafei Moslems, who predominate along the coast, share that part of the country with small communities from the other side of the Red Sea – Somalis, Dankilis and Ethiopians – and their outlook might be said to reflect this more cosmopolitan experience. The Zaidi highlanders of the north are rather more inward-looking, operating a strongly tribal system with a measure of autonomy, led by the tribes of

Terraced agriculture in North Yemen.

Hashid, Baqil and Zaraniq. As one moves north, into Sadaa for example, guns begin to become noticeable, slung over the shoulder and carried in addition to the traditional *Jambia* or dagger, which every adult male throughout North Yemen wears in his belt. The daggers are essentially a sign of economic status and virility but the guns serve as a constant reminder of the unsettled history of the north – the power base of the deposed royal family during the civil war and republican Yemen's living political link with the conservative Arab regimes elsewhere in the peninsula and the Gulf.

As for town and country differences, one clear example is the custom of veiling for women. Women in Sanaa, or even girls from the age of eight, either cover their faces completely with black or coloured cloth or swathe their heads tightly in black so that only their eyes are seen. In the villages, where women work in the fields, such customs are not observed.

Culture and history

The two halves of Yemen – North and South – have been split since 1839 when the British occupied Aden (then Yemen's southern port) and set about concluding special pacts with each of the 30 or so sultanates, sheikdoms and emirates which then made up the southern hinterland. At about the same time the Ottoman authorities were once again attempting to tighten their grip on the northern part of the Yemen and reabsorb it into the Ottoman Empire, having allowed it to drift into semi-autonomy after first defending it from rival international powers in the 16th and 17th centuries. Deserted Turkish forts dotted about the country are relics of this spasmodic Ottoman domination.

North Yemen has thus been a politically separate unit for almost 150 years (even though its chief northern and southern boundaries remained vague until only some 40-50 years ago) but the Yemenis themselves have never grown wholly accustomed to this fact. Mobility between the North and South has remained a fact of life over the years. Refugees from the Imams' dictatorial rule and migrant labourers in search of work headed for Aden. And in more recent years, critics of the radical government in Aden attempted to bring about its downfall from the North. Since 1972 both halves of the country have begun officially to work towards reunification – a process that both sides seem to think completely logical no matter how tricky or long-term. It is within this context that Yemen's 3,000-year history should be surveyed.

Beyond its recent turbulent past, the most widely-known feature of Yemen's history dates back to the period from the tenth to second centuries BC, the time-span of the Kingdom of Sheba (or Saba). Balkis, the renowned Queen of Sheba, who was said to have visited King Soloman, is believed to have come to power around 997 BC. The remains of her temple and the great dam at Maarib (the capital of Sheba, sited east of Sanaa) are still extant – a testimony to the architectural genius of the Sabaean people. The original dam, a colossal 650 metres long and 60 metres wide at the base, was still being relied upon until 542 AD and the markings on its stonework recount the details of the repair operations it underwent.

The theocrats of Sheba were replaced in 115 BC by the Himyarite dynasty, from whom the modern Imams claimed descent. With the rise of the Himyarites, the capital of the country moved to the central city now known as Dhamar and it was in the fourth century, towards the end of their reign, both Judaism and Christianity came to Yemen. An outburst of friction between the two religions provoked an invasion from Christian Ethiopia in 525, but Ethiopian domination lasted only 50 years, giving way to forces from Persia who absorbed Yemen into their Sassanid kingdom. This again only

Yemeni tribesman.

208

lasted until 628 when the governor of the 'province' was converted to Islam and the two main branches, Shafei and Zaidi, began to evolve and establish themselves side by side. The next major incursion was not until the arrival of the Turks in 1517, but by then the inhabitants of Yemen were sufficiently tightly-knit and independent-minded to prevent the invaders from having any more than nominal authority. When a second attempt was made to subjugate the centres of power in the mid-1800s, opposition was as fierce as ever and when the Zaidi leader, Imam Yahya, succeeded in driving the Turkish troops out of the country once and for all in the early 1900s he was able to capitalise on this achievement to assume the secular title of king and consolidate his position as ruler of the whole of North Yemen. Thus began half a century of tyranny with no obvious contemporary parallel in the Middle East. Maintaining themselves in power by purchasing tribal loyalties, holding hostages, murdering their relatives, barricading themselves in impregnable castles and subjecting the country to a policy of total isolation, Yahya and his son and successor Ahmad managed to keep Yemen in the Middle Ages until it was finally dragged away from them by the rising of tide of local discontent. Yahya was assassinated in 1948 but his assassins, divided on the issue of a constitution, were unable to hold out against tribal forces who saw to it that Imam Ahmad was installed in his place. Ahmad in his turn miraculously survived numerous assassination attempts and finally died in 1962 from a combination of natural causes. But his departure marked the beginning of the end of the monarchy. Ahmad's son Badr, a would-be reformer, floundered amid conflicting pressures from all sides and only eight days after his accession his Commander-in-Chief, Abdullah al-Sallal, shelled the palace and proclaimed the Yemen Arab Republic, with himself as President. As was the case in 1948, however, tribal forces rallied round the royal family and within a week a royalist government-in-exile was functioning from across the border with Saudi Arabia.

The country then sank deep into a state of civil war which can only be said to have come to a decisive end in 1970, when King Faisal of Saudi Arabia finally recognised the republican regime in Sanaa and that regime reciprocated by co-opting a former royalist to their number. In the years since then Yemen has leaned gradually further and further back towards its powerful northern neighbour and, consequently, towards the west. Major steps in this direction were taken by Colonel Ibrahim al-Hamdi who was president from the time of his bloodless *coup d'etat* in 1974 to his own assassination in October 1977. Subsequent regimes have continued along the same lines. There has been sporadic political upheaval. An upsurge of conflict with South Yemen occurred in early 1979, but this subsided later in the year. In May 1980 both countries agreed to establish joint economic projects and to coordinate their development as a step towards unification and an agreement was signed with the PDRY in December 1981. However, fighting broke out again in 1982 and, although the agreement remains in principle and commercial and administrative cooperation between the two countries has increased it is unlikely that a full merger into a single Islamic state will be achieved in the forseeable future. In 1984 exploration work revealed commercially viable quantities of oil in the country. The exploitation of oil in North Yemen could have a number of far reaching effects. Indeed, the future shape of political, social and economic development in North Yemen depends to a very great extent on the country's nascent oil industry.

The fact that Yemen was brought out of a state of the severest economic and political under-development only to be plunged back into the economic chaos wrought by war has left deep scars. In many ways, however, there are features of the Yemen's daily life that would be unlikely to change, whatever the prevailing economic or political climate. One such feature is the habit of chewing *qat* – a locally-grown shrub bearing shoots that have a narcotic effect. Every afternoon virtually every male adult in the country indulges in this habit and all activity comes to a halt as cheeks stuffed with wads of masticated qat leaf begin to bulge and eyes glaze over in a qat-induced trance. The general slowing-down effected by the drug is reflected in some of the traditional Yemeni dances, in which the performers link arms and sway slowly and rhythmically. When women dance among themselves they wear vivid colours, scarves woven with gold thread and valuable jewellery in which gold, silver coins and amber beads predominate. For the men too, the *jambia* and its sheath, sometimes made in intricately-worked silver, are a form of ornament. Although it is rarely used in anger, the dagger is occasionally drawn in dancing and either brandished or, in a show of virtuosity, made to slice the air within a hair's-width of the dancer's exposed forearms or thigh.

Economy

The economy of North Yemen has long been dependent on the remittances sent back home every month by more than a million Yemeni men working abroad, particularly in Saudi Arabia and the Gulf. These remittances have become the country's primary source of revenue. But there is a high price to be paid for this source of cash. While Yemenis abroad ease Saudi staffing problems they are creating massive labour shortage problems at home and this in turn exacerbates local inflation – making Yemen a very expensive place.

Inflation is further fuelled by the flood of cash, which, instead of being channelled into productive investment, is spent (understandably for a population of seven million which found itself in 1962 with no more than three hospitals and a serious lack of schools) on washing machines, refrigerators, cassette recorders and Japanese-made motor bikes. Added to this is the fact that the neglect of the country's agricultural potential and the turning over of more and more land to qat (now that more people have the money to consume it in greater quantities) means that the bulk of Yemen's food needs have to be imported from abroad through a severely congested infrastructural network.

General Information

Government

North Yemen is a republic. The President Col Ali Abdullah Saleh heads the Military Command Council in the name of the people.

Language

Arabic is the official language. English is the most commonly used foreign language although some Russian is used in business dealings. Outside the capital of Sanaa, or the country's main port town of Hodeida, little other than Arabic is spoken or understood.

Religion

North Yemen is an Islamic state. The majority of the population are Moslem, mainly Zeidis, a Shia sect, in the north of the country and Shafei, a Sunni sect in the south. Very few of the once numerous Jewish population now remain.

How to get there

By air: Yemenia Airways is the national carrier.
By road: Road access from Saudi Arabia or South Yemen could be dangerous and is not recommended.

There are no railways in the Yemen but cargo vessels call at Hodeida, the country's major port.

Entry regulations

All foreigners must obtain visas to enter the country, except nationals of Egypt and Syria. An exit permit is required by all. These can be obtained from Yemeni missions abroad.

Vaccination against cholera, typhoid and polio is recommended but not essential. Travellers from infected areas are required to have an international yellow fever vaccination certificate.

Customs regulations

There is no limit on the amount of foreign or local currency imported or exported.

Personal effects are admitted free of duty. Visitors can take in, duty free, 200 cigarettes or half a pound of tobacco and one pint of perfume or cologne. Foreigners may import 2 pints of alcoholic beverages.

Climate

Climate varies with altitude. The coastal plain is hot, humid and dusty for most of the year. The highlands are more agreeable in summer and very cold in winter. Most of the rain falls between July and September.
What to wear: Lightweight clothing is advisable in the coastal plain all the year round. Winter clothing is necessary November to April in the highlands.

Currency

Yemeni Riyal (YR) divided into 100 fils.

Business hours

Friday is the weekly holiday.
Government offices: 0800-1330.
Business firms: 0800-1230 and 1600-1900.
Shops: 0800-1300 and 1600-2100.
Banks: 0800-1200, Saturday-Wednesday, 0800-1100 Thursday.

Public holidays

First day of Ramadan*, 7 April 1989
Corrective Movement, 13 June 1988
Eid al-Fitr*, 7-9 May 1989
Eid al-Adha*, 14-17 July 1989
Hijra*, 4 August 1989
Al-Ashoura*, 13 August 1989
Revolution Day, 26 September 1988
Prophet's birthday*, 13 October 1989
The dates of the Moslem holidays, marked with an asterisk, are only approximate as they depend on the sightings of the moon.

Consulates/Embassies in Sanaa

Algeria: POB 509, Ring Rd, Sanaa. Tel. (2) 247755.
China, People's Republic: Az-Zubairy St, Sanaa. Tel. (2) 275340.
Czechoslovakia: POB 2501, Safiya Rd, Sanaa. Tel. (2) 247946.
Ethiopia: POB 234, Az-Zubairy St, Sanaa. Tel. (2) 72825.
France: POB 1286, Al-Bounia, Sanaa. Tel. (2) 73196. Telex 2248.
German Democratic Republic: POB 15, 26 September St, Sanaa. Tel. (2) 270065. Telex 2236.
Germany, Federal Republic: POB 2562, Outer Ring Rd, West Hadaa, Sanaa. Tel. (2) 72818. Telex 2245.
India: POB 1154, off Az-Zubairy St, Sanaa. Tel. (2) 241980. Telex 2578.
Iran: POB 1437, Sanaa. Tel. (2) 206945. Telex 2241.
Iraq: POB 498, South Airport Rd, Sanaa. Tel. (2) 244122. Telex 2237.
Italy: POB 1152, 65 Gamal Abd an-Nasser St, Sanaa. Tel. (2) 72792. Telex 2560.
Japan: POB 817, Ring Rd, West Safiya, Sanaa. Tel. (2) 79930. Telex 2345.
Jordan: POB 2152, Customs Lane, As-Safiya, Sanaa. Tel. (2) 241794. Telex 2703.
Korea, Democratic People's Republic: POB 1234, Qiyada St, Sanaa. Tel. (2) 223504. Telex. 2603.
Kuwait: POB 17036, Hadda Rd, Sanaa. Tel. (2) 208086. Telex 2481.
Lebanon: POB 2283, Al-Lakama St, South Safiya, Sanaa. Tel. (2) 240437. Telex 2438.
Libya: POB 1506, Ring Rd, Sanaa. Telex 2219.
Morocco: POB 10236, West Safiya, Sanaa. Tel. (2) 247964. Telex 2299.
Netherlands: POB 463, Hadda Rd, Sanaa. Tel. (2) 215626. Telex 2429.
Oman: POB 105, Hadda Rd, Sanaa. Tel. (2) 72313. Telex 2253.
Pakistan: POB 2848, Ring Rd, Sanaa. Tel. (2) 248812.
Romania: POB 2169, Hadda Rd, Sanaa. Tel. (2) 247921. Telex 2361.
Saudi Arabia: POB 1184, Zuhra House, Hadda Rd, Sanaa. Tel. (2) 240429. Telex 2420.
Somalia: POB 101, Hadda Rd, Sanaa. Tel. (2) 247842. Telex 2610.
Sudan: POB 517, Hadda Road, Sanaa. Tel. (2) 241811.
Syria: POB 494, Hadda Rd, Sanaa. Tel. (2) 247750. Telex 2335.
USSR: POB 1087, 26 September St, Sanaa. Tel. (2) 72353.
United Arab Emirates: POB 2250, Ring Rd, Sanaa. Tel. (2) 248777. Telex 2225.
United Kingdom: POB 1287, Haddah Rd, Sanaa. Tel. (2) 215629. Telex 2251.
USA: POB 1088, Beit al-Halali, Sanaa. Tel. (2) 271950. Telex 2797.

Transport

By air: There are occasional flights linking Sanaa, Taiz and Hodeida airports.
By road: Travel between three main cities is by taxi or shared taxi. There is also a regular inter-city bus service between the three main cities. It is advisable to fix the fare before the commencement of the journey. Self-drive hire facilities are available.

Hotels

NAME	ADDRESS	TELEPHONE	TELEX
SANAA			
Ramada	PO Box 999	215212	2301
Sheba	PO Box 773	272202	2551
Sheraton	PO Box 21407	237500	2222

Accommodation and food

There are three hotels catering for visiting businessmen, and many other less expensive establishments.

Sanaa

One of the most impressive things about Sanaa, the capital of Yemen, is that virtually all its buildings – old and new – conform to the typical style of architecture. It is not just a few special houses which have white decorations on their exterior walls and decorative arched windows. It is the majority of houses and government office blocks. Each house, designed to be inhabited by one extended family, is usually seven to eight storeys high with its own central stairway and special plumbing system. The lower storeys are generally built in stone and those above in brick and the whole structure, with its solid door at ground level, is designed to keep intruders out. As for interior decor, one of the most accessible examples is the Dar al-Hamd – a former palace of a relative of the Imam which has been turned into a hotel without loss of low doorways, stone staircase, multiple windows or sculpted white walls. A similar building is the Rawdah Palace outside the city which is also an hotel but which is generally used for the benefit of Yemeni Airline crews.

On a less secular note, Sanaa itself also boasts 45 mosques, some of them among the oldest in the Moslem world, the great mosque of Aroua dating back to the seventh century. These are not always freely accessible to non-Moslem visitors. Visitors to the city should try to see the Sanaa museum, remembering the building is usually closed to the public on Friday. At such times, however, there is always the main *souq* of Sanaa, the Bab al-Yaman, situated around a gate in the ancient city walls. Here the shops are no more than tiny kiosks – wide enough to accommodate one salesman and barely more than one customer at a time. Daggers, jewellery and candlesticks are among the goods on display – occasionally piled in a dusty heap and sometimes coming not from Yemen but from Syria and India or other foreign parts. The best time to visit Bab al-Yaman on a weekday is the late afternoon. And this is also perhaps the ideal moment to leave Sanaa and drive 10 km to the Wadi Dhahr so as to see it while the afternoon sun is casting dappled light and shade over the idyllic valley scenery. A favourite picnic spot is on the edge of the rocky precipice that overhangs the spread of cultivated greenery below, but the Dar al-Hajjar (the palace on the rock) in the valley itself should also be visited, even though a long climb is involved. Rather nearer Sanaa, at only 5 km distance, are the gardens and orchards of Hadda, where special facilities for tourists have been built. Again near the capital stands the ghost town of Kawkaban with its white stone palace standing at nearly 3,000 m above sea level.

Taiz

The fact that Yemen's various rulers have opted for a series of different capitals at different times means that there are many different places of interest dotted around the country – Maarib, the small but picturesque town of Jibla, Dhamar, Zabid and so on. But the second capital of Yemen today has come to be Taiz, situated at four hours' drive south of Sanaa at a height of nearly 2,000 m, which makes for generally warmer weather than Sanaa. Taiz was a centre of commerce and scholarship in the period from the 13th to 15th centuries. Overlooked by Mount Sabr and the citadel of Al-Kahira, Taiz is encircled by a city wall and houses two important palaces (one now a museum) and the beautiful Sharafiya mosque.

Downtown Sanaa – two local men sporting the traditional jambia, or dagger.

YEMEN PDR

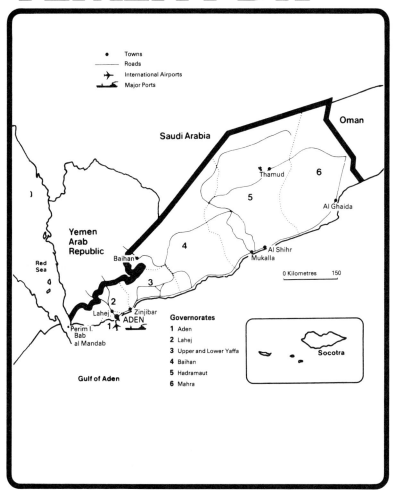

Towns
Roads
International Airports
Major Ports

Saudi Arabia

Oman

Thamud

6

5

Al Ghaida

Yemen
Arab
Republic

Baihan

Al Shihr
Mukalla

Red
Sea

4

0 Kilometres   150

3

2

Lahej   Zinjibar
ADEN

Governorates

1 Aden

Perim I.
Bab
al Mandab

2 Lahej

3 Upper and Lower Yaffa

4 Baihan

5 Hadramaut

Socotra

6 Mahra

Gulf of Aden

Area: 336,869 sq km
Population: 2,365,000 (latest official estimate)
Capital: Aden

215

The People's Democratic Republic of Yemen, also known as South Yemen, and formerly as Aden or South Arabia, has an area of 336,869sq km and a population of 2.3 million.

The country combines a wide variety of attractions: unspoilt sandy beaches, spectacular mountain villages and scenery, and the historic architecture of the Wadi Hadramaut. Among Yemeni handicrafts are silver and gold jewellery, basket weaving, Yemeni textiles, and the fruits of the Indian Ocean – corals, sharks' teeth and turtle shells. Yemeni coffee, *mazqul*, made from the husks of coffee beans and spices, and the mincemeat and pepper dish known as *haradha*, are among local culinary specialities.

Hillside villages and towns

The mountains of Yemen have been the site of a settled agricultural population for over two and a half millenia. The pre-Islamic settled civilisations Minaean, Sabaean and Himyarite have left behind a rich archaeological legacy. Today over 60% of the population of South Yemen work in agriculture. There are several thousand fishermen and women. Most of the rest work in towns; only a small percentage, along the edges of the northern desert, are nomads. The rural population rely on the infrequent rains for the water needed to produce their wheat and sorghum, and for their animals.

The area known as Democratic Yemen is that over which Britain extended control between 1839, when the port of Aden became part of the British Empire, and 1967, when the country gained independence. It is today divided into six Governorates, or provinces. The First Governorate consists of Aden the capital, plus the republic's islands. Much of the population of Aden has come, in the past decade, from the Yemeni hinterland and from the countryside of North Yemen. There are also substantial immigrant communities from Somalia and from India. The Second, Third and Fourth Governorates cover the southern part of the historic Yemeni heartlands, the rest of which is now included in the Yemen Arab Republic to the north. Here the peasants live in compact villages and still wear the traditional clothes of the area, the Yemeni kilt or *futa* for men, and the coloured dresses for women. Whereas women in the towns often wear the black drape or *chador*, this is much less common in the countryside.

The Fifth Governorate covers the area formerly known as the Hadramaut, a region which has relied for centuries on money sent by families who migrated abroad to East Africa, Singapore and Indonesia. The beautiful curved port of Mukalla, and the three architecturally rich towns of the Wadi Hadramaut in the interior (Tarim, Shibam, Seiyyun) are the products of this long relationship with the outside world. In the sparsely populated Sixth Governorate, one can find many native speakers of the pre-Arabic language Mahri. This is a language with no accepted written form, and is closely related to Socotri (spoken in the island of Socotra).

Culture and history

The religion of all Yemenis is Islam and small mosques and graves of holy men and women can be found in many parts of the country. At the same time there is a powerful literary tradition, which has taken the form of short stories and of oral poetry. There is also a lively theatrical activity in the towns, and a revival of Yemeni literature, music and dancing has been part of the nationalist revival of the past few decades.

An important part of traditional Yemeni society has been the chewing of the narcotic green leaf *qat*, an activity normally carried out by men for several hours in the afternoon. Since 1976 chewing of qat has been officially limited to Thursday and Friday, but it is illegal on other days. However, such legislation is almost impossible to enforce.

Prior to independence on 30 November 1967, Democratic Yemen was ruled by Britain. In the years just prior to independence, the country was the site of a bitter three-sided conflict between the colonial power and the two nationalist groups, FLOSY and the NLF. In the end the NLF (National Liberation Front) was victorious, and since 22 June 1969, when the radical wing of this organisation came to power, the country has been undergoing a process of radical change. Most land, property and businesses have been nationalised, and the NLF, with its associated mass organisations, has developed a single-party system, inspired by theories of 'scientific socialism'. Health and education in the towns and even more so in the rural areas have been improved drastically. A mass literacy campaign was launched in the 1970s, and the law relating to the family reformed to remove practices inimical to women.

Since independence Democratic Yemen has received economic aid from a variety of sources: from the Soviet Union, China, Cuba, the German Democratic Republic and other communist states, from the UN agencies and the World Bank, and from Kuwait, Qatar, Abu Dhabi and Saudi Arabia. Ties between the Soviet Union and South Yemen continue to be strong. Between 1976 and 1978 the Soviets transferred their naval base from Berbera to Aden, as relationships with Somalia collapsed and Soviet involvement continued to grow in revolutionary Ethiopia. The PDRY caused much consternation in the Moslem world when it publicly applauded the intervention of the USSR in Afghanistan. Closer to home, fighting broke out between South and North Yemen in early 1979. Inter-Arab diplomatic activity was intense following the outbreak of fighting and a ceasefire was negotiated after mediation by Saudi Arabia and the Arab League. Although hostilities have died down, scuffles between the two countries – which operate under totally opposing sets of social and political beliefs – continue. In January 1986 a combination of factors led to a military battle in Aden between President Ali Nasser Muhammad's supporters and his opponents in the ruling party. Thousands of casualties and the destruction of much of the harbour area and military equipment resulted. The emergent regime of Haidar Abu Bakr al Attas has, however, been at pains to reassure its neighbours of its keen desire to pursue a policy of peaceful co-existence.

Economy

The political turmoil of January 1986, when the regime of Ali Nassar Muhammad was overthrown has caused considerable economic upheaval in South Yemen. It is calculated that 60% of the active population of the country are engaged in agriculture. The sector contributes about 12% of the country's gross domestic product (GDP).

The Aden Refinery Company – a partnership between the Yemeni National Petroleum Company and Saudi Arabia national oil company, Petromin – is the country's only large industrial complex. The refinery – with a capacity of around 8 million tons per year – was badly affected by the closure of the Suez Canal in 1967. In recent years it has been running at about 50% capacity. Although the government has given priority to oil exploration the PDRY still has to import all the petroleum refined on its territory. South Yemen is currently one of the poorest Arab countries although some progress has been made in industrial development, often with the help of foreign cooperation. Cotton is still an important source of export revenue but the great hope for the country's economy is the fishing industry. Output is already good but, it is believed, can be increased by 250% with better equipment. Already prawns and lobsters are exported to the USA and Europe, and cuttle fish to Japan. Two fish canning plants have been established in the country, with another planned to go into production shortly.

General Information

Government

Socialist Republic. President Haidur Abu Bakr al Attas took office on 24 January 1986.

Languages

Arabic became the official language after independence but English is still widely spoken in urban areas.

Religion

Predominantly Moslem (Sunni/Shafi). There are small Christian and Hindu communities.

How to get there

Alyemda is the national carrier.
By sea: Passenger ships on tourist cruises occasionally stop at Aden Port.
By road: The only land link used by visitors is the road between Aden and Taiz, in the Yemeni Arab Republic. Driving time is three to five hours, exclusive of customs stops.

Entry regulations

All visitors to the PDRY are requested to register with the Central Registration Office of the Ministry of the Interior within 48 hours of arrival. They must be in possession of return or onward tickets.

Photography of topics other than government buildings, the port, and military areas is officially permitted, but visitors are advised to use their cameras only after consultation with an official guide.

All movement by foreigners between governorates is restricted. Prior permission must be obtained from the relevant authorities. Tourism outside the First Governorate is confined to groups.

A certificate of smallpox vaccination is necessary. Yellow fever and cholera certificates are required for those coming from infected areas. Precaution against malaria and polio is advisable.

Customs regulations

Any amount of foreign currency may be brought into the republic. It must be declared on a customs form when entering, and all exchanges should be registered with a relevant form. These are checked on departure against the original declaration.

Normal tourist baggage is exempt from tax. Visitors may bring 200 cigarettes, 50 cigars or 250 grammes of tobacco, two litres of alcoholic drinks, one litre of perfume and presents to a value of YD20.

Climate

Rainfall varies from 300 mm on the coast to 350 mm in the mountains. Temperatures in the summer rise to well over 35°C and from October to March vary from 20°C to 32°C. The best time of the year to visit is between mid-October and mid-April. In the winter the nights can be cold in the mountains.
What to wear: Lightweight clothes are preferable at all times; dress is nearly always informal.

Currency

Yemeni Dinar (YD), divided into 1,000 fils.

Business hours

Most government offices and businesses are open 0800-1300, 1400-1600, with half day on Thursday, and closure on Friday. It is advisable to concentrate visits in the period before 1300.

Press

No daily English language newspapers are published in Aden. The highest circulation daily (20,000) is the Arabic Ar-Rabi "Ashar Min Uktubar" (14 October) POB 4227, Crater, Aden, not published on Saturday.

Public holidays

New Year's Day, 1 January
Worker's Day, 1 May
First Day of Ramadan*, 7 April 1989
Corrective Move Anniversary, 22 June
Eid al-Fitr*, 7-9 May 1989
Eid al-Adha*, 14-17 July 1989
Hijra*, 13 August 1989
Al-Ashoura*, 4 August 1989
National Day, 14 October
Independence Day, 30 November.
The dates of the Moslem holidays, marked with an asterisk, are only approximate as they depend on sightings of the moon.

Transport

By air: Alyemda operates flights to all governorates. The main internal airfields are in the Fifth Governorate, at Riyan near Mukalla, and at Ghuraf, near Seiyyun.

By road: There is a surfaced road from Aden to Mukalla (500 km) built with aid from the Peoples Republic of China and another from Shihr to Sayhut. Other roads are under construction. In 1987 studies were completed for the construction of three roads to link Aden with al Baha, Dhalaa and Dhabous, at a total cost of $30m.

Taxis are available in Aden with fares fixed in advance. Collective taxis and buses also link the different sectors of the city. There is no rail transport.

Accommodation

Aden has only one international class hotel: the French-managed Frantel (P.O. Box 6111. Tel: 42911. Tlx: 2319).

Consulates/Embassies in Aden

Algeria: Lenin Quarter, Khormaksar, Aden. Tel. 32858.
Bulgaria: 136 Whitehall Gardens, Khormaksar, Aden. Tel. 32499.
Chine, Peoples Republic: 145 Andalus Gardens, Khormaksar, Aden. Tel. 32783.
Cuba: 36 Socotra Street, Khormaksar, Aden. Tel. 32107.
Czechoslovakia: Qasem Hilal Street, Khormaksar, Aden. Tel. 32101.
Ethiopia: Abdullah as-Saidi Street, Ma'alla, Aden. Tel. 32655.
France: Sayhut Street, Khormaksar, Aden. Tel. 33511.
German Democratic Republic: Radfan Street, Khormaksar, Aden. Tel. 32011.
Germany, Federal Republic: 49 Abyan Beach Road, Khormaksar, Aden. Tel. 32162.
Hungary: Portland Building, Tumnah Street, Khormaksar, Aden. Tel. 32671.
India: Premjee Chambers, Tawahi, Aden. Tel. 22445.
Iran: Al Madinah al Baida, Khormaksar, Aden. Tel. 31361.
Iraq: Miswat Street, Khormaksar, Aden. Tel. 32345.
Italy: 22 June Street, Tawahi, Aden. Tel. 23281.
Japan: POB 1186, Steamer Point, Aden. Tel. 24426.
Korea, Democratic Peoples Republic: Sayhut Street, Khormaksar, Aden. Tel. 32074.
Kuwait: Plot 52, Abyan Street, Khormaksar, Aden. Tel. 32880.
Libya: Embassy's Quarters, Khormaksar, Aden. Tel. 32777.
Pakistan: 34 Qasem Hilal Street, Khormaksar, Aden. Tel. 32702.
Romania: Muhammad Abdu Ghanem Building, Socotra Street, Khormaksar, Aden. Tel. 32366.
Saudi Arabia: Socotra Street, Khormaksar, Aden. Tel. 32540.
Somalia: Britannic Court, Dolphin

Square, Ma'alla, Aden. Tel. 24621.
Sudan: Aden.
Sweden: Khormaksar, Aden.
USSR: Abyan Beach Road, Lenin Quarter, Khormaksar, Aden. Tel. 32792.
United Kingdom: 28, Shara Ho Chi Minh, Khormaksar, Aden.
Viet Nam: 110 Awadh as Saidi Street, Khormaksar, Aden. Tel. 32711.

Aden

Aden is the largest urban district in the republic. During its history the capital has known great changes. Its strategic position has made it an historic fuelling station and, thanks to plentiful supplies from artesian wells, a traditional watering hole. With the opening of the Suez Canal and the revival of the Red Sea route, Aden, which had been a free port since 1853, enjoyed probably its greatest period of prosperity. Although when the Portuguese first rounded the Cape of Good Hope in 1498, Aden was already an important port of call for ships from India *en route* for Red Sea destinations. The city falls into several districts. **Tawahi,** or Steamer Point, includes the ship passenger landing area, free trade shops, and hotels. It includes some ministries, the presidential residence, the Port of Aden Authority building, and the Central Committee offices. **Maala,** dominated by the blocks of flats along Madram Street, includes the main docks, and a growing industrial establishment. **Crater,** the oldest part of Aden, is bounded on three sides by the barren rocks of the volcanic structure and can be approached only along the coast or through a pass from Maala. It contains old Adeni houses and the *souq.* **Khormaksar,** on the peninsula linking the volcanic area to the mainland, includes the main embassies, the airport, and residential villas. On the mainland are the districts of Shaikh Othman Mansura, and poorer residential areas with some

industrial plants. Further around Aden bay are two isolated areas: Madinat al-Shaab, site of Aden University and of the Ministries of Education and Foreign Affairs, and Bureika, comprising the refinery and a population of around 20,000.

There are a number of tourist sites to visit in Aden. In Crater there are the Tawila Tanks, ancient water storage units, surrounded by a pleasant garden; the Aidrus Mosque; the Minaret; and Sira Island. In Shaikh Othman the Kemisri Gardens, believed to have been laid out by a Persian merchant, are open to the public. There are three museums: Archaeological Museum in Tawahi, the Military Museum of the Revolution in Crater, and the Ethnographical Museum, in the garden of the Tawila Tanks.

Tax-free shops can be found in Tawahi and Khormaksar. Shops in Tawahi sell Yemeni handicrafts, at fixed prices. In Crater, around the main market square, can be found many interesting shops. In Streets Two and Three in Section A, Yemeni gold and silver work is sold.

Elsewhere there are spice and perfume shops. Incense *(bukhur)* grown in Yemen for millenia is still sold in small round plastic boxes: but don't forget to buy the charcoal and pottery containers needed to burn it. Basketware, brightly coloured mats and traditional Yemeni textiles are also widely displayed.

Beaches for swimming are found about 5 km along the coastal road beyond Tawahi. Entrance to the Gold Mohur Club requires a ticket, while that to the Yemeni Club next door costs 250 fils per day. There is also a swimming club at Bureika which requires a card to enter. **Tourist information:** The sole body responsible for tourism is the Public Corporation for Tourism, which is part of the Ministry of Culture and Tourism. The Corporation's address is: PO Box 1167, Aden, People's Democratic Republic of Yemen. Tel: Aden 23603.

YOUR COMMENTS

Your comments are very welcome indeed. We depend on you, our readers, to help us keep the *Traveller's Guides* as up-to-date and accurate as possible. We hope you'll use this handy form to tell us what you have learned as you've travelled around Africa, so that we may pass along your observations to our other readers in the next edition.

THE EDITOR

_____

Country visited: _____

Date: _____

Remarks: _____

_____

_____

_____

_____

_____

_____

_____

_____

_____

_____

_____

_____

Please send this form to: The Editor, *Traveller's Guide to the Middle East*, IC Publications, PO Box 261, London WC2B 5BN, UK.
Thank you.

YOUR COMMENTS

Your comments are very welcome indeed. We depend on you,
our readers, to help us keep the *Traveller's Guides* as up-to-
date and accurate as possible. We hope you'll use this handy
form to tell us what you have learned as you've travelled around
Africa, so that we may pass along your observations to our
other readers in the next edition.

THE EDITOR

_____

Country visited: _____

Date: _____

Remarks: _____

_____

_____

_____

_____

_____

_____

_____

_____

_____

_____

_____

_____

Please send this form to: The Editor, *Traveller's Guide to the Middle
East*, IC Publications, PO Box 261, London WC2B 5BN, UK.
Thank you.

YOUR COMMENTS

Your comments are very welcome indeed. We depend on you, our readers, to help us keep the *Traveller's Guides* as up-to-date and accurate as possible. We hope you'll use this handy form to tell us what you have learned as you've travelled around Africa, so that we may pass along your observations to our other readers in the next edition.

THE EDITOR

_____

Country visited: _____

Date: _____

Remarks: _____

_____

_____

_____

_____

_____

_____

_____

_____

_____

_____

_____

_____

Please send this form to: The Editor, *Traveller's Guide to the Middle East*, IC Publications, PO Box 261, London WC2B 5BN, UK. Thank you.